D0754354

3 0050 01476 7247

INDIVIDUALISM AND WORLD POLITICS

Individualism and World Politics

Edited by

Michel Girard
Département de Science Politique de la Sorbonne
Université Paris 1
Paris

First published in Great Britain 1999 by
MACMILLAN PRESS LTD
Houndmills, Basingstoke, Hampshire RG21 6XS and London
Companies and representatives throughout the world

A catalogue record for this book is available from the British Library.

ISBN 0–333–71559–4

First published in the United States of America 1999 by
ST. MARTIN'S PRESS, INC.,
Scholarly and Reference Division,
175 Fifth Avenue, New York, N.Y. 10010

ISBN 0–312–21571–1

Library of Congress Cataloging-in-Publication Data
Individualism and world politics / edited by Michel Girard.
p. cm.
Includes bibliographical references and index.
ISBN 0–312–21571–1 (cloth)
1. Individualism. 2. International relations—Moral and ethical
aspects. I. Girard, Michel, 1946– .
JC571.I4875 1998
327.1'01—dc21
98–16553
CIP

This book is printed on paper suitable for recycling and made from fully managed and
sustained forest sources.

10   9   8   7   6   5   4   3   2   1
08   07   06   05   04   03   02   01   00   99

Printed and bound in Great Britain by
Antony Rowe Ltd, Chippenham, Wiltshire

Contents

Notes on Contributors

Jean-Pierre Colin is Professor of International Relations at the University of Reims. His main research interest is in studying the political function of law in international relations. He has published many articles or contributions, notably on collective security, neutrality and Francophonie.

Dominique David is Senior Research Fellow at the Institut Français de Relations Internationales. He has published extensively on strategic thinking, French strategy, and European security. He is also Professor at the Military Academy of Saint-Cyr and teaches in the Department of Political Science of the Sorbonne at the University of Paris 1.

Michel Girard is Senior Lecturer in International Politics in the Department of Political Science of the Sorbonne at the University of Paris 1. His research interests are international relations theory and methodology, foreign policy and European integration. He has published many articles on these subjects. He is the editor of *Les individus dans la politique internationale* (1994) and co-editor of *Theory and Practice in Foreign Policy-Making* (1994).

Jacques Herman is Professor in the Department of Political Science at the University of Louvain la Neuve. His teaching and research interests are in methodology, and he is working at the moment on chaos theory and politics. His last book is *Incertitudes sociétales* (forthcoming).

Jean Klein is Professor of International Relations in the Department of Political Science of the Sorbonne at the University of Paris 1. His interests are in disarmament and international security. He has published extensively on these subjects. He is the author of *Sécurité et désarmement en Europe* (1987) and of *Maîtrise des armements et désarmement* (1991).

Anna Leander is Assistant Professor at the Central European University, Budapest College. Her recent research and publications are in international political economy and international relations theory. She has published many articles in these fields.

Marcel Merle is Emeritus Professor of International Relations in the Department of Political Science of the Sorbonne at the University of Paris 1. His numerous books include *La politique étrangère* (1984), *Les acteurs dans les relations internationales* (1986), and *Sociologie des relations internationales* (1988).

Michael Nicholson is Professor of International Relations at the University of Sussex. Originally a graduate and Ph.D. in economics from Cambridge University, he moved to peace research and international relations. His main work has been on theoretical topics and formal theory, and recently includes *Rationality and the Analysis of International Conflict* (1992) and *Causes and Consequences in International Relations: a Conceptual Study* (1996).

James N. Rosenau is University Professor of International Affairs at the George Washington University. His recent writings include *Along the Domestic–Foreign Frontier: Exploring Governance in a Turbulent World* (1997) and *Turbulence in World Politics: A Theory of Change and Continuity* (1990); as well as co-authorship of *Thinking Theory Thoroughly: Coherent Approaches to an Incoherent World* (1995).

Susan Strange is a pioneer in the field of international political economy, and her *States and Markets* has been translated into Japanese and Chinese. She is currently Professor at the University of Warwick. Before that she taught at the European University Institute and at the London School of Economics and Political Science. Other books include *The Retreat of the State* (1996), *Rival States, Rival Firms* (1991) with John Stopford, and *Casino Capitalism* (1986).

1 Individuals, Individualism and World Politics
Michel Girard

INDIVIDUAL AND INDIVIDUALISM

Just like the notion of individualism to which it is related, that of the individual is saturated with meanings, the idea as well as the word being heavily weighted with history.[1] As early as the seventeenth century, the concept of the individual, heir to the *individuum* of medieval scholasticism (the somewhat mediocre special case from which it was thought no safe deductions could be made), started to be applied particularly to the human person.[2] At this time also the individual was thought of as an abstract item, distinct in nature from political society and its variable structure.[3] The 'community of individuals' and the 'social body' (or 'individual' and 'collective' units) then formed an antinomic couple which a long philosophical tradition was to work on by giving it multiple faces which left their mark on thinking for a long time.[4]

Since then, this outline of the individual has been filled in in a thousand ways, but most of the doctrines and political and social analyses which gave it a specific usage ran counter to a logical contradiction – there can only be a general thought of individuality at the paradoxical price of sacrificing any strictly individual singularity. Therefore, most of the viewpoints with an idealist orientation show the individual (most of the time in the singular) as a generalizing abstraction in which any singularity is easily negated or abolished. For Hegel, for instance, the individual is a world, that of the spirit, only in so far as it is to be found, in an objective form, in the historical reality of the spirit of a people going way beyond the simple individual.[5] In just as abstract a way, in our time, the anthropologist Louis Dumont proposes a purely theoretical (*idéel*) individual, defined as a moral being totally independent from society and a characteristic product of 'modern ideology' and 'egalitarianist individualism'.[6] As far as more realist or positivist conceptions of man and society are concerned, which should in principle be more inclined to respect objective singularities, they sometimes talk about individuals in the plural, but usually tend to subordinate them closely to wider political and social entities. Needless to say that, in this context where holism is dominant, theoretical individualism often gets short shrift. For instance, in two very different and, it is true, hardly individualistic registers, Marx and Durkheim both sketch out an actual individual who is a kind of anti-Robinson Crusoe because he is essentially determined by historical or social laws of a much larger scale than his own. Likewise, less holist thoughts, which mingle individual determinations and social causality in more balanced constructions, such as those of the sociologists Max Weber and Talcott Parsons, often tend to give the individual an abstract and refined form leaving out most of his or her specific characteristics, in order to keep their discourse sufficiently general.

If one wishes to take the analysis of the individual and individualism a step further, it is advisable at least to start distinguishing between the different meanings that these words may receive. The notion of individual is undoubtedly neither unequivocal nor universal. As for the notion of individualism, it can conceal as many meanings as the rainbow can reveal colours.

The word 'individual' does not always designate a person, but can also be understood as meaning a unitary, if not always singular, case of a general category or of a collection constituted of various elements: states, international organizations, coalitions, etc. In international political analysis, instead of the notion of the individual, 'normal science' rather refers to that of the 'actor' (meant, in a vague way, as an autonomous authority endowed with a capacity of decision and action).[7] This 'actor', who for the most part is only a pseudonym for the individual in the international relations scholars' language, is not necessarily a person, and when it is one, it is almost always a political leader. But officials such as heads of states and governments and all their delegates or substitutes are undoubtedly much more than, and very different from, pure and simple persons, in spite of appearances to the contrary which allow ordinary people to become identified with the living symbols that they embody. On the too well-lit forestage where they have to constantly parade their public image, their personal individuality cannot really show itself other than in the alienating form of a semblance. The remarkable attention brought to bear on them by many scholars, joined with that of the media and the general public, contributes to a large extent to their transmutation into objects of identification or points of reference for the ordinary people who are the ones they govern.

Even when the individual referred to in the discourse is actually a person, the degree of singularity or particularity which he is then allowed is still, as we have already been able to see, very variable. Between the abstract, ideal-typical individual, almost totally devoid of singular characteristics, and the real individual who is socially and historically located, is there more in common than there are differences? Whatever the case, all the individuals examined in this volume will be persons.

Likewise, all human beings in the world are not individuals to the same extent and in the same way, because forms of political and social individualization can vary greatly from one society to another, from one social category to another, from one gender to another. In this respect, the modern or post-modern male individual of developed western societies is a richly endowed heir. He reaps the fruit of hard work which continued over a long period through the intermediary of institutions, practices, ideas and sensitivities in order to valorize his person as such, by distinguishing it clearly from the collective units he belongs to or to which he refers, without however always setting his person against them or assuming that it can do without them.[8] In more traditional societies, where processes of individualization can be of a lesser intensity and of a different nature, the notion of the individual still makes sense, but designates very different realities. In spite of a fairly universal movement of extension of liberal capitalist economic logic, of a spreading of democratic structures and of a promotion of western ideas and values generally associated with modernity, hierarchical, collective and ritualized forms often continue to prevail over individualizing and egalitarian logics, or to coexist with them, producing much less individualized human beings, apart from certain privileged elites, generally perceived as 'westernized'.

The notion of individualism can therefore also be understood in many different ways. In the spectrum of such possibilities, a distinction should at least be made between three major meanings.[9] The noun, and even more its adjectival form 'individualistic', can first mean an existing state of affairs, relating to the field of empirical realities, in which institutions, ideas, behaviours, processes or people are strongly individualized. Even if the two notions usually share relations of complicity, this *empirical* or factual individualism needs to be distinguished from *normative* individualism which seeks to valorize some idea of the individual. Whether ontological, ethical or political, normative individualism can always be analysed as an endeavour to legitimize an ideal form of the individual. As for *methodological* individualism, it is defined as the epistemological choice of explaining social science phenomena from the behaviour of individuals involved in these phenomena, which are always understood as effects emerging from aggregated individual causes. Defined in such a way, methodological individualism is in principle separable if not from empirical individualism, at least from normative individualism.

WORLD POLITICS

In a world made up of differentiated and relatively stable political units, politics inevitably presents two sides, much like the two sides of a coin. One of them – domestic politics[10] – is turned inwards, while the other – international or world politics – is directed outwards. These two spheres, by definition, cannot be separated nor reduced to one another. The multiple boundaries which separate these two political spheres – internal and external – are undoubtedly much more indistinct and complex than the territorial borders of modern states,[11] but they do not seem easy to abolish. In fact, as long as there are cities, empires or states, these political entities will probably be condemned to maintain with one another an ambiguous relationship of inevitable interdependence and ignorance.

This congenital partitioning of politics in a world made up of a multiplicity of states and societies is fraught with consequences. It allows in particular a fundamental polarization of all possible visions of world politics between two extreme and antinomic positions, each defined according to those two confronting sides of politics.

According to a first conception – positive, intrinsic and narrow, appealing to those who are fond of clarity and tradition – international politics includes all political phenomena which affect relations between political units. Therefore what is international is all that is either external to states or interstate. This outlook is in perfect harmony with the traditional identification of politics with the government of men and states.

In a second definition – negative, extrinsic and broad – international politics embraces the heterogeneous mass of all political phenomena which extend in a significant way beyond the sphere of domestic relations. What is international or worldwide, then, is anything which is not exclusively internal and, since nowadays nothing ever seems to be solely domestic, everything tends to become 'global'. This second definition is more likely to seduce the adventurous or the idealists, and suits better those who dream of putting an end to the tragic bipartition of politics. It is in total agreement with an extensive meaning of the word 'politics', understood as the exercise of a power which is not necessarily of a public or governmental nature.

Between these two conceptions of international politics, the difference is not only quantitative – one of them being simply broader than the other – but also qualitative, because they are strictly speaking incommensurable.[12] The history of international relations theory during this century can largely be interpreted as a long duel, sometimes subtle and often confused, between these two understandings of world politics. Advocates of the first thesis logically tend to defend the specificity of international political analysis, while defenders of the second one demonstrate a clear inclination to base it on the common law of political science or social sciences. As a matter of fact, the majority of international relations minds are undoubtedly divided between these two outlooks and affected by a dangerous strabismus, which is like an implicit mark of professional recognition. This strabismus is often openly discussed, whether to justify the prescription of a monocular vision with orthoptical purpose, or to be assimilated as a theoretical comfort device with no curative pretensions.[13]

Claiming to take an interest in the role of individuals in international politics almost inevitably means abandoning the intrinsic and interstate definition of things, in which there does not seem to be a place for individuals other than political leaders, and adopting instead the extrinsic outlook according to which anything which is not solely domestic politics can be declared international or, better still, global. At first sight this conception seems in a better position to leave scope to individuals, even though a careful scrutiny demonstrates, as we will see later on, that a large majority of the theories inspired by this school of thought are in fact holistic. This broad understanding of world politics is all the more tempting to those who are interested in individuals since supporters of the narrow conception immediately reject very strongly any individualistic point of view. For instance, for most classical thinkers who remain attached to the core logic of the realist tradition, the very idea of introducing the individual, the ordinary citizen, the indivisible unit of the domestic sphere, into the international political order already represents a mixture of styles or an incongruity close to mental confusion. However, even if it were more inconvenient or incongruous, the question of the place and role of the individual probably deserves to be raised in the political order of interstate relations just as it should in that of extra-domestic relations.

INDIVIDUALISM AND WORLD POLITICS

The central theme of this book may appear astonishing, or even preposterous, to some readers, because up to now individuals as such have never formed a very common category in international political analysis. The great discretion of the individualistic point of view in the huge contemporary literature devoted to international relations seems to result from a converging body of ontological and epistemological reasons which, without always being very obvious, have none the less largely managed to impose today this common 'truth' – with regard to international politics, the individual is by definition not part of the agenda, or even to be discussed at all.

However, this apparent exclusion of any individualistic outlook in international politics should not mislead one to the point of holding it as the fruit of a long-established wisdom. When one thinks carefully, the question of the individual never really ceased to stimulate international political reflection since states which we recognize as modern started to form in Europe. During the Renaissance and at the beginning of the Classical Age, concern for the individual seems to have been widespread with those who sought to submit the relations between princes to the jurisdiction of reason, or tried to think about war in order to procrastinate it more easily. Between the seventeenth century and the end of the eighteenth century, the rights of people became the rights of states, but the enigma of the individual, now declared offside in international politics, nevertheless continued to haunt moral consciences and political thoughts. It is by pure optical illusion that we convince ourselves of the virtually total disappearance of any individualistic point of view in international relations analysis during the last two centuries. The interstate view, which has made it a matter of principle to forget about the individual, was far from being able always to assert itself everywhere, and when it succeeded in dominating, it did not manage to do so without difficulty or division. The virtually total disappearance of individuals from our understanding of world politics is in fact a recent phenomenon which dates back less than half a century. This theoretical shift had indeed been made possible by an epistemological overturning which, for its part, dates back to the Age of Enlightenment.

'There is no war between men: there is only war between states.' This statement, which may today seem paradoxical, held Jean-Jacques Rousseau's attention, who commented on it on two occasions.[14] It is in total accordance with his views about politics, and fits the spirit of his time. The comments of the philosopher centre around the opposition, traditional in his thought, between society and the natural man, that is to say in the political order between the political body and the individual.[15] According to Jean-Jacques Rousseau, man in his natural state is a peaceful and gentle being, with 'limited faculties', who has 'a limit to his force and size fixed by nature and which he cannot exceed'. 'However much he may elevate his ideas, he always remains small.' The state on the contrary has no limitation, 'the size which is the state's is unlimited', the state can increase in size endlessly, all the more so since 'its security, its conservation require that it becomes more powerful than any of its neighbours'. The conclusion seems to anticipate, two centuries ahead, the realist conceptions of someone such as Raymond Aron: 'The state of war is natural between powers' and war occurs 'between two powers', with no place for the individual. In Jean-Jacques Rousseau's argument, a vision of international politics organized by a compelling classificatory logic becomes very clear – there is a difference of scale between individuals and states which is equivalent to a difference in nature. The two scales of size are incommensurate; and power politics, which are of the dimension of states, consequently cannot be of the dimension of men. There can be no more logical way of explaining to the individual-citizens the reasons for their exclusion from the sphere of international politics. The philosopher confirms in fact this tendency to put the individual offside on a collective mode in a famous text in which he expresses the view that 'the external exercise of Power does not suit the People', and that the latter should refer back to its leaders as far as external action is concerned.[16] How could one not see an enigma in the fact that the same thinker who justified the individual-citizen and modern democracy in the internal order rejected them so totally in the external order?

Between the death of Grotius and the moment when Jean-Jacques Rousseau justified a general measure of exclusion, hardly more than a century went by – just the amount of time needed for the *jus gentium* to become almost exclusively the law of states. According to the thinker from Leiden, all the laws regulating international relations should indeed be arranged according to persons just as much as states. Of course, the somewhat abstract humanity which preoccupied him could not in his view be made up of very individualized beings, but persons were already by principle sufficiently singular and valorized to deserve, at the price of a slight anachronism of vocabulary but not of idea, the term of individuals. By examining international politics, the century of Grotius seems to have conceived for the individual, still in childhood, a promise which the Age of Enlightenment could not, or would not, keep. This epistemic reversal of historical importance still constitutes nowadays a mystery which is all the more disturbing because it undoubtedly contains part of the secret of the intellectual origins of our modern vision of the political world.

It would be unwise to imagine that the views of Jean-Jacques Rousseau were shared by everyone during the following 150 years. Because of a modern rewriting of the history of international political ideas, to which we are indebted as much for historical omission or ignorance as for hegemony of the realist credo, we are sometimes too easily convinced that the interstate point of view completely dominated perceptions about international politics during the nineteenth century. However, the philosophical and moral tradition inaugurated by Kant, the liberal-radical school of thought illustrated by Cobden, the 'utopian' socialist approach represented by Proudhon, the 'scientific' socialist analysis promoted by Marx, or the different trends of Christian universalism, for instance, have contributed to keeping open – much like a regret – the question of the place and role of the individual in world politics. In the twentieth century, the completion of the expansion of the world, the development of individualistic and universalist values, the progress of democracy, the amazed discovery of great internationalist mobilizations transcending national borders, and the powerfully destructive experience of the First World War even contributed to the strong comeback, during the years 1918–30, of an idealism which rather favoured individualistic logics. But this was to be vigorously denounced by one of the founding fathers of the modern realist science of international politics as early as 1939.[17]

It was especially after the Second World War that the interstate paradigm of realism appeared to become for a while hegemonic, because of the total discredit of idealist themes due to the absolute atrocity of the conflict and the compelling ideological imperatives of the Cold War. Everyone knows that conceptions of the realist kind successfully claimed the legacy of a supposedly 'classic' tradition – dating back to Hobbes or to Machiavelli – and decided in favour of dealing mainly with states within the realm of international politics. At the same time, as far as individuals were concerned, realist authors were almost exclusively interested in heads of states or governments and in their various substitutes. In their views, apart from these state-men, these living symbols raised way above ordinary mankind, there were never many individuals worthy of attention.

This almost total suppression of the individualistic point of view was far from reaching an end when, starting from the 1960s, the realist approach was rivalled and partly overtaken by functionalist, systemic and structuralist conceptions which were even less favourable to the taking into account of individuals. Even the transnationalist constructions of the 1970s and following years developed holist conceptions and referred to individuals as minor actors, tolerated on the international scene only on the condition that they remained subject to larger entities (firms, trade unions, foundations, churches, NGOs, etc.) within which it was recommended that they fade away in silence at the first interjection. Likewise, in conceptions claiming to be part of the world society paradigm, individuals are often presented as abstract units merged in the collective categories they belong to. This virtual omission of the individuals was not challenged either by the wide spreading of the rational actor paradigm, although inspired by a liberal and individualistic tradition, which came from international political economy and games theory. Indeed, this paradigm has virtually only been applied to states and other major collective actors, treated as the unavoidable individual-actors of any international political analysis.

The significant reappearance of individuals as such in the landscape of international political theory only dates from the end of the 1980s. And even then, this comeback first took place in very discreet ways, whether on the side of critical theory or on the side of feminist studies.[18] As far as the post-modernist view is concerned, it appeared to restore the individual only the better to deconstruct the subject and promote the problematical notion of an individual who is not a subject.[19] In 1990, James N. Rosenau, basically quite isolated, published a book about world politics in which individuals occupy an absolutely central position.[20] Building on his previous works,[21] the writer, who obviously took much inspiration from chaos theory, places individuals at the heart of a fracture of historical importance from which would originate unprecedented turbulence affecting world politics. Out of the three 'parametric transformations' which are to explain in his view the now almost uncontrollable character of global political dynamics, that of the 'individual parameter' is by far the most decisive.[22] This 'individual parameter', which tries to synthesize several political dimensions of our western modernity, is thought to have been much disturbed during the last decades, mostly by the effects of the micro-electronic revolution. The result for individuals seems to be a general phenomenon of erosion of loyalties, a progressive replacement of habits of passive submission by active processes of adaptation, as well as a considerable increase of analytical skills and capacities for emotional investment regarding world politics. The fact that a writer so well-known for his previously firm commitments to behaviouralism and structuro-functionalism became, at least partly, converted to theoretical and methodological individualism may foretell the emergence of a new intellectual climate in which individuals will once again be allowed to be considered in international political analysis.

METHODOLOGICAL INDIVIDUALISM IN INTERNATIONAL RELATIONS

The large majority of political thinkers in international relations, just like most sociologists in the field of sociology,[23] reject the idea that methodological individualism, which seeks to bring the analysis 'down' to the level of the individual, could be of any help at all in the study of macro phenomena. Considered to be acceptable in the analysis of small molecular clusters formed by restricted groups and organizations of limited complexity, the resort to the individual unit is usually challenged for the study of macromolecules, to which most of the studies of these scholars are devoted. In an intellectual situation in which international studies give great preference to analyses of the macro level, as is the case nowadays, it is true that a double difficulty crops up for the individualistic outlook. On the one hand, taking individuals into consideration seems to be an unwarranted and useless approach. On the other hand, trying to put the individual units in the macroscopic context of world politics seems to constitute too ambitious a venture to be feasible.

It is not certain that the situation has changed dramatically since J. David Singer stood up in 1961 against the unfortunate tendency of international relations scholars to mix in their studies concepts of different levels of analysis and to go from one level to another as easily as if they were taking a lift without any stable focal (or storey) point.[24] Global system, IGO, region, coalition, nation, public policy, social classes, elites, and individuals were the main 'departments' between which the scholars of the time moved about in a disorderly manner to do their scholarly shopping. Driven by the laudable desire to tidy up a little in order to see things more clearly, Singer laboured none the less under a misconception, which is still today fairly widespread, about the disjunction of level of analysis and unit of analysis.[25] An analysis on the macro level can, without repudiating itself in any way, bring in a unitary element of small size – for instance taking into account this or that renowned Soviet dissident in the general analysis of East–West relations during the 1970s. Likewise, an analysis on the micro level can without incoherence (but not without difficulty) take into consideration large-scale unitary elements. For that matter, many international studies dealing with small-scale objects do not fail to proceed in this way, if only to escape the easy criticism of being too narrow. It is nevertheless the case that, in an analysis whose level is on a certain scale, it is not easy to use pertinently and rigorously elements of a very different size scale. In such conditions, can one wonder that in the field of international relations a certain conventional wisdom is easily and wrongly convinced that methodological individualism presents a prospect which is almost always maladjusted?

What is more, the usefulness of an analysis of the individualistic kind may seem questionable to those who believe, in accordance with the ontological positions embedded in their reference theories, that the decisive factors of international politics lay mostly in supra-individual phenomena. Although it is true that granting individuals a significant causal value is not essential to turn them into an object of analysis, methodological individualism can still seem to present a gratuitous choice for all those who think that the truth of world politics phenomena lies elsewhere. Suppose that one were fully convinced that methodological individualism can be totally separated from ontological or theoretical individualism,[26] they would still need to be convinced of its interest or of its usefulness in terms of research strategy. Can its ambition be any more than merely adding interesting but secondary details to what we already know? Would it not be more profitable, and therefore a priority, to develop holistic analyses, which, for lack of explaining everything about something limited, try to explain something about everything?

If 'normal' science in international relations managed to convince itself that methodological individualism can neither be inappropriate nor unnecessary, it would still need to be convinced that the undertaking is possible. Indeed, the elucidation of the megamolecular subject matter of international politics starting from the individual units seems at first to be a rather excessive project. Although methodological individualism has managed to provide enlightening insights into local or regional phenomena, such as the congestion of traffic, the behaviour of 'free riders', or the zealous sabotage of organizations by 'svejkism',[27] it has proved so far so absent in the field of interpretation of international politics that precedents and models are rare.[28] Located at both ends of the long scale of sizes, the international system and the individual cannot be put in communication with each other without many mediations, levels or stages. From emergent effects to emergent effects, the chain which can lead from real individual units, their ideas, their motivations and their behaviours to the heavy physics of international processes looks almost as hazardous to reconstitute as the human genome structure. However, from a scientific point of view, the difficulty of an approach should not be enough to discredit it.

A revived interest in methodological individualism in the field of International Studies would undoubtedly be likely to introduce a salutary breaking off with the most conventional discourses of the discipline, which sometimes seem so enmeshed in their usual holistic categories that international political analysis unfortunately resembles a repetitive catechism ritually manipulating its favourite stereotypes of the moment. Of course, holistic analyses – which seek to study the characteristics of the complex sets which form organic-type bodies – can be extremely interesting,[29] but we have to admit that anything which can contribute to the disintegration of their familiar 'holons' is likely to be of great help to the scholars, who might be more in danger than they believe of a dogmatic intellectual sclerosis. Therefore, trying to disaggregate the state, especially from its external side, can lead to many discoveries, notably that of the untenable character of the too substantialist and juridical-institutional conception that many analysts still have nowadays around the world. Likewise, the disintegration of IGOs, multinational firms, and other various organizations (international regimes, nations, societies, groups, etc.) which inhabit the bestiary of standard international political analysis could allow us to foresee, beyond the apparent simplicity of macro sets, the inextricable complexity of inter-individual networks and the aggregation processes which pass through them. With a paradoxical backlash, the transition from holistic 'complexity' (often thought in rather simplistic terms) to the only apparent 'simplicity' of the individual offers a precious opportunity of rediscovering the actual and stupendous complexity of political phenomena.

In the end, the best favour which the individualistic approach could do for international relations scholars is undoubtedly to disorientate them by making them leave at times their usual surroundings of macro-political generalities of which they are too fond, whether in an intuitive and literary mode or in a formalist and scholarly manner. While they may not be easier to observe and apprehend than macro phenomena, micro-political processes and their emergent effects in international politics provide curious minds with the promise of a luxuriant *terra incognita*, neighbouring the workplaces of historians, anthropologists and sociologists who are also interested in individual phenomena. As long as it does not lead one astray into naive descriptivism or subjectivist illusions, taking individuals into account in international political analysis can then provide international relations scholars with what they are obviously very much in need of nowadays – a huge terrain for empirical research which could be used both as a principle of reality and as a space of discovery.

RETURNING INTERNATIONAL RELATIONS TO INDIVIDUALS

Although it is true that, at least for several decades, individuals as such have been very much excluded from international politics and from most of the profane or scholarly ways in which people see them, the change is that the persons concerned do not seem today ready to accept nor recognize this state of things as easily as in the past. Is it, as so many people following James Rosenau like to believe, because the nature of world politics has changed dramatically before our eyes; or is it rather because the opinion we all have about world politics has been affected, mostly without our knowing, by profound modifications?

The recent development of interest in the individual in international politics lies visibly at the intersection of many modern and post-modern evolutions which are not always confined to advanced societies – the almost universal progress of social processes of individualization allowing the multiplication of personal micro-strategies; the frantic publicity promotion of values and models of behaviour related to the ego; the slow, unequal but inevitable introduction of the reserved sphere of international politics at the heart of the 'public space' debates; the better perception of the inextricable complexity of international problems and issues introducing a loss of and search for meaning; the imposition, in minds and facts, of the supremacy of liberal institutions and neo-classic type economic processes; the transmutation of political actions into media-covered shows always in search of leading figures; the individual allergic reactions caused by the perfecting of the dysfunctional rule of bureaucratic apparatuses; the disillusion, which sometimes turns into a little complaisance, in front of a world which is judged too indifferent to the ethical preoccupations of the subjects. Are these evolutions sufficient to assert the profound novelty of the present political moment on a global scale? The theme of a radical and recent change in the existing state of things assuredly constitutes a standard argument, especially in the political or social field, for all promoters of theoretical 'novelties' who do not wish to undertake too harsh a criticism of established conceptions. According to the famous expression by Alexis de Tocqueville, a new world calls for new ideas. Presupposing the originality of the present political world is all the more likely to appeal, since it flatters spirits by showing them how incredibly lucky they are to live in their own historical time, especially the youngest of them, who are all the more naturally tempted to think that the world is new to them, since for certain they are themselves new to the world.

However, the reality of things may in fact have changed less than the opinion that we have about it. In a world where numerous forces work towards endlessly perfecting the work of individualization, inevitably more and more people, if they are interested in international politics, come to feel a certain uneasiness towards a situation ignoring individuals, in which they can neither easily recognize their own world, nor subjectively find themselves. There is always some legitimate pleasure in identifying with a picture, even that of world politics, and in getting the confirmation, through a symbolic mark, that our own presence counts and makes sense. It is obviously one of the major appeals (and maybe dangers) of the individualistic approach that it searches for a version of the world which would not be totally alienating for the ego. Bringing together men and world politics by showing them world politics not as a performance of which they are at best occasional spectators, but as a very complex set of processes of which they are sometimes the agents, sometimes the actors – this could be the programme of a scholarly community concerned with not isolating itself completely from its contemporaries by shutting itself in an ivory tower maybe more suited to serving corporatist interests than strictly scientific ambitions. Restoring a space of visibility and significance to the benefit of contemporary individuals in order to reinstate them in the history of world politics, which is also their own history, would contribute to ease the post-modern 'ill-being' which tends to turn them into non-caused causes without a cause, lost Robinsons who have run out of political society and ideals, subjects both free and powerless of a history which has become from now on aimless, and of a world society whose advent seems unlikely to almost everyone.

Anti-individualism during the time of triumphant realism, just as most subsequent theoretical phases, had greatly contributed to the pronounced marginalization of the ethic of international relations, to the current deterioration of ethical ambition into rather trivial pragmatism, and even to the invention of ethical systems which can do without the subject at all.[30] A return to the individualistic outlook would constitute a necessary, if not sufficient, condition for the re-emphasis on the personal ethical point of view in thought and action in international politics. 'Empirical' or 'scientific' theory and philosophy (generally referred to as 'normative theory') form from now on two largely separate universes in international relations maintaining limited and often difficult relationships. Their lasting reconciliation, which does not seem to be the most likely hypothesis for the moment, would require at the very least that the ethical subject find its essential counterpart in theoretical constructions as well as empirical studies – that is, an identified or identifiable individual.

PLAN AND AMBITIONS OF THIS VOLUME[31]

Each of the following chapters seeks to provide the reader with an opportunity to carry the reflection further on one of the aspects of the subject. Chapters 2 to 5 – respectively written by Michael Nicholson, James Rosenau, Jacques Herman and Anna Leander – bring out and examine thoroughly some of the theoretical and methodological problems raised by the individualistic outlook in international relations. Chapters 6 to 10 – by Marcel Merle, Susan Strange, Jean Klein, Dominique David and Jean-Pierre Colin – study the place and role of individuals in particular spheres of world politics.

As is suggested by Michael Nicholson's contribution, Chapter 2, the infinitesimally small singular individual can influence the infinitely big global system only under special conditions which do not seem easy to gather. However, the hypothesis of turbulence can show a glimpse of the increase in possibilities of influence and action of individuals starting from the 'switch points' of the international system or of its sub-systems. It is usually very difficult nowadays to predict whether an individual action can have important effects or, on the contrary, insignificant consequences on the course of world politics. For the time being, the question still seems to be related to an ontological or meta-theoretical choice which does not belong to the field of demonstrable facts.

As for James Rosenau, in Chapter 3, he essentially builds on his own works to state again that citizens represent 'key variables in world politics', and provides us with a typology of four fundamental types of citizenship resulting from the 'self–environment orientation' taken by each citizen. Reasoning upon typical individuals and their relations with their society and the collective categories to which they belong, the author takes up a point of view which seems to hesitate between individualism and holism. His analyses, which are full of insight, often let us see the emergent effects which can result from the orientations of the citizens as well as the influence of collective or global developments on a particular form of citizenship.

By seeking in Chapter 4 to keep count of the epistemological and methodological problems raised by the individualistic outlook in international relations, Jacques Herman makes a useful contribution. An interesting point, among others, of his work is to suggest that the obstacle of the antinomic tension between the micro level and the macro level can be overcome by distinguishing between a larger number of levels of analysis. Therefore the problem is no longer opposing one level to another or seeking in vain to reduce one to the other, but linking all levels with each other. This is in fact what a number of empirical studies have been trying to achieve for a long time. Moreover, the writer is convinced that new formal paradigms such as those stemming from catastrophe theory, autopoiesis theory and chaos theory really could shed light on the analysis of the complex relations between the individual and the system.

In Chapter 5, Anna Leander undertakes a thorough investigation into the prolific literature devoted to international questions by feminist studies. She also reveals the extent to which these works have been influenced by the theoretical circumstances specific to international relations and social science. Indeed, feminist approaches, although not much disposed to accept the downgraded status of sub-discipline of a sub-discipline which they are often awarded, have demonstrated, at least for a time, a certain tendency to follow intellectual trends which did not really tend towards individualism. However, because of the importance taken by normative debates, the already varied landscape of feminist studies has grown richer with the contribution of critically individualist approaches which try to reconcile the dimension of universality which is essential for the ethical subject, and respect for individual differences in gender, in political choice, in culture or in nationality.

In order to integrate the individual dimension in the analysis of world politics, it is necessary, contrary to a whole tradition of thought, to forget for a while about states-men, who are the target of so many scholarly anxieties which often remain enmeshed in the appearances dictated by politics and at its profane service. Rather than taking an interest in political rulers, it seems sensible to examine closely the case of people who find themselves in a position of exception because special circumstances seem to project them directly into the world political space where they can put forth their action or display their commitment. How could one abstain from observing these units, offered in an almost experimental situation, at this privileged time when, escaping from the crowd, they can seem to free themselves, at least in a certain proportion and for a while, from the attraction forces of their original macromolecule? This is true about the disarmed prophets which Marcel Merle analyses at length in Chapter 6 to reveal that Machiavelli's abrupt formula is far from always being confirmed.

It seems very appropriate to examine closely the forms of identification, the allegiances and the behaviours of individuals who, without being altogether nondescript, are closer to the ordinary standard, because one can suppose that they contribute to secretly weaving the fabric from which the monumental clothes of international politics can be cut out. In this line of thought, Susan Strange briefly mentions in Chapter 7 the conflicts of allegiance experienced by managers of multinational firms. After having restated the core ideas expressed in her previous works, the author turns to corporate diplomacy and to the way in which it affects the future of many individuals.

As for Jean Klein, he examines in Chapter 8 a particular form of mobilization of scientists against nuclear war. His careful description of the Pugwash movement shows how a rather limited group of people, not all of them being celebrities, could exert an influence, difficult to determine with any precision, but undeniable, on the policy of the great powers in the field of nuclear disarmament. The writer is confronted here with a methodological problem on a very general level – in a world of complex relations, where cause and effect relationships are numerous, multi-levelled and of different orientations, how is it possible to isolate (and evaluate) on a macro level the emergent effects caused by certain micro phenomena, and by these alone?[32]

Undoubtedly the analysis of such an extreme international political situation as war is likely to disclose, with the simplifying distinctness which characterizes extreme cases, what can be the place and role of individuals in international politics. Dominique David analyses in Chapter 9 the position of the individual in modern strategies and defence systems. He shows how the reduction of the space allocated to the individual in war, which started very soon after the First World War and the invention of the 'unknown soldier', continued during the course of this century, especially in the nuclear age. The individual is present in modern war only in a partial and residual way and, by an alarming paradox, sometimes sees in Europe and elsewhere a war from which he had been very much excluded get closer to him.

In Chapter 10, Jean-Pierre Colin wonders about the relations between the individual and humanitarian law. In the sphere of *jus in bello*, humanitarian law constitutes nowadays a legal monument erected to the benefit of the individual. Indeed, this complex and perfected structure, which clearly comes close to a *jus cogens*, carries very far the protection of individuals, civilian and military, during armed conflicts; to the point where states, although joint authors of this law, are now embarrassed by it in the case of conflict. Contemporary humanitarian law proves that the individual can from now on be subject to a consecration, equal or superior to that of war or of the national interest. Such a situation may well owe less to the goodwill of states and their leaders than to the emergence of individualistic aspirations stemming from individuals.

This collection of essays is the fruit of shared curiosity and friendship. The result of a project which gradually took shape over the years and with meetings in Paris, London, Washington, Florence or Louvain la Neuve, this volume aspires at least to help clarify ideas, and at best to contribute to opening new horizons for theoretical reflection and empirical investigation. Readers alone will be in a position to decide how matters stand.

NOTES

1. An introduction to the semantic history of the word 'individualism' may be found in Steven Lukes, *Individualism* (Oxford: Blackwell, 1973) pp. 1–42.
2. See Norbert Elias, *La société des individus* (Paris: Fayard, 1991) pp. 207–15 or *Die Gesellschaft der Individuen* (Frankfurt/Main: Suhrkamp Verlag, 1987).
3. See Lukes, op. cit. pp. 73–8.
4. For a very short outline on the weight of the philosophical background of this antinomy in contemporary debates concerning the micro–macro connection, see J. C. Alexander and Bernhard Giesen, 'From Reduction to Linkage: The Long View of the Micro–Macro Debate' in Jeffey C. Alexander, Bernhard Giesen, Richard Münch and Neil J. Smelser (eds), *The Micro–Macro Link* (Berkeley: University of California Press, 1987) pp. 3–4.
5. See Jean Hyppolite, *Introduction à la philosophie de l'histoire de Hegel* (Paris: Marcel Rivière, 1968) pp. 19–20.
6. See Louis Dumont, *Essais sur l'individualisme: Une perspective anthropologique sur l'idéologie moderne* (Paris: Esprit/Seuil, 1983) pp. 27 and 274.
7. The notion of the agent (a non-autonomous actor who can be acted just as much as, or more than, he can act), which forms a conceptual pair with that of the actor, is used less frequently, and then in theoretical writings rather than empirical analyses.
8. On this point, we very clearly part company with many authors and in particular with Louis Dumont, who relies on his analysis of the boldest

individualistic features of what he calls 'modern ideology' to postulate a relentless antinomy between the individual and society. His thinking turns individualism (and the individual) ultimately into an absolute
opposition whose other term is holism (or society). In this analytical
construction which reproduces a brutal and commonplace ideological
structure, the individual is inevitably defined by contradiction with society
or independently from it, as a 'moral, independent, autonomous and
(essentially) non social being'. See Dumont, op. cit. pp. 273–4. A definition of the individual marked to such an extent by individualistic
ideology can undoubtedly be more useful in the field of demarcation
and interpretation of ideas than in that of empirical analysis of international political phenomena, which is our concern here.

9. Our distinction resembles, although with different formulations and
probably some slight differences, that proposed by Pierre Birnbaum
and Jean Leca as editors in their presentation of *Individualism: Theories and Methods* (Oxford: Clarendon, 1990). See also R. Bhargava,
Individualism in Social Science: Forms and Limits of a Methodology
(Oxford: Clarendon, 1992).

10. We will consider the terms 'world politics' and 'international politics'
as strictly equivalent, although common use has introduced in most
cases a difference in meaning between the two. A well-established
semantic and conceptual polarization, which reflects a well-known
antinomy, leads to a distinction between 'interstate politics', 'international politics', 'world politics', and 'global politics'. It should be
noted that realist and neo-realist authors who are under the semantic
influence of the interstate approach talk about 'international politics'
but feel very reluctant to talk about 'world politics' and naturally prefer to ignore 'global politics'.

11. J. N. Rosenau proposes the notion of 'frontier'. See James N. Rosenau,
*Along the Domestic–Foreign Frontier: Exploring Governance in a Tur-
bulent World* (Cambridge: Cambridge University Press, 1997).

12. Thus an absence of additivity which can be confirmed by the characteristics of the residue left when unwisely subtracting the 'smallest'
(the interstate) from the 'biggest' (the extra-domestic): i.e. the de-
scribable but politically unintelligible odds and ends of transnational
phenomena, if one tries to examine them without reference to states.

13. An example of the first type, which is a plea in defence of the explanation of international politics by specific and systemic interstate causes,
can be found in Kenneth Waltz, *Theory of International Politics* (Reading,
Mass.: Addison-Wesley, 1979) chs 2, 3 and 4. For an example of the
second kind, which seeks to theorize the bifurcation of world politics
into two worlds, see James N. Rosenau, *Turbulence in World Politics:
A Theory of Change and Continuity* (Princeton: Princeton University
Press, 1990).

14. See Jean-Jacques Rousseau, 'L'état de guerre' in *Ecrits sur L'Abbé de
Saint-Pierre, Oeuvres Complètes, III* (Paris: Bibliothèque de la Pléiade,
Gallimard, 1964) pp. 604ff and *Le contrat social, Oeuvres Complètes,
III*, ditto, I–IV pp. 356–7.

15. The modern or 'individualistic' meaning of the word *individu* seems

to have been well-established in France as early as the middle of the eighteenth century.

16. See Jean-Jacques Rousseau, *Lettres écrites de la montagne, Oeuvres Complètes, III* (Paris: Bibliothèque de la Pléiade, Gallimard, 1964) pp. 826–7.

17. See Edward Hallett Carr, *The Twenty Years' Crisis, 1919–1939* (London: Macmillan, 2nd edn, 1949) chs 2 to 5.

18. See for instance a study inspired by critical theory about the relations between men who are citizens and those who are not in the theory of international relations: Andrew Linklater, *Men and Citizens in the Theory of International Relations* (London: Macmillan, 1982). On the unwilling and late rediscovery of individualism by feminist studies, see in this volume Chapter 5 by Anna Leander.

19. On the relative subversion of the subject in post-modernism, see Pauline Marie Rosenau, *Post-Modernism and the Social Sciences: Insights, Inroads, and Intrusions* (Princeton: Princeton University Press, 1992) pp. 42–61.

20. Rosenau, *Turbulence in World Politics*, op. cit.

21. See especially 'The Tourist and the Terrorist' in James N. Rosenau, *The Study of Global Interdependence* (London: Frances Pinter, 1980) pp. 73–105.

22. This 'individual parameter', both disturbed and disturbing, is defined according to a constellation of four elements supposed to be closely linked – feelings of loyalty on the part of individuals towards the collective categories to which they belong, their behaviours of submission to the holders of authority, their ability to analyse world politics and its scenarios, and lastly their 'cathectic' ability to be moved by an external problem, even a remote one.

23. See Raymond Boudon, 'The Individualistic Tradition in Sociology' in Alexander, Giesen, Münch and Smelser (eds), op. cit. pp. 45–70.

24. See Joel David Singer, 'The Level of Analysis Problem in IR', *World Politics* 14 (1961) pp. 77–92.

25. On this point, see Heinz Eulau, *Micro–Macro Dilemmas in Political Science* (Norman, Okla.: University of Oklahoma Press, 1996) pp. 124–5. In fact, level of analysis and unit of analysis are two very different notions, but they are almost always related, often in an intuitive and rather vague manner, to a same scale of size, which has the effect of seeming to link them together ('micro unit for micro level' or 'meso level for meso unit', and so on).

26. The absolute separation of these two forms of individualism is only really tenable if we assume that a methodological concept can even be exempt of any ontological denotations and connotations. For pleas in defence of this, see contributions by Raymond Boudon and Jon Elster in Birnbaum and Leca (eds), op. cit.

27. On this particular form of individual disengagement, see F. G. Bailey, *The Kingdom of Individuals: An Essay on Self-respect and Social Obligation* (Ithaca: Cornell University Press, 1993).

28. The research and the systematic collection of all elements of analysis in international relations which come from an individualistic

methodological approach, even in an embryonic or imperfect way, would undoubtedly be a very useful prerequisite.

29. For a close analysis of holistic thought in social science, see D. C. Phillips, *Holistic Thought in Social Science* (Stanford: Stanford University Press, 1976).

30. See Klaus-Gerd Giesen, 'Entre décisionnisme et structuralisme: La précarité de l'éthique individuelle dans les théories des relations internationales' in Michel Girard (ed.), *Les individus dans la politique internationale* (Paris: Economica, 1994) pp. 25–38.

31. Apart from Chapter 5, not previously published, all chapters in this work are repetitions, often substantially rewritten, of the chapters of a book published in French: Michel Girard (ed.), *Les individus dans la politique internationale* (Paris: Economica, 1994). Chapter 6 is a translation of the original text. Chapters 3 and 7 have been revised. Chapters 4, 8, 9 and 10 have been substantially rewritten. Chapters 1 and 2 were almost totally rewritten, and can therefore be considered as new pieces of work. Chapters 1, 8 and 9 were translated from French by Delphine Wharmby, and Chapter 6 by Ania Thiemann.

32. To the well-known phenomena of combination or composition which characterize situations of multi-causality in a simple and homogeneous space, we can also add here the less well-known phenomena of aggregation or emergence, which are characteristic of complex and heterogeneous spaces offering several distinct levels to the analysis.

2 Individuals and their Influence on the International System
Michael Nicholson

INTRODUCTION

How far individuals can influence the behaviour of the international system, or indeed the domestic political system, is a perennial issue of debate. In many ways individuals feel buffeted about by a system which is impersonal and impervious to any views they may have as to its operation. Even in democratic societies, individuals often feel helpless, perceiving themselves either as the victims of venal and scheming politicians or alternatively of politicians who themselves appear to have little control over the system in which they ostensibly hold power. The disillusionment with politics which many journalistic commentators claim to detect is perhaps the result of the feeling that the system is out of the control of any individual or group whether within the formal political structure or outside it.

However, whether the system is out of control or 'turbulent' is a matter of analysis. They are not necessarily the same thing. This increase in turbulence in the international system has been noted and analysed by James Rosenau.[1] A more optimistic view than that reported in the first paragraph is that the increase in turbulence has made it possible for individuals outside the formal political structure to have greater impact on the behaviour of the system than was earlier the case and that this possibility is being exploited. Political and social activism outside the established political structures can be more effective. In this paper I shall examine to what extent this claim is justified and what are the conditions for effective action by individuals and groups both within and without the formal political system.

However, the concept of the significance of an individual in the international system is itself ambiguous. I suggest three different ways in which individuals can be significant. First is the case of an individual who has a role within a political system such as Prime Minister or within another actor such as a multinational corporation. To what extent can an individual within the role make a difference, or are all Prime Ministers, Presidents and so on essentially creatures of their roles with very little ability to transcend them, however much they may wish to? Does it matter who is Prime Minister or, for that matter, who is Pope? Similarly is the managing director of a multinational corporation, who derives power from the role in the firm, able to make much difference? The second case is that of the individual who is outside the political system but trying to influence its behaviour. In this case, I regard an individual as not necessarily literally a single person. It could be a group such as Greenpeace which has few economic resources compared with the other actors they are trying to influence. What significance do they really have? They appear to have put issues on the political and economic agenda but perhaps these issues would have appeared anyway. The third case is of the individual who is working outside the central political system but who is trying to replace the system by revolutionary or quasi-revolutionary means. Thus we can ask whether Gandhi as an individual made a difference to Indian independence or the Ayatollah Khomenei to the Iranian revolution. Would a substitute Gandhi have been forced to do the same sort of things, and did what Gandhi did make any real difference to what happened? These different ways in which individuals can be relevant raise related but different points which I shall elaborate.

There is another type of individual which does not fall into any of the classes above, namely the individual person, such as George Soros or Rupert Murdoch, who has resources comparable to the other actors such as states with which they are dealing. They are actors in their own right. Their influence is direct and not due to their role within an organization. I shall not deal with this other class of actor beyond saying that it seems clear that they do have an influence.

Basically my argument will be as follows. The power of individual actors varies according to the sort of social system they are operating in. I emphasize social system in that I am not referring to the political system alone but the whole social system of which it is a part. Some social systems are stable in structure such that there is relatively little freedom of manoeuvre. The basic pattern of the behaviour of the system will be much the same irrespective of the actions of a single actor within it. A competitive market in an established product is of this form. It does not mean that an individual has no influence; they might modify the product somewhat, for example. However, anything they do can only have a small effect on the behaviour of the system in question. There are other social systems which are less stable in that the overall pattern of behaviour can be significantly altered as a consequence of relatively minor variations in the inputs. 'Minor variations' can be interpreted as the actions of a few individuals. Famine relief systems are possibly of this nature. Finally, I argue that, even in the case of basically stable systems, where in general individuals have little influence, there can be 'switching points' where the system is poised between two very different forms of behaviour. It can move onto one pattern rather than another as a consequence of minor differences in behaviour on the part of the actors. International crises are sometimes examples of this, where a basically stable pattern of relationships between some states is interrupted by a brief unstable period where the result could be determined by such things as the personality of the actors.

As there is great scope for ambiguity, I shall clarify some terms. I can restate some concepts from earlier in this vocabulary. A political actor is an organization such as a state which has in some sense a corporate identity. Multinational Corporations, the UN, the World Bank and the Vatican are all organizations in this sense. They have large resources as compared with an individual. An individual actor is an actor whose resources are small. Hence, political and individual actors are defined in terms of one another. However, as mentioned before, an individual actor is defined more broadly than a literal individual human being, though individuals in the conventional sense are included within it. It is a useful definition inasmuch as there is a discontinuity in resources, though there is almost certainly an ambiguous middle ground. The questions we posed at the beginning can be restated. First, how important are individual actors occupying roles directly within political actors in altering what would otherwise have been the decisions of the political actor? Secondly, how important are individual actors in contexts where they are operating at the same level as the political actors but trying to effect the behaviour of the political actors from the outside and perhaps in conflict with them? The third is when individual actors are trying to displace political actors by replacing them. We are particularly concerned with the problem of whether the significance of individuals in either context has increased in recent decades due to the increase in turbulence. We shall concentrate on the first two of these questions.

First I shall approach the problem obliquely and discuss an example to illustrate the conceptual problem of individuals acting within structures. The underlying debate revolves around the question of how much freedom of action the individual has and how much is dictated by the social system or systems of which they are a part. Consider the case of Hitler. Was it because of his decisions that the Second World War broke out at the time and in the way it did, or would it have happened anyway as a consequence of the underlying social forces within the domestic political system or in the international system? If the latter, when was the outcome determined? At Versailles? Or at the Big Bang? Much of the debate about the problem assumes Hitler as an individual was crucial. In their classic dispute over the origins of the Second World War, both A. J. P. Taylor (1971) and Hugh Trevor-Roper (1971) take it for granted.[2] However, it is arguable that in fact Hitler had little freedom of manoeuvre. He did what he had to do, both internally and externally, in order to maintain his power (which does not mean that it was not temperamentally congenial to him). There were many rivals for the role of dictator of Germany who would quite readily have replaced him had Hitler not ruthlessly put them down. Like him, they would have followed the policies of external expansion and internal repression involving a particularly savage anti-Semitism. These were popular and brought general approval. Thus, the argument runs, whoever had been in power, they would have had to follow more or less the policies Hitler followed or they would have found themselves ejected from office. Given the mores of the time, this means they would have been executed. Thus, the combination of the internal political and economic system and the external international system determined the outcome, and Hitler was a mere pawn of these systems.[3] Machiavelli argued that the Prince should recognize the constraints of the system conceived of as other actors (though admittedly he did not phrase it in quite this way). Hitler followed Machiavelli's precepts.[4] The difficulty with these two views of the rise of Nazism is that it is not clear what sort of evidence we would need in order to choose between them. A few more facts are unlikely to help. Our theories of social systems are still inadequate to tell us how much the structure of the system matters and how much individuals matter in determining the direction a system takes. This issue exemplifies some of the problems which face us in trying to decide the individual's influence on the international system, though we are more concerned with people in less formal political roles. This paper aims to clarify some of the issues involved, though it does not solve them.

MORE ON THE INDIVIDUAL

In the conventional and everyday sense of the word, an 'individual' is an individual person. We are using it more broadly in the present context to mean a social grouping outside the formal political system, or the 'establishment' of people who might be expected to have influence on the political system. Earlier it would not have been thought that such groups would have an influence on the international system. Thus a pressure group such as Greenpeace has had some impact on policies and raised a number of issues to the political agenda which, one suspects, would not have been noticed, or at least not as quickly. However, while some individual people have been important within such organizations, they are typically not the creation of one individual person without whom the organizations would not have existed. Had any single individual leader of Greenpeace fallen under a bus, the organization would still have operated in its general form. However, a small group of like-minded individual people were necessary to get the organization going and provide the energy and special resources to get it moving. One can imagine a world without Greenpeace or without an effective Greenpeace. I shall treat Greenpeace as an individual in this broader sense and similarly such organizations as Amnesty, Oxfam, the Peace Movement and so on.

In non-structural accounts of the international system, whether realist or pluralist, the individual always did have a role. In the extreme case of absolute monarchy, the individual, namely the monarch, clearly was extremely important. Similarly the monarchs' advisers had important roles such as the grand Cardinals of France, Richelieu and Mazarin. The Tsar of Russia was likewise an individual of importance as were his wife and the dreadful Rasputin. In later years dictators took over the role and Hitler and Stalin were people of enormous influence. In less autocratic regimes, even full democratic regimes, the individual is accorded significance, so

Roosevelt, Chamberlain and so on all had influence within their respective societies and, in these cases, on the world at large. Churchill, in the 1930s, probably had some influence where his role in the political structure of the day is ambiguous, though by most standards he was an insider.

This, however, is only part of the problem. The people in this sort of analysis who have influence have it by virtue of the position they have acquired or inherited within the orthodox confines of the relevant political system. They may be able to manipulate the roles they are in, but they are roles none the less. One question about individuals is how much roles are manipulable such that it is significant which individual holds the position in that they can make significantly different decisions. A second question is rather different. In the modern world, can people who have no established roles, whether formal or informal within a political system, influence the behaviour of the international system? Rosenau's analysis implies they can. However, it is not clear from Rosenau's analysis whether the holders of roles have greater or lesser freedom of manoeuvre than before.

WHAT DOES 'HAVING AN INFLUENCE' MEAN?

We need to consider more carefully what it means for anyone to have influence on the international system or indeed any other form of social grouping. We can restate the issue as asking when are decisions genuine in that someone or some group can decide to do A instead of B, where A and B have significantly different consequences. They must have the ability or resources to bring the decision about. If we talk about a decision we must talk about a decision taker which, at least in the normal usage of the words, must either be an individual or a small group. Only a strict structuralist would claim that decisions are totally determined by the structure of the system and hence are always pseudo-decisions where the consequences are pre-determined. Those who are not complete structuralists believe that decisions are at times real and have consequences which could have been otherwise. Hence individuals or individual groups have always existed. Thus the question needs re-stating. In recent times have the individual would-be decision-makers which have existed in pluralist societies who are outside the normal political structure become important actors in a way they have not been before?

Clearly if we say that individuals have influence we mean that they can do something which will make a difference. Had they refrained from doing it, something other than the actual consequence would have happened. This is almost trivial. However, it does imply something about the system they are in. It means that the system they are in is not totally determinist, for if it was, nothing they did would make any difference. However, nor must it be totally random, for they must have some knowledge of the likely consequences of an act otherwise one has no basis for choosing one course of action rather than another. Thus, there must be some degree of structure to the system. It might be an uncertain system such that a decision-maker is choosing between alternative probability distributions but there must be some basis for thinking that one course of action will lead to one distribution and another lead to another where the two are noticeably different from each other. If a system is too turbulent, we are in trouble. We may know that individually our actions will make a difference, but if we have no idea what this difference will be we are as powerless as if they made no difference at all. If the weather system is chaotic in the sense of chaos theory,[5] which seems to be the prevailing opinion, then it might be the case that my singing in the bath will provoke a hurricane in the West Indies in six months' time (a sort of debased butterfly effect). However, there is no way of my knowing this, or of anyone else knowing it either. In fact, there is no way of knowing even in retrospect. My singing is as likely to stop a hurricane as start one, but as there is absolutely no way of my knowing there is no basis for making a rational choice. If I dwell on my awful powerless power, I shall only become deeply neurotic and perhaps behave in ways which might have goodness knows what further consequences for the weather system, but more predictable effects upon the micro-social systems of which I am a part. Hence, to have influence, we must be able to alter the future state of affairs in a way which is to some extent predictable.

There are three points of clarification I wish to make here. First, the basic question is whether one or a small group of actors can make a large difference to a system of which they are only a small part such as the international system. In the small micro-systems such as a family of which they are larger parts, people can and presumably do make a big difference irrespective of the degree of influence possible on larger structures. It is consistent to regard the big system as predominantly structurally determined, while believing that the individual has a large role in small groupings.

Secondly, to say that an individual has a small influence on a system does not mean small influences are not worthwhile. Thus, sending blankets to victims of a war has an influence – it keeps people warm, though in proportion to the number of blankets sent. It is perfectly consistent to argue one has the influence at the level of individual actions which yield proportional results, while believing in a broadly structuralist view of social systems in which, for example, no individual can end a war (or only under the special circumstances discussed below). Finally it follows from the first argument that the general issues of determinism and free will are not relevant to the argument. The argument is not about total determinism but about the constraints on choice in a world in which there is some freedom of decision.

STRUCTURES AND CHOICES

Models of social systems can be broadly categorized into two. Those where the structure is dominant and which dictate the behaviour of the individual actors (in Kaplan's terms these are system-dominant[6]) and those where decisions can really make a difference (subsystem-dominant). The first of these encompasses holist views where it is argued that the behaviour of the system cannot even in principle be understood by some sort of aggregation of the individual actors and those which are system dominant but nevertheless not holist. That is, though the aggregate of the system determines the behaviour of the system, nevertheless the aggregation is in the last analysis that of the behaviour or characteristics of the individuals in some possibly complex aggregative sense. This is the form of systems dominance found in the classical model of perfect competition or in international relations in the Waltzian system.[7]

We can restate the issue of structure and decision. Consider the concept of a decision. Clearly there is some degree of constraint on the options a decision-maker in the international arena can in fact choose from, which is dictated by the environment. These constraints are partly physical, partly dictated by other actors in the international system, and partly dictated by domestic actors who are normally peripheral to the international system such as divisions within domestic political parties. (We may wish to say that these are international actors also inasmuch as they have influence outside their purely local concerns.) The constraints imposed by this environment we can call the system. The question is how much the system constrains the decision-maker. Even in very free environments there must be some constraints. On the other extreme, it is possible that constraints determine everything and there is no freedom of decision. The disagreements concern how tight these constraints are and how variable they are in different situations. Unfortunately it is not easy to see how this issue is decidable or how it could be decided, but I shall leave that problem aside here. I will argue, however, that the degree of constraint varies very radically in different systems.

I shall classify the number of types of system which are of interest for the present argument into three. The Type 1 system is the system exemplified by the model of perfect competition in economics (or the Waltzian model in international relations). Each actor in the system is constrained by the actions of all the actors behaving together in the system. The group of actors effectively if unconsciously determines the rules of the system. If actors do not follow the rules they are forced out of the system or are penalized in some way because of their failure. In system Type 2, many opportunities for certain sorts of behaviour are offered in a context where there are many potential actors who can move into the system. Thus, the opportunities are almost bound to be taken up. In general we would expect these systems to be stable in the sense that small variations in the inputs into them lead to small changes in their behaviour. However, this point will be dealt with in more detail later. System Type 3 is a variant of the second in which the system offers opportunities but where the number of potential actors is small and thus they may not be taken up. It is this last type of system which is particularly relevant to the present problem. We shall return to it in the next section after elaborating the different forms.

System Type 1: A classic case is the model of the perfectly competitive market. If there are a large number of actors in a market, with cost conditions given by other markets and the technical factors of production, then the price, quality produced and so on will be determined. The model is analysed in terms of stylized decision-making processes where businesses try and maximize profits. A firm which fails to do so will go out of business. The choice facing an actor in such a system is between the two rather extreme alternatives – to maximize profits in accordance with the rules of the system or find oneself ejected from the system. Real life may not be quite so stark, but the point that decision is restricted is a valid one. Notice that this is not to say that one cannot explain the behaviour of markets in terms of the individual actors, but that it is trivial to do so if the market is truly perfect. Clearly the individual is left out of account in that there is essentially no range of decision available for them to choose from. The 'captains of industry' are merely pawns enslaved to the system. When there are imperfections, which is normal, the analysis of individual firms is restored to a place of interest and importance. Waltz's analysis of the international system is rather similar. The actions of the individuals as a group determine the system, and it is only in terms of the system that the behaviour of individual states can be understood properly. It follows that, even if the state is ruled by an absolute monarch or an absolute dictator, the range of choice is very limited and even these privileged individuals have no effective control over the system. Other actors who have no role within the political system are even more excluded from influence.

System Type 2: In the Type 1 system we assumed there were actors who were compelled by the forces of the system to behave in certain ways. New actors can enter such a system of course, but the centre of interest is on how the system behaves when it is in operation. We shall now consider the case where a broader social system permits various sorts of activities and opens the opportunity for system change. Further, the circumstances are such that there are many potential actors, so that some will almost certainly participate in the change. The British economic and social system in the last decades of the eighteenth century was in just such a position. The conditions were such that an Industrial Revolution was possible. Individuals did not decide to have an Industrial Revolution: it was the consequence of large numbers of people pursuing narrower goals. The structure of the economy and society was such that various decisions were possible or had consequences which would not have occurred at other times. Various technical discoveries were possible in the Middle Ages and may indeed have been made. However, they had no practical consequences. Capital was not available, nor was transport sufficiently developed or safe from attack for the sort of large market necessary for industrial production to develop. Given those structures, which emerged from a whole range of other decisions about totally different issues, the decisions followed rather naturally. They were taken by a lot of people and no individual made very much difference. If James Watt had not invented the steam engine someone else would have done, and the history of the Industrial Revolution would have been substantially unaltered.

Another case, closer to the subject matter of this paper, is that of the nineteenth-century expansion of the European powers into less economically developed parts of the world such as Africa, and the intensification of the expansion into other parts such as the Indian sub-continent. One explanation of this is in terms of the Hobson/Lenin theory of imperialism as a consequence of the falling rate of profit on capital as more capital was accumulated. Even if this explanation is not accepted in its purest form, it would seem a remarkable coincidence that a number of states should feel the urge to be expansionary all at more or less the same stage of economic development. For the most part the urge for expansion did not initially come from governments but from trading and commercial interests. In some cases, such as that of the British, the governments watched the processes with some concern in case they were going to cost a lot of money. It was only later that empires became symbols of macho-nationalism and enthusiastically backed by governments. Once again, though, we have a system which provided a lot of opportunities, the internal economic systems which provided the push factors, and many people who were in a position to take advantage of those opportunities. The structures of the social system determined both opportunities and the opportunities available to grab them. What one individual failed to do, another individual would step in and do.

Both Type 1 and Type 2 systems appear to lead to highly structured, possibly deterministic systems. I shall qualify this later, but it is certainly the case that the general direction of their development is primarily determined by the characteristics of the system and very little by any small interference such as would be possible for an individual to interject. This is not true of Type 3 systems. As they are of direct relevance to our basic problem, I shall now devote a section to them.

FLEXIBLE SYSTEMS

Type 3 structures are variants of Type 2, but the differences are significant. Type 2 involved structures in which there were many opportunities and many people who had a powerful interest in taking them, so the result was more or less inevitable. In Type 3, the opportunities are there but there is a shortage of people who have powerful motives to take them up. For example, chronic famine has been widespread in the world but it rarely attracts much attention. However, when attention is drawn to a particular famine then something can be done. Thus, the individual Bob Geldof and Live Aid did manage to have an influence, where it is by no means clear that if Geldof had not acted someone else would. It is arguable that this did not effect the political structure of the world but it did have some affect on the lives of the people in question. On a longer-term basis such organizations as Oxfam and Christian Aid raise consciousness and funding for the alleviation of physical distress and, modestly, for some sort of development. Other organizations such as VSO (Voluntary Service Overseas) add to development in a way which would probably not be done if it were left to the formal political processes alone.

Other individual groups which might be said to have broader political influence while lacking a formal role are groups like Amnesty. Amnesty is not an integral part of the political system and one can imagine a world in which it did not exist. Political repression is a part of the internal systems of many states. It could go unnoticed, but a small group of individuals keeps many issues on the political agenda even if it frequently inconveniences and annoys both those who practise the repression and those who find their profitable intercourse with such regimes embarrassed when the abuse of their supposed ideals is pointed out. For organizations like Amnesty to exist at all, and certainly for them to have influence, requires in itself certain sorts of structures. Thus, it requires some societies to act as a base which is comparatively pluralist and permits embarrassing organizations to function and acquire a few necessary resources. The issue of resources should not be neglected, as they in practice consist mainly of voluntary or poorly paid labour and grants from benevolently inclined foundations which are nevertheless likely to be limited in resources as compared with governments (particularly if they are promoting activities which are challenging to governments). However, pluralism does not guarantee that such organizations exist; it merely permits them. It is in just such circumstances that individuals can act in ways which influence the international system.

THE PROBLEM OF UNCERTAINTY

Following Rosenau, I am accepting that the world consists of many more actors than hitherto. Further, these actors are heterogeneous in kind. In the nineteenth century, many major features of the international system could be described adequately in terms of states interacting with each other as interpreted in the realist theory of the international system. Even then the centrality of states can be disputed. Imperialism was only partly a state or inter-state phenomenon, and many aspects of the international political economy cannot be explained in this way. Nevertheless states were important; and furthermore the system as a whole was simpler. Broadly the smaller number of actors in a system and the more homogeneous they are, the more orderly is the system as a whole and, in a weak sense, more predictable. Thus, in the nineteenth-century international system, when decision-makers took decisions, they had some general idea what the consequences were likely to be.

The present-day international system is much more complex and, at least partly because of this, it is less orderly and predictable. Not only are there many more actors but the actors are very diverse. States themselves are very different, ranging from liberal Western such as the Scandinavian states to revolutionary Islamic such as Iran. There are big difficulties in mutual comprehension. States are also much more numerous than in the nineteenth century, or even in 1945. Further there are economic organizations of many different sorts including the multinational corporation, campaigning organizations such as Amnesty, religious groupings such as the Roman Catholic Church and so on. Thus the range of interactions is much broader than in the nineteenth century. This is indeed what we mean by turbulence in the international system. It partly comes because entry into the system, in the sense of being able to interact directly with the major actors and sometimes effectively, is much easier. Not only are there more actors doing lots of different things but the whole network of relationships which any single actor should notice becomes more complex with many alternative states. One immediate example is the break-up of the Soviet Union, which has replaced the relatively simple structure of the Cold War days with many actors whose behaviour and interactions are scarcely known. However, another aspect of turbulence is uncertainty. The sheer size and range of the interactions in the present international system means that it is harder for a decision-taker to predict the consequences of any action. As I stressed before, effective action means not only that it is possible to take a decision which has significant consequences but that one should know what those consequences are. Thus, though it is easier for individuals to enter and to act within the current international system than in earlier times, the uncertainty reduces the efficacy of the actions, and indeed the actions of all other people within the system. This is what I shall call the paradox of participation.

Because of the greater turbulence in the system it is much easier for actors, including individuals in my definition of individuals, to enter the system and participate and have some impact on the more established actors. However, this itself makes for a problem. The increased number of actors and their very different natures means that there is greater uncertainty in the system. Hence they have less influence because there is greater difficulty in knowing just what the consequences of their actions will be.

The increase in turbulence and uncertainty can work in more than one way as far as the significance of individual groups external to the formal political system is concerned. Though individuals may be less able to cope with overall systemic uncertainty very well because of lack of resources, this may not matter very much. They can specialize in particular issues and both draw attention to problems and have a shrewder understanding of the options available and the probabilities of the various alternatives. Thus in some relevant subsystem they can cut down the uncertainty by simply knowing more about the subsystem. In some cases, such as those of standard forms of technology such as computers, information superhighways and the like, traditional organizations such as state or large state-blessed corporations undertake this. However, in many cases where there is no obvious profit in terms of money or power to the actors, it is left to other organizations. The environmental movement, particularly in its earlier days, was a good case in point. Essentially the environmental movement drew attention to some questions which no official body was geared up to ask. The questions were not in the domain of orthodoxy. In such cases individuals, in the broader sense of individuals, were able to make an impact in that the questions, once asked (or at least when asked a few thousand times), required at least some sort of response. An example of a protest movement which failed to secure the sorts of policy shift they demanded was the various European anti-nuclear movements both in the 1950s and 1980s. This could be described as saying that the appropriate bits of the international system were at that stage of Type 1 and insensitive to small perturbations in the system.

We can extend this notion. Inasmuch as the world is more complex it is harder to understand as a whole. It may not be inherently more uncertain,[8] but the fact that there is more to understand means that for anyone trying to understand everything as a whole, each bit of it is more uncertain for them in that they have not the opportunity to find out everything necessary about it. This leads to the opportunities for specialization, whether in geographical areas or in issues such as deep-sea fisheries. The specialists can assess the uncertainties much more effectively simply because they know more about the matters in hand. This applies also to funding organizations such as the various charitable trusts. They can specialize or hire specialists on issues which traditional political organizations cannot operate on or are not constructed to put on their agendas. Resources can then be allocated to problems which would otherwise go unsolved or perhaps even unnoticed. Hence more organizations, including informal ones, become significant. In a simpler world, the actors within the main political system could cope with all they needed to, particularly if they had a comparatively pliant and docile domestic constituency. With the greater complexity this has altered and more significant roles are being taken by individuals outside the conventional political structure.

This argument implies that individuals may have greater impact in specialist areas than political actors, though this is not necessarily the case. Clearly, in this regard, the political actors can behave like the individual actors and get more information about subsystems so as to reduce uncertainty in them. They may be less imaginative in doing so in novel areas, but they are good at doing so in more established areas. Within technological areas, for example, political actors tend to be rather good. However, one way for individuals to gain influence is to operate from within rather than in conflict with a political actor. Thus there is the rise of the epistemic communities. These are the groups of specialists in some particular area such as the environment who derive a common code of values due to studying and being concerned about the same range of issues. Peter Haas has studied environmental agreements in the Mediterranean and attributes the surprisingly high agreement amongst some very different and often mutually hostile regimes to the fact that the epistemic community dominated the discussions.[9] The various states were willing to accept that much of the debate was technical and leave it to the experts. However, these experts were much closer in their values about what they wanted to achieve than the politicians in more obviously political areas. They tried to keep the discussions as non-political as possible and to a large measure succeeded. This was in effect the influence of individuals within the political actors on the political actors' decisions. The epistemic community might be partly in and partly out of the political system. Thus, though the Pugwash movement (nuclear disarmament) was generally outside the political actors there was some degree of overlap. People who had been involved in the Pugwash were often also involved as individuals within governments, though sometimes at a later stage.

How influential individuals are within political actors sometimes depends on the sophistication of the political actors themselves. Thus in the case of some economic actors such as the oil companies, it is clear that the effective work of campaigning organizations has forced them to become much more sophisticated about such things as environmental issues and to acknowledge the significance of some of the objections to their activities. As far as states are concerned, there are big differences. Broadly the larger and richer states can take on board the complexities of the increasingly turbulent world. However, they are often prodded into activity both by individuals within and without the system which at times take the form of epistemic communities. Poorer states with smaller and over-burdened bureaucracies have greater difficulties. For this reason they may be more susceptible to the influence of individuals operating within the political system. Haas argues this in the case of the Mediterranean. The bureaucracy was only too willing to be relieved of a set of problems by the individuals and give them a lot of leeway. The more established bureaucracies, such as that of France, were much less ready to do so. It is possible that this is a general phenomenon, though I have no further information on it.

In summary, the increase in uncertainty in the international system due to turbulence affects the individual as an influence on the international system in contrasting ways. The increase in complexity and uncertainty makes all decision-taking less effective inasmuch as the consequences of decisions are harder to predict, particularly on a large scale. This is true of political actors and individual actors. However, the increase in holistic uncertainty increases the analysis of subsystems with a reduction in uncertainty in these more limited cases (which, like the environment, can still be significant). It is arguable that individual actors, whether working outside or inside the political actors, have an advantage here, so their relative position is improved by turbulence. This is perhaps particularly true in terms of putting new items on the agenda.

STABLE SYSTEMS AND 'SWITCH POINTS'

Type 3 systems give one form of structure in which individuals might make some difference to the behaviour if, as seems plausible, such systems are represented in the international scene. However, we should not give up too readily on the other types of system. There may be conditions where they likewise become sensitive to minor events.

Let us consider the following possibility. Suppose some social systems are by and large stable in the sense that small changes in the behaviour of one part of the system produce similarly small changes, but no more than small changes, somewhere else. Thus a single actor, certainly outside the formal political structure, can have only a little effect on the whole system. If this is the case, structural explanations are sufficient for most phenomena. However, there might be occasional points in the system where it is unstable and where a minor change in behaviour can have major consequences. I shall call such situations 'switch points'. There is nothing in the nature of either Type 1 or Type 2 systems which prohibits such behaviour. International crises, or some of them, might represent such switch points. Intuitively one feels this was the case with the Cuban Missile Crisis. The counter-factuals which would have resulted in nuclear war are many and all too credible. This picture of the structure of some international systems is very plausible, consistent with a lot of common-sense views of social systems.

Many dynamic models – that is, models in which changes and rates of changes in one period are determined by various features of preceding periods – involve 'switch points' of this sort where behaviour is qualitatively similar on one side of some boundary but takes on a very different mode at the other side of that boundary. A classic case in our discipline of international relations is the unstable version of the Richardson arms race model.[10] It involves just such boundaries where, on one side, the system moves off into an explosive arms race, while on the other it goes to disarmament. Safely on either side of the boundary, the behaviour of the arms acquisitions process is comparatively insensitive to minor changes in the initial position the system happens to be in. However, close to the boundary a small shift in the initial conditions can alter the behaviour of the system from one form of behaviour, say a disarmament pattern, to the radically different behaviour of explosive arms race or, of course, vice versa. Catastrophe theory[11] is a well-known class of mathematical model where such switches are central to the enterprise. Near such switching points, small changes in the details of the model, such as the personality of the decision-maker, or the influences on the decision-maker, can make a great deal of difference, and decision-making plays a central role. Posed in this way it suggests that we are dealing with governmental decision-makers, that is, the established decision-makers in the political system. However, if the behaviour of the system is very sensitive to the precise decisions, influences on those decisions, such as from pressure groups, can themselves be significant. Richardson himself believed the arms race system was at such a point in the 1930s and endeavoured to point it out, though he was regarded as a mad professor and ignored.[12] The wise mandarins of the British Foreign Office of the day were not well-versed in the intricacies of differential equations, though admittedly some scepticism was understandable. Whether Richardson was right or wrong in his analysis is still unclear. His general analysis has a lot to be said for it, though most scholars would be sceptical of his interpretation of the situation in the 1930s. The point, nevertheless, still holds. Some systems which are generally stable in the sense of being hard to shift are very sensitive to shifts at other points, as it is at just such points that the influence of small groups of individuals can have a great deal of effect.

Another instance of this is the internal situation in the former communist states. The economies having performed in a very dreary manner and in many cases verging on collapse, governments were open to any set of economic ideas available, particularly if they were markedly different from the ideas they had known so far. There were many options available but advocates of rather extreme and rapidly imposed free market solutions won the day. A small number of individuals advocating such solutions in the West appear to have been well-organized and supremely confident in their beliefs, and did have an important influence on the economic development (or lack of it) in the former Soviet bloc. Though I have no formal model of this process at this point, this is interpretable as a switch point where a system could have gone in a number of different ways according to relatively small shifts in the initial conditions.

CONCLUDING REMARKS

Though I think the significance of individuals and informal organizations has greatly increased in the modern world it is not without some precedent. When Einstein wrote to Roosevelt about the potentialities of an atomic bomb he was in the same situation of knowing a possible question which was not part of the range of questions which the political system at the time was capable of asking.[13] The experience of the Second World War made political systems only too adept at asking such questions in later years, namely the questions about technology. Now there are other types of questions which need posing but which neither the political system nor the conventional economic system can pose, and which therefore become the purview of individual. I believe this tendency has vastly increased, but it is not a total novelty.

One of the features which it is fashionable to point to in the current international system is a speed of communications which makes it possible for us to be aware of events immediately and watch the shelling of Sarajevo and similar occurrences as they happen. This is a factor which gives individuals a greater influence over some classes of events, but it can be exaggerated. The mere fact that we see events in real time, while making them more vivid, is not the only thing. Past atrocities were well publicized, as when Gladstone, admittedly an establishment actor, stumped Britain to denounce the Bulgarian Massacres, creating indignation rather like that at events in the former Yugoslavia over a century later. There was clearly a time-lag, but the indignation was just as great. Earlier, William Russell had broadcast the dreadful conditions of soldiers in the Crimea through his dispatches to *The Times*. The lack of immediacy did not stop them having a great impact. It may be that it is sometimes important in that it is necessary to correct some problem, but it is not clear that immediacy is more than one factor in giving us an understanding of the world beyond our doorstep.

This chapter is not very helpful as a set of recommendations to political activists, social revolutionaries or even funding agencies with an optimistic view of the future of the human race. The implication of the argument is that they look for opportunities which would otherwise go unnoticed. This is a reasonable enough proposition, but hardly a startling insight into the human condition. They might also look for systems which are close to a switch point or may get there in due course. The second recommendation is less self-evident than the first, and is easier said than done. Our knowledge of social systems is still woefully inadequate. Whether a social system such as the international system has a switch point anywhere and whether, at any particular time, we are near it, is something we know little about. The lack of knowledge has provoked a fashionable scepticism about whether such knowledge is possible. I believe it is, but this is an act of faith. Anyone with ambitions for altering the nature of the international system so that it functions in a more benevolent manner needs to consider as a central question which needs to be answered the issue of where small inputs can result in large outputs. In the meantime one can only plunge on in the hope that one is close to such a point. The turbulence argument suggests that there may be more of these points than there were before. This does not make their identification in advance any easier, though perhaps it means that we are more likely to trip over them by accident.

NOTES

1. James N. Rosenau, *Turbulence in World Politics: A Theory of Change and Continuity* (London: Harvester Wheatsheaf, 1990).
2. A. J. P. Taylor, 'How to Quote: Exercises for Beginners' and Hugh Trevor-Roper, 'A. J. P. Taylor and the War' and 'A Reply' in Esmonde M. Robertson (ed.), *The Origins of the Second World War: Historical Interpretations* (London: Macmillan Press, 1971).
3. Alan Bullock, *Hitler, a Study in Tyranny* (New York: HarperPerennial, 1991) and J. P. Stern, *Hitler: the Führer and the People* (Berkeley: University of California Press, 1975).
4. This argument does not abolish the problem of moral responsibility. Hitler took the decisions he did because he believed in them. He was not obliged to be the Führer. He survived because he held beliefs, almost certainly genuinely, which were widely popular. That these beliefs were structurally required by anyone hoping to remain in power in 1930s Germany does not excuse Hitler from the responsibility for these

beliefs and their appalling consequences. That the alternatives might not have led to his short-term survival does not alter the moral issues involved.

5. J. P. Mason, Mathias, and J. H. Westcott, *Predictability in Science and Society* (London: The Royal Society and the British Academy, 1989).
6. Morton A. Kaplan, *System and Process in International Politics* (New York: Wiley, 1957).
7. In fact, I am not quite sure that Waltz would particularly like this characterization, though he accepts and indeed introduced the analogy of the international system with the perfectly competitive economic system. See Kenneth Waltz, *Theory of International Politics* (Reading, Mass.: Addison-Wesley, 1979).
8. Concepts of 'inherent uncertainty' in referring to a system need handling with care, though I think the meaning is clear in this context. I discuss such issues in more detail (and more carefully) in Michael Nicholson, *Formal Theories in International Relations* (Cambridge: Cambridge University Press, 1989), ch. 4.
9. Peter Haas, *Saving the Mediterranean: the Politics of International Environmental Cooperation* (New York: Columbia University Press, 1990).
10. Lewis Fry Richardson, *Arms and Insecurity* (Pittsburgh: the Boxwood Press, 1960) and Nicholson, op. cit., ch. 8.
11. Tim Poston and Ian Stewart, *Catastrophe Theory and its Application* (London: Pitman, 1978) and René Thom, *Structural Stability and Morphogenesis: an Outline of a General Theory of Models* (Reading, Mass.: W. A. Benjamin, Inc., 1975).
12. Oliver M. Ashford, *Prophet – or Professor? The Life and Work of Lewis Fry Richardson* (Bristol and Boston: Adam Hilger Ltd, 1985).
13. C. P. Snow, *Variety of Men* (London: Macmillan, 1967) and Stern, op. cit.

3 The Skill Revolution and Restless Publics in Globalized Space

James N. Rosenau

To argue that individuals at the micro level are central to the course of events at the macro level of global politics is to evoke doubt and disbelief. Many analysts reject the proposition on the grounds that it does not really matter what individuals do at the micro level, that macro-level processes can be described, analyzed, and predicted without recourse to the conduct of citizens, that in world affairs the latter are, in effect, mere servants of the former. Put more elegantly, some contend that accounting for the behavior of citizens only completes our mental pictures of international politics by adding detail to our understanding of it. The attribution of causal power to individuals, such reasoning concludes, serves our moral consciences, but that is a far cry from servicing the requirements of cogent empirical inquiry.

The fact that this rejection of the micro-level proposition persists in the face of an extensive elaboration of the case for treating citizens as key variables in world politics[1] suggests that the case is flawed, or that it has not been adequately made, or that those who cling to the rejection are so deeply embedded in macro approaches as to be incapable of ascribing any causal power to micro phenomena. Lest either or both of the last explanations of the persistent rejection is sound, the initial task here is to restate briefly the core premises underlying the view that micro–macro interactions do matter, and then to undertake further elaboration by identifying four kinds of citizenship that can introduce variability into the processes whereby micro dynamics contribute to macro outcomes on the world stage.

Put differently, it is time to turn the table on the skeptics. The case for taking individual behavior seriously may be flawed, but the flaws have not been persuasively advanced. It is not enough simply to assert that systemic processes at the macro level are sufficient to explain macro outcomes. To be sure, if variations in the macro sources of these processes can be systematically linked to variations in the processes themselves and then to variations in the macro outcomes, there is no reason to examine micro phenomena. But propositions and findings descriptive of these links are conspicuously scarce in the literature on world politics. Rarely, if ever, do macro-level analyses account for enough of the variance to offset the proposition that unrecognized micro dynamics are at work.

So, if nothing else, it is time to give the skeptics pause, to make them so uncomfortable about their dismissal of the micro level that they are impelled to restate and defend more fully their strict macro perspectives. If they are resistant to probing the micro level empirically, at least they can clarify their theoretical bases for ignoring it.

CHALLENGING THE SKEPTICS

Stripped to its essentials, the case for viewing individuals as crucial to world affairs rests on four equally important premises. One is that citizens have become more analytically and emotionally skillful; and a second is that this skill revolution at the micro level matters, that through perceptual and aggregative processes citizens are shaping macro outcomes more extensively than they have in the past.[2] The third is that the macro system of world politics has entered a period of prolonged turbulence that is especially vulnerable to micro inputs.[3] The fourth is that new political space is being created by the dynamics of change[4] – what can aptly be called "globalized space"[5] – that enables individuals, on their own, to alter the life of their communities.[6]

Perhaps through no fault of their own, skeptics have misconstrued these premises in several significant ways: they have equated skills with information; they have thought in terms of individuals acting alone rather than collectively; and they have underestimated the extent of the authority crises that are part and parcel of the transformations presently sustaining global turbulence.[7] Accordingly, skeptics find it easy to dismiss the relevance of micro actors by highlighting the great gaps in peoples' information about world affairs (noting the proportion of poll respondents who are unable to identify the capital of Pakistan always seems a winning blow), and/or by stressing that the single person has neither adequate access to or influence in the political process to impact significantly upon it, and/or by noting the historical pattern wherein governmental authority is always being challenged. Accurate as these observations may be, however, they have little to do with the underlying argument.

To become more analytically and emotionally skillful is to be able to construct more elaborate scenarios, to discern more causal relationships, to be readier to accept complexity, and to have a greater capacity for focusing any emotions evoked by the perceived scenarios[8] – irrespective of the amount of information one may possess. What counts is not the capital of a country, but the capacity to trace events into and out of the capital regardless of its identity. One does not need to know the capital of Pakistan – indeed, one can be misinformed about its name and location – in order to grasp ominous stirrings in distant places and appreciate how these can trace a path to one's doorstep and pocketbook. To be sure, it may be the case that the more information people have, the more are they able to frame goals, sift alternatives, and make decisions; but analytic skills also derive from a host of sources and experiences unrelated to levels of information. Political wisdom can be acquired through families, work situations, and community crises – to mention only its more conspicuous sources.

It is not difficult, therefore, to make a strong case for viewing "the judgment of the general public ... under some conditions ... [as] equal or superior in quality to the judgment of experts and elites who possess far more information, education, and ability to articulate their views."[9] To fall back on the skimpy-level-of-information reason for rejecting the relevance of micro phenomena in world politics is thus to avoid confronting the challenge. Compared to the impressive indicators of effective citizen activities that mark the recent history of most countries of the world, the alleged information barrier comes close to being a rationalization for elitist perspectives.[10]

Similarly, reliance on the loneliness of individuals in an ever more complex world is profoundly misleading as a basis for dismissing the micro level. The individual does appear to be increasingly isolated and removed from the centers of societal power, and his or her solitary actions such as voting may well not make much of a difference; but this loneliness is beside the point. What counts are the processes whereby citizens join together to aggregate their preferences and actions through collective behavior. The presumption of increasing micro relevance rests squarely on the understanding that people, being more analytically and emotionally skillful and thus better able to assess where, when, and how collective action can be effective, are increasingly ready to pool their resources on behalf of shared goals. There is, I believe, overwhelming evidence that this greater readiness has become a permanent feature of the political landscape in a world rendered turbulent by the transformation of three of its prime parameters.[11] In town squares throughout eastern Europe, for example, citizens converged in 1989 to concert their energies against communist rule and, as a result, they toppled governments and hastened the end of the Cold War.[12] Much the same happened shortly thereafter in South Africa, except in this case the institutions of apartheid were toppled by a combination of collective actions in the country and concerted efforts abroad to press businesses and governments to withdraw support that helped sustain apartheid. To be sure, in Tiananmen Square and Rangoon comparable protests ended abruptly as the Chinese and Burmese governments turned the military on their own people, but the subsequent conduct of both governments with respect to human rights suggests a continuing fear that the capacity for collective action remains viable in both countries.

Some analysts have questioned whether the spate of collective actions were a temporary phenomenon, soon to be followed by citizens lapsing back into an earlier passivity;[13] but there is no evidence of a let-up in the resort of restless publics to collective actions as the first decade of the post-Cold War period comes to an end. On the contrary, if anything, the variety and duration of collective protests appear to have expanded considerably. Recent episodes in Korea, Canada, Yugoslavia, and Mexico are illustrative in this regard. In Belgrade citizens from all walks of life marched in the streets days after day for weeks protesting the canceling of local elections, and their prolonged efforts forced concessions from the Milosevic government that wrongly presumed the marches would peter out.[14] Korea, too, has been marked by continuing strikes protesting a new labor law, but in this case the protests were "not so much about gains in wages and working conditions as about protecting them," because the new law made it easier for companies to dismiss workers.[15] Likewise, in several Canadian cities "Days of Action" protests against budget cuts surprised the Canadians themselves, since they "do not easily take to the streets; it's just not their way." Indeed, as the same observer put it, "Deference to authority [in Canada] is declining, and Canadians are growing feistier as they seek control over their lives."[16] And in Mexico City "public demonstrations have become the voice of choice," with protests marches being so commonplace – 1,522 in the first nine months of 1996 – that "the right to free assembly has become insufferable."[17]

Nor are these recent examples the only basis for anticipating that the skill revolution and a growing proclivity for collective action is not a temporary phenomenon. Not only are systematic data now available that depict the expansion of elite skills across epochs and cultures,[18] but the accelerating pace of globalization points to continuing sources of uncertainty for people – for those in the middle classes as well as workers and those below the poverty line – that are sensitizing previously quiescent publics to distant scenarios that can so seriously alter their lives as to make them ever readier to engage in collective action. The aforementioned cases of Korea and Canada would seem to be good indicators of a straightforward consequence of globalizing dynamics. Indeed, the protests in Korea were interpreted as people "taking a stand against the global economic forces that brought investment and prosperity to low-wage Korea and now threaten to take it elsewhere."[19] Macro theories of international relations have yet to allow for the ways in which globalization may arouse publics,[20] but it may not be long before the insecurities fostered by mobile capital flows so pervasively agitate individuals at the micro level that macro theorists will have to broaden their lenses and refocus their concerns. In effect, they will have to allow for an acceleration and further globalization of the skill revolution.

The permanence of the collective-action pattern points up the danger of underestimating the extent of the authority crises inherent in this period of global turbulence. For the pattern reflects the transformation of the parameter wherein public agencies are less and less able to achieve the compliance of those over whom they have jurisdiction. Put simply, in all parts of the world national governments are becoming weaker while subnational and transnational organizations are becoming more coherent and effective.[21] Indeed, not only is today's news filled with accounts of citizens engaging in collective actions that challenge established authorities, but it is also pervaded with reports of them defying their own leaders. A front page of the *New York Times* is illustrative: on June 6, 1992, it carried a story from the Earth Summit in Rio that described "pressure from environmentalists in their own countries" as the reason several countries signed the biodiversity treaty,[22] another that quoted Serbian leaders as repeatedly insisting that the Serbian irregular forces spearheading the onslaught on Sarejevo "were not under their control,"[23] and still another report about the Haitian army, whose commanding general "is no longer in control of all his forces."[24]

In sum, the global context in which citizenship is claimed and practiced is especially intrusive in the present era. With people, economies, cultures, and polities becoming ever more interdependent, the larger forces playing upon citizens everywhere are sometimes liberating and sometimes constricting; but at all times they are relentless, complex, and substantial, often demanding adaptive responses even as they also invite habitual acquiescence.[25] The resulting crises of authority and legitimacy that pervade every region and continent pose difficult and unfamiliar challenges for modern citizens. Today their identity, their ethics, and their conduct are in question as the dynamics of change alter the boundaries, norms, and goals through which they relate to their fellow citizens. They now have more skills with which to cope with these challenges, but many of them appear to have lost their way politically, as if they are practicing what might be called citizenship without moorings.[26]

ALTERNATIVE CITIZEN ROLES

If it is thus reasonable to presume that the aggregation of preferences and actions of increasingly competent and restless citizens at the micro level are increasingly consequential for the conduct of world politics at the macro level – or if the reader is at least given pause in this regard – the analytic task becomes one of exploring possible systematic links between micro variations and macro outcomes. How, that is, might shifts in the conduct of citizenship contribute to corresponding changes in the conduct of societies, states, and international relationships? Here we seek to probe this question by differentiating among four types of citizenship that people in any society can practice on the basis of what I call their self–environment orientations. The core hypothesis underlying the analysis is simple: to the extent major shifts occur from one type of citizen orientation to another, so will traces of these shifts be manifest in the institutions and policies of macro collectivities and their relationships.

By a citizen's self–environment orientation is meant the appraisal people make of the relative worth of themselves and their societies. As can be seen in Table 1, by dichotomizing between high and low appraisals of both self and society, four distinct types of citizens can be identified. Those who are inclined to treat their own needs as far more important than those of society practice what can be called self-centered citizenship. Persons who have the opposite tendency and place society's needs well ahead of their own practice either of two forms of citizenship: those who have an incremental approach to societal problems practice altruistic citizenship, whereas those who proceed from an inflexible image of what societal life ought to be practice ideological citizenship. People who are skeptical about the responsiveness of macro politics to micro inputs or for other reasons attach little political significance either to their own or society's needs and are thus disinclined to enter the public arena, practice what can be regarded as apathetic citizenship. Finally, individuals who are deeply invested in the realization of both their own and society's needs are likely to practice a democratic form of citizenship. This balanced form approaches the democratic ideal in the sense that citizens are not unmindful of their own interests even as they recognize the necessity of also accommodating to the processes and goals of the larger collectivities to which they belong.

While self–environment orientations derive primarily from the way in which citizens assess the value of their interests relative to those of society, they are also shaped by a crucial perception, namely, how the individual perceives the interactive processes that sustain micro–macro relationships. The causal strength of micro factors relative to macro dynamics is never self-evident. Whatever may be the objective bases of micro–macro interactions, the interpretation of them can vary widely, from the total cynic who believes individuals can exercise no influence over the course of events to the unmitigated optimist who sees macro institutions as keenly responsive to micro inputs. It follows that cynics are likely to be attracted to forms of citizenship wherein minimal consequence is attached to actions at the micro level; they just cannot believe that anything they may do in the political arena matters, a belief that may well be so powerful as to offset the values they attach to their own or society's interests. Contrariwise, optimists are likely to be drawn to citizenship practices consistent with their view that societal institutions are malleable, that what they do counts. Strong convictions

Table 3.1 Four types of citizenship

Priority Attached to Society	Priority Attached to Self	
	Low	High
Low	PASSIVE or ALIENATED	SELF-CENTERED
High	ALTRUISTIC or IDEOLOGICAL	DEMOCRATIC

about political issues, in short, can be moderated by views of how the political process functions.

Neither the cynic nor the optimist, however, can be oblivious to the spectacular ways in which micro actions have been converted into macro outcomes in recent years. As previously noted, protesting citizens filling town squares have, more often than not, produced concrete and visible results in the form of revised policies and collapsed governments. And there is good evidence that such outcomes in one country embolden people elsewhere and that this contagion effect is a major factor in the rapidity with which change has come to the former Soviet empire, South Africa, and many other parts of the world. Never before, perhaps, has the sense of subjective competence felt by citizens everywhere been so thorough-goingly stimulated. They have literally witnessed, both in person and through television, micro stirrings reshape macro institutions.

Accordingly, while self–environment orientations can never be more than subjective appraisals developed through personal experience, society's socialization processes, and the impact of class, economic, political, and other objective circumstances that prevail at any moment in time, under globalizing conditions of rapid change new objective circumstances are likely to foster new self–environment orientations and shifting practices of citizenship. Our focus, in other words, is on the interaction of subjective orientations and objective circumstances. The latter are presumed to exert sufficient pressure on the former to foster pronounced patterns worthy of analysis, but this is not to predict the citizenship behavior of particular individuals. Because self–environment orientations are a product of personal experience and early socialization as well as prevailing realities, and not a little because the familiar moorings on the political landscape have become unhinged, there are bound to be some people who deviate from the expected pattern even though the pattern itself is likely to persist as long as there is no major alteration in the objective conditions which conduce to it. Whatever objective realities may prevail, in other words, any of the self–environment orientations can be practiced.[27] Although objective conditions may be favorable to a balanced, democratic citizenship, for example, some people will nevertheless by disposed toward ideological or apathetic forms of political involvement.

To note the subjectivity that underlies how people conduct themselves in the political arena is to remind ourselves of the difficulties that attach to probes into the micro underpinnings of political systems. We can recognize and trace the macro patterns, and these may well become so habitual as to endure for decades, but even so they rest on subjective foundations that are capable of great volatility in times of enormous change such as presently prevail.

The skill revolution constitutes a major source of the volatility fostered by global turbulence. As the analytic skills of citizens expand, so does their capacity to identify their own interests, to evolve scenarios of how the course of events will culminate on their doorstep, or to otherwise cope with the welter of complexity churned by the parametric transformations. For some of those mired in apathetic and ideological inclinations, their new-found skills are likely, other things being equal, to wrench them out of their habitual orientations and render them more ready to engage in either self-interested or democratic forms of citizenship. In some cases, on the other hand, the expanded skills may foster a greater sense of futility over the ability of micro actors to shape macro outcomes and thus move some self-interested and democratic citizens away from politics and into passivity and apathy.

In a like manner the worldwide authority crises that mark the present era are likely to have micro consequences irrespective of the type of citizenship people practice. Other things being equal, for example, the more citizens get caught up in the volatility of such crises, the more are they likely to redefine their self–environment orientations and undertake new forms of behavior in the political arena. In effect, the shifting lines of authority in their environment leave them with little choice but to reconsider how they want to conduct themselves.

New conceptions of territoriality are still another consequence of global turbulence that can be traced in all the citizenship types. With authority undergoing relocation "upward" toward transnational organizations and "downward" toward subnational collectivities, the meaning of territory – of geographic space to which historical and cultural significance is attached – is no longer as compelling as it once was. As a result, citizens of every orientation are subject to altered claims on their loyalties and, other things being equal, are thus more ready to redefine the balance between their own and society's interests.

But other things are rarely equal. Just as crises which lead to the relocation of authority can vary in their intensity, scope, and direction, so can the dynamics of the skill revolution be varyingly applied. Hence, in order to take note of the systematic under-pinnings of such variabilities, we need to look more closely at how each of the citizenship types has been affected by the cascading changes brought on by global turbulence, before turning to the question of how large-scale shifts in self–environment orientations can feed back as systematic agents at the macro level.

Self-Centered Citizenship

The distinguishing features of this manner of relating to the political arena are the high value attached to one's own interest and the low concern for the welfare of any larger collectivity. Most people are, properly, keenly attentive to their own needs and wants, ever ready to seek a minimum degree of comfort for themselves and their families. In this sense self-interests are a prime source of the power that propels political issues and sustains political processes. But many people are also preoccupied with the more encompass-ing systems to which they belong, partly because their own welfare is tied to the stability and progress of the larger system and partly because they also care about the values to which their societies are committed. Except as noted below, however, these larger concerns are essentially irrelevant to those who practice self-centered citizenship. Their focus on themselves is so extensive as to preclude appreciation of, and participation in,[29] macro institutions.

This is not to imply, however, that self-centered citizens are necess-arily inclined to advance their interests by exploiting the larger system. Such individuals can certainly be found in every corner of the world. Whenever possible, they cheat on their taxes, avoid regulations, disregard efforts to conserve resources, limit pollution, and so on through a long list of actions that could make a contribution to the welfare of their communities. They are the free riders of societies and, as such, their collective impact serves to exacerbate macro tendencies toward stalemate and fragmentation. If the larger society is unstable and incapable of addressing and resolving its major problems, self-centered citizens could care less as long as the disarray does not undermine their livelihood. If their way of life is endangered by societal disarray, of course, their keen attention to their own goals will lead them into momentary concerns for the macro system and to actions designed to preserve the status quo through which they have benefited.

It follows that as societies become increasingly fragile and unable to retain an underlying value consensus or institutional coherence, so will more and more individuals be inclined to restructure their self-environment orientations in the direction of self-centered citizenship. Indeed, the individual can be viewed as the ultimate subgroup, and it would not be difficult to amass evidence that this form of subgroupism has become increasingly rampant on a worldwide scale. One indicator along these lines is the difficulty that many military establishments are encountering in recruiting and retaining personnel.[30] Another, even more pronounced expression of self-centered citizenship is readily apparent in the rush to make money in liberalized economies, a pursuit that is often carried out oblivious to the well-being of others and, indeed, not infrequently takes the form of criminal behavior.

Nor are the tendencies toward self-centered citizenship confined to mass publics. Leaders in all walks of life are giving voice to subsystem values and neglecting to stress the virtues of whole-system cooperation and coherence. Rare today is a leader who speaks of the need to maintain balanced self-environment orientations. Rare are leaders who resign their position rather than yield to subgroupist impulses.[31] Rare are the heads of state or prime ministers who articulate a vision which stresses that societies cannot move forward without compromises in which people give up some of their personal needs on behalf of larger aggregates. Put differently, gross leadership failures throughout the world have undermined socialization processes and contributed to the emergence of new generations lacking the values necessary for whole-system progress and persistence.

While global turbulence may well be swelling the ranks of self-centered citizens at an exponential rate throughout the world, it needs to be stressed that not all of them are free riders. Some are self-centered, so to speak, by default. Due to the dynamics of turbulent change, they have no larger system for which they feel any attachment and to which they can devote their energies. They are not apathetic about the political arena, but either they are confused as to where they fit in it or they have been drawn into lines of work or lifestyles that transgress the traditional boundaries of politics. Instead of being free riders, they are either lost riders whose political homes have been swept away by authority crises or jet-set riders whose political homes have been transformed by an ever more globalized economy and the expanding webs of an ever more intricate global interdependence.

With governments weakening and subnational groups becoming more demanding, and with the established boundaries of political communities thus being called into question or overthrown, it seems likely that more and more citizens will lose their bearings. They may be inclined to care about the well-being of a larger system, but they no longer know what that system is and thus are compelled, by default, to practice self-centered citizenship. A quintessential illustration of such lost riders is provided by this comment in a letter to the editor of a Russian newspaper: "I am a citizen of a nonexistent state, and I don't know where I live. Is it the Commonwealth of Independent States, or is it the Russian Federated Republic? Is it Siberia, and is it the Sovereign Republic of Altai?"[32]

Similarly, although for entirely different reasons, jet-set riders have had to default to their own self-interests. In their case the larger national communities to which have been attached are less and less salient the more they become ensconced in new, transnational roles that orient them to see the world as their bailiwick. The product of ever greater interdependence and the globalization of national economies, these roles require their occupants to focus on concerns that extend well beyond national boundaries and that obscure the values into which they were originally socialized. Since there are no reasons to anticipate a slowing down of the pace of globalization, the ranks of jet-set riders seem bound to become more numerous, as the following account of the variety of new, transnational roles implies: "Commercial pilots, computer programmers, international bankers, media specialists, oil riggers, entertainment celebrities, ecology experts, demographers, accountants, professors, athletes – these compose a new breed of men and women for whom religion, culture, and nationality can seem only marginal elements in a working identity."[33] Put in terms of self-environment orientations, these new global roles have not only loosened their occupants from the psychological constraints of territory, but to a large extent they have also liberated them from the responsibility of worrying about the welfare of political communities.

Not all self-centered citizens, however, have been comfortable with their new roles in the global economy. For some the shedding of territorial commitments and responsibilities is worrisome, as if they retain their democratic self-orientation even though their line of work no longer contributes to their prior society. Consider, for example, the case of Americans who moved from long-time jobs in Detroit's automobile industry to comparable positions in Japanese firms producing Japanese cars in the United States. Consisting of designers, engineers, salespersons, public relations specialists, and manufacturing experts, these "Detroit expatriates" who committed their professional lives to the Japanese have apparently been increasingly confused by their citizenship as US–Japanese automotive competition intensifies. "Cast into a neutral space in terms of patriotism," they speak of "evenings when my wife and I look at each other and I think, 'I wish I could be doing this for an American company.'"[34] Yet, despite their concern that their new positions may seem like a betrayal, most of the expatriates are eventually able to accept and rationalize the political implications of their new positions. Some see their work as having helped the US by prodding its automobile industry into adopting higher standards. Others view themselves as having contributed to the creation of US jobs that offset Detroit's losses. Still others regard themselves "as ground-floor participants in the borderless economy, their positions in the industry transcending such quaint notions as them-against-us."[35] As one of them put it, "I could feel the shrinking of the globe in a very personal way. It's been overwhelmingly exhilarating."[36]

Whatever may be the extent to which self–environment orientations are turning in self-centered directions on a global scale, the result is a further weakening of governments and other institutional mechanisms for realizing collective goals and maintaining social order. Such is the central dynamic of macro–micro interactions in the present era. The macro arrangements work less and less well, thus turning micro actors inward, all of which further reduces the effectiveness of the macro arrangements.

Altruistic Citizenship

It will be recalled that this is one of two forms of self–environment orientations in which citizens treat society's needs as considerably more urgent and important than their own. It involves an incremental approach to the political arena, a focus on particular issues which come to be viewed as so salient or threatening as to warrant putting personal concerns aside, or at least achieving a perceptual convergence in which personal satisfactions are equated with societal goals and needs. In this sense, in the sense that such individuals come to focus so intensely upon larger problems that they ignore their own immediate interests, it is an altruistic form of citizenship. It is driven not by ideology in the sense of being a blueprint for society, but by a concern with one problem or issue at a time.

The quintessential expression of this form of citizenship is to be found among those who participate in social movements. The feminists, the environmentalists, the anti-war activists – these are people for whom a single set of issues is all-encompassing. They tend to have enough personal resources, or to be so ready to place societal concerns over their own, that they have or make the time necessary to engage in a wide variety of activities on behalf of their issue-based goals. For some of them the issue-oriented incremental approach becomes so much a way of life that they turn to new issues if and when the old one is resolved. An example here are members of the peace movement who moved on to environmental preoccupations when the end of the Cold War reversed the global arms race.

To a large extent transnational rather than national or subnational concerns serve as the driving force of altruistic citizenship. All the issues that sustain modern social movements involve global problems and thus the movements become informal networks of like-minded citizens in different parts of the world who communicate and converge episodically as the issues that draw them together surge and wane on the global agenda. It follows that altruistic citizens, like some of their self-centered counterparts, tend not to be oriented toward specific societies. But unlike self-centered citizens, the altruistic types have no sense of loss with respect to their political homes. Rather, their home takes on a global cast as they develop allegiances to issue outcomes. And their convictions along this line, reinforced by movement members elsewhere in the world, lead them to believe that micro actions can have desirable collective outcomes, that governments can be moved if enough people share in their efforts to bring about change. Indeed, it is reasonable to presume that no other form of citizenship stimulates deeper beliefs in macro–micro interactive processes than does the altruistic form. The image of a movement member engaging in protest behavior that leads them to be physically removed by police exemplifies the depth of their perception that micro actions can have cumulative consequences.

It seems plausible that the transformative consequences of global turbulence have also greatly enlarged the ranks of altruistic citizens. With governments weakened and lines of authority obscured, social movements have flourished with the onset of turbulence.[37] People are attracted to them because the movements are, so to speak, picking up the slack brought on by the globalization of national economies and the bifurcation of world politics into multi-centric and state-centric worlds.[38] Since interdependence issues such as environmental pollution, famine, AIDS, currency crises, terrorism, the drug trade, and the ozone gap cannot be addressed, much less managed, by governments alone, and since the informal structures of social movements are well suited to transgressing the boundaries that inhibit states from resolving these types of issues, individuals predisposed toward self–environment orientations that attach greater value to the environment than the self are likely to gravitate toward the transnational networks which social movements offer their members. Self-centered orientations, in short, are not the only form of citizenship spurred by globalization and the parametric transformations that have accompanied the onset of worldwide turbulence.

Ideological Citizenship

Although for very different reasons, there is a second type of person who attaches much greater importance to societal needs than to personal ones. Unlike the incremental approach of the altruistic citizen, the ideologue has a vision of the total society and is inflexible with respect to the basic principles on which the vision rests. Ideologues are more than ready to sacrifice their personal well-being on behalf of their larger blueprint. The image of an Iranian fundamentalist throwing himself into battle and seeking martyrdom on behalf of Islam captures well the extent to which the self–

environment orientation of ideologues is skewed in favor of the environment. It also highlights the large extent to which ideologues have faith in the processes through which micro actions can serve macro goals.

Of all the citizenship types identified here, it is probably the ranks of the ideologues that have been most diminished by the onset of global turbulence. The ever greater complexity of societal life, the dynamics of globalization, the pervasiveness of authority crises and the unmistakable tendencies toward political stalemate – not to mention how the collapse of the Soviet Union revealed the falsities of communism – have all contributed to a flight from rigid ideological formulations and a worldwide readiness to cast self–environment orientations in a more pragmatic context. To be sure, some personality types still cling to the rigidities that sustain ideologues and thus all societies will always have their ideological wings. In the present era, however, it seems likely that these wings will be small even as they will doubtless continue to be vociferous.

And how have the disaffected ideologues restructured their self–environment orientations? As indicated by trends in the former Soviet Union, many have turned toward a balanced set of orientations and come to subscribe to democratic citizenship practices. More accurately perhaps, such people were always predisposed in this direction even as they underwent the socialization processes of communist regimes. Accordingly, the collapse of communism made it easy for them to give expression to their underlying inclinations.

On the other hand, there is also considerable evidence that the transition to democratic practices have proven difficult, even impossible, for many in those lands that have thrown off the communist yoke. The heady first days and months of freedom have been followed by the realities of an economy in shambles and the lures of ethnicity. Learning to accept the consequences of democracy – votes that produce undesired results, debates that seem interminable, competitive programs that seem confusing – is not easy under the best of circumstances and thus requires huge leaps under horrendous conditions. And given the absence of an elite capable of articulating extensive experience in democratic procedures, it is hardly surprising that many in the former Soviet empire have moved quickly through democratic self–environment orientations and come to adhere either to apathetic or self-centered orientations.

Apathetic Citizenship (Passive and Alienated)

Notwithstanding the incentives to active citizenship that the skill revolution and other dynamics of global turbulence have highlighted, there remain many people in all parts of the world who attach little importance to either their own or society's needs insofar as these can be served through action in the political arena. This self–environment orientation, however, derives from several contradictory sources, with the result that it is possible to differentiate between two basic types of apathetic citizenship, one that we shall call passive citizenship and another that can be labeled alienated citizenship. The former is, so to speak, the truly apathetic citizen who attributes no causal strength to collective action at the micro level and no readiness on the part of macro institutions to attend to his or her needs. Such people are, thus, oblivious to the political arena. They neither care about it nor follow its developments. Alienated citizens, on the other hand, are no less ready to see themselves as lacking influence through collective action or to view society as unresponsive to their needs, but they differ from the passive citizen in that they are not so much oblivious to the political arena as they are disgusted by it. That is, they care and at some level they tend to believe that their alienation conveys a message which may eventually be heard by the society's leadership. The alienated citizen, in short, engages in a form of active passivity, contradictory as such a characterization may seem.

A host of factors operate to encourage and sustain passive citizenship. The poor and downtrodden, long suppressed in the relentless rigors of poverty, have little reason to hope that society will be responsive to their needs and, thus, they have even less reason to believe they can do anything about their plight. Passivity thus becomes a way of life, not only because the resources needed to be active in politics are lacking, but also because the spirit lags. Under these circumstances, the skill revolution is of no consequence. Passive citizens have no reason to enlarge their skills and thus either resist or avoid the powerful stimuli that the skill revolution has to offer.

It may also be that passivity becomes a way of life for some people who live well above the poverty line but who have used their new-found skills to extend their belief that the world is too complex to change. Such people may have a modicum of the resources needed to participate in collective action even though they have become habituated to passivity by virtue of the assumption that collective action at the micro level is futile. Citizens of this sort do not become alienated in the sense of actively detesting the political arena. They are, rather, truly passive because they have long since presumed the political world is essentially irrelevant to their daily routines.

In the case of alienated citizens, however, futility is moderated by caring and passivity is offset by indirect involvement. Normally their behavior consists, for all practical purposes, of inaction and detachment, but it is also a studied inaction and detachment because their orientation is to follow the course of events and derive therefrom reinforcement for their alienation. Most importantly, on occasion their convoluted form of caring can actually lead to action, to staying away from the voting booth, casting blank ballots, avoiding rallies, or otherwise seeking to make known their alienation through nonparticipation. Indeed, sometimes town squares remain empty because leaders have urged their followers to engage in collective action wherein the macro sum of micro actions is a conspicuous avoidance, a message that the political arena has gaps because they chose to remain outside it.

Still another reason for the pervasiveness of apathetic citizenship is the worldwide dearth of effective leaders who can rouse people out of their doldrums. Confidence that micro actions can produce collective outcomes is, presumably, subject to variability, depending in part on whether the case for it can be persuasively voiced. Yet, such voices are hardly a salient aspect of the political landscape in this turbulent era. As previously noted, the ranks of leaders throughout the world are so pervaded with those who focus on narrow interests that few are concerned to make politics seem meaningful to those who have either lost hope or are alienated. To be sure, there is no dearth of leaders who seek to capitalize on fear, racism, and territorial attachments among apathetic citizens as means of enlarging the ranks of their followers, and to some extent such manipulations do result in stirrings among the apathetic. And there are also some leaders who seek support by offering themselves as no-nonsense outsiders who can break through governmental stalemates and produce effective cures to society's ills, and again these tactics can lead to momentary inroads into the ranks of the apathetic. But the messages of outsiders are not geared to an enduring break with apathy. They are only palliatives, temporary expedients that are ill-designed to initiate basic alterations in self–environment orientations.

None of this is to say that the several forms of apathy presently at work on a global scale constitute a major pattern. The skill revolution and the successes of collective action in recent years have surely inhibited tendencies in these directions. As noted above, in some countries these products of global turbulence have induced a swing toward self-centered citizenship on the part of many who might otherwise be apathetic. Elsewhere the alienated have been moved to join social movements and engage in altruistic citizenship. Still others have employed their enlarged skills to derive hope from the downfall of communism and renewed their faith in democratic practices. To be sure, there are also signs that alienation and apathy are on the rise as politics and politics leaders descend further into disrepute. As will be seen, such a pattern is perhaps especially discernible in the United States. Still, such a trend must be viewed in the larger context of authority crises and enhanced skills that stimulate people into a greater readiness to experience the full measure of their citizenship. It is hard to remain outside the political arena while parametric transformations are rendering the world ever more turbulent. The moorings of citizenship may have been loosened, but the impulse to be politically anchored persists.

Democratic Citizenship

Since recent years have been witness to a widespread turn away from authoritarian toward democratic governments, it is tempting to conclude that there has been a corresponding tide in the direction of democratic citizenship. As previously implied, however, it is easier to establish formal institutions that adhere to democratic procedures than it is to evolve self–environment orientations which sustain and enlarge support for those procedures. Clarity about the intent and meaning of these procedures, and the processes of socialization through which they become habitual lines of thought for citizens, take decades to evolve. And in the course of their evolution a variety of intervening events can undermine the core values that need to be grasped. So there is little certainty that newly established democratic institutions at the macro level can take full root at the micro level, as the people of the former Soviet empire are presently demonstrating.

Put differently, the values associated with achieving a balance between self and societal needs are complex and delicate. They necessitate being prepared to favor process over outcome and thus to accept unwanted outcomes to which a majority subscribes. They require a readiness to be sensitive to the needs of the larger collectivity precisely at those times when one's own interests may be at stake. They demand an ability to resist corruption and other forms self-interested behavior which might undermine equity and curtail deliberative forms of decision-making. And they are also founded on an understanding that the rights of minorities need to be protected. Such values are not easily maintained without any prior experience in democratic ways.

Nor is the preservation of balanced self–environment orientations a simple matter for those whose cultures have long been inured to democratic principles. In a globalizing world marked by pervasive uncertainties, not to mention the onset of tense international situations or the influx of large numbers of immigrants, even those most committed to democratic values can be sorely tempted to accept short-cuts, emergency measures, restricted liberties, martial law, and a host of other procedures which compromise their commitments to open and equitable procedures.

Given the authority crises fostered by the parametric transformations of this turbulent era, moreover, the practices of democratic citizenship can be subjected to enormous pressures. In the absence of clear-cut lines of authority and the presence of paralyzed or otherwise ineffective governments, individuals in the majority can all too easily begin to forget the principles that accord protection to minorities. No less important, they can begin to loose touch with the democratic value that differentiates between being heard and being heeded by public officials and thus start to reject political processes that fail to yield their preferred outcomes. And all of this is especially the case if the leadership of democratic societies begins to compile a record of deception, self-serving corruption, and a host of other actions that can make micro actions seem irrelevant to macro outcomes and thereby erode public appreciation of democratic values and procedures.

On the other hand, it is noteworthy that the aforementioned recent episodes of collective action in Yugoslavia and Korea had their roots as much in concerns about democratic processes as they did in self-serving interests. The continuing marches in Belgrade, to repeat, focused on the canceling of the outcomes of local elections by the central government, while the strikes in Korea were a response to the secret way in which the new labor law was adopted as well as to the contents of the law. Despite all the difficulties of adjusting to the nuances of democratic citizenship, it would seem, the foundations of democratic procedures have become increasingly salient and appreciated in places where they have not long been practiced.

In sum, while the challenges to democratic citizenship have always been severe, today they seem particularly intense and subtle. More than that, the challenges are everywhere, or at least wherever governments are faltering and change is overwhelming.

RESTLESS PUBLICS AS SOURCES OF GLOBAL TURBULENCE

As the foregoing analysis makes clear, the onset of global turbulence has had major consequences for the way in which people everywhere balance their own needs off against those of their larger societies. Most citizens at every point on the self–environment continuum are in motion, either searching for a new balance or struggling to reaffirm the old one. Like their ships of state, the anchors that tie citizens to core values have become unhooked, leaving their commitments adrift and their sails buffeted by cross-cutting winds. The inner need to maintain macro attachments and political identities persists, but the foci of the attachments and identities have been increasingly obscured by transformative events. There are no moorings on to which people can readily latch.

Assuming, therefore, that the world's publics are restless and that this micro restlessness can have discernible macro consequences, we can now turn to the central question of how global politics might be affected by large-scale shifts in various self–environment orientations. Some linkages seem reasonably obvious. If the trend toward self-centered citizenship continues and gathers momentum on a worldwide scale, it seems probable that national governments will become increasingly stalemated and paralyzed. Similarly, if the trend toward altruistic citizenship acquires more and more adherents, transnational social movements are likely to become increasingly salient, thus further weakening national governments and hastening the processes whereby authority is being relocated in "upward" directions. Likewise, if apathy and alienation at the micro level spreads within and between societies, the world may well witness a spate of demagogues taking advantage of the disarray and coming to power and turning to authoritarian rule at home and confrontation abroad. Finally, if the delicate values that sustain democratic citizens are reinvigorated and capture the attention of large publics in every part of the world, it can be reasonably anticipated that governments will break out of their stalemates and effectively address both the domestic and international problems currently prominent on the global agenda.

While these four scenarios portend very different consequences for world politics, the chances are that the long-run outcomes will not be so clear-cut. The dynamics are in place for all four of the shifts in self–environment orientations to occur simultaneously, thus sustaining the turbulence that accompanies the absence of any central global tendencies. And a long-term persistence of turbulent conditions may well be desirable. Since two of the scenarios – those involving a predominance of self-centered or alienated citizens – are essentially noxious, it could well be argued that continued turbulence is the least risky and most easily achievable equilibrium.

In any event, whichever scenario or combination of scenarios proves most viable, the fact of their relevance serves to demonstrate the original contention that the micro level of world politics does have consequences for the conduct of macro collectivities and their relationships. The course of events, it seems clear from the perspective advanced here, is bound to be affected by the stirrings and demands that are presently at work in the homes and jobs of people everywhere. A world in which citizenship is without moorings is a world in flux, a world in which pervasive uncertainties can give way to predictable and enduring patterns only as people begin to use their new skills to the advantage of both themselves and their societies.

NOTES

1. For an elaborate development of the argument that citizens are key variables in world politics, see James N. Rosenau, *Turbulence in World Politics: A Theory of Change and Continuity* (Princeton: Princeton University Press, 1990). Extensions of the argument are set forth in James N. Rosenau, 'The Relocation of Authority in a Shrinking World,' *Comparative Politics*, Vol. 24 (April 1992), pp. 253–72, and James N. Rosenau, "Citizenship in a Changing Global Order," in Rosenau and

E. O. Czempiel (eds), *Governance without Government: Order and Change in World Politics* (Cambridge: Cambridge University Press, 1992), pp. 272–94.

2. Rosenau, *Turbulence in World Politics*, chs 7, 9, and 13.
3. Ibid., chs. 1, 5, and 10.
4. See Rosenau, *Along the Domestic–Foreign Frontier: Exploring Governance in a Turbulent World* (Cambridge: Cambridge University Press, 1997).
5. See Rosenau, "Material and Imagined Communities in Globalized Space," a paper presented at the Conference on Internationalizing Communities: Australia, Asia and the World, convened at the University of South Queensland, Toowoomba, Australia (November 30, 1996).
6. For example, see how a single student persuaded a New Hampshire town to reverse its policies toward a national holiday: Sara Rimer, "An Effort to Honor Dr. King Moves a Mostly White Town," *New York Times*, January 20, 1997, p. 1.
7. Rosenau, *Turbulence in World Politics*, chs 8 and 14.
8. For recent discussions of emotional skills, see Daniel Goleman, *Emotional Intelligence* (New York: Bantam Books, 1995), and Joseph LeDoux, *The Emotional Brain: The Mysterious Underpinnings of Emotional Life* (New York: Simon & Schuster, 1996).
9. Daniel Yankelovich, "You Can Argue with Einstein," *The Responsive Community*, Vol. 1 (Winter 1990–1), p. 78.
10. For a provocative discussion of how elite perspectives may also prevent academics, journalists, public officials, and other observers from discerning how well citizens employ their analytic skills – "We perhaps have trouble taking citizens seriously because they do not theorize in the specialized vocabulary of theory" – see Manfred Stanley, "Taking Citizens Seriously," *Kettering Review*, December 1990, pp. 30–8 (the quote is from p. 34). That conceptual and methodological barriers inhibit adequate measurement of shifting levels of analytic skills is also evident in literacy research. See, for example, Daniel A. Wagner, "World Literacy Research and Policy in the EFA Decade," in Symposium, "World Literacy in the Year 2000," *The Annals*, Vol. 520 (March 1992), pp. 12–26.
11. For an extensive discussion of the three parameters and their transformation, see Rosenau, *Turbulence in World Politics*, ch. 4.
12. Rosenau, "The Relocation of Authority in a Shrinking World."
13. This query is fully explored in Sidney Tarrow, "The Globalization of Conflict: Isn't This Where We Came In?" a paper presented at the Annual Meeting of the American Political Science Association (Washington, DC: August 1991).
14. See, for example, Jane Perlez, "All Walks of Life Protesting in Belgrade," *New York Times*, December 31, 1996, p. A10.
15. Andrew Pollack, "Thriving, South Koreans Strike to Keep It That Way," New York Times, January 17, 1997, p. A1.
16. Anthony DePalma, "Protesters Take to Streets to Defend Canada's Safety Net," *New York Times*, October 26, 1996, p. 3.

17. Molly Moore, "Fighting Wrongs with a Gridlock of Protests," *Washington Post*, December 2, 1996, p. A18.
18. Cf. Rosenau and W. Michael Fagen, "Increasingly Skillful Citizens: A New Dynamism in World Politics?" a paper presented at the Joint Conference of the Japan Association of International Relations and the International Studies Association, Makuhari, Japan (Sept. 20–2, 1996).
19. Pollack, "Thriving, South Koreans Strike to Keep It That Way," p. A1.
20. Mary Durfee and James N. Rosenau, "Playing Catch-Up: IR Theory and Poverty," *Millennium*, Vol. 25, No. 3, pp. 521–45.
21. Rosenau, *Turbulence in World Politics*, chs 8 and 14.
22. James Brooke, "Britain and Japan Split With US on Species Pact," *New York Times*, June 6, 1992, p. 1.
23. Michael T. Kaufman, "Yugoslav Denies Involvement of Belgrade in War in Bosnia," *New York Times*, June 6, 1992, p. 1.
24. Barbara Crossette, "US Is Discussing an Outside Force to Stabilize Haiti," *New York Times*, June 6, 1992, p. 1.
25. Rosenau, *Turbulence in World Politics*, pp. 228–36.
26. A cogent account of the many consequences that may follow when citizens are deprived of their political moorings can be found in Bruce Weber, "Many in the Former Soviet Lands Say They Feel Even More Insecure Now," *New York Times*, April 23, 1992, p. A3. For an inquiry into the same dynamics as they are unfolding in the United States, see Rosenau, "Citizenship Without Moorings: Individuals' Responses to a Turbulent World," a paper presented at the Annual Meeting of the American Sociological Association (Pittsburgh: August 23, 1992).
27. It should be noted that each set of orientations is an ideal type. As is evident in Table 1, the varying forms of citizenship represent extremes on continua. In fact, of course, people tend to combine their self and societal concerns and are thus located at various points along each continuum. It is only for analytic purposes that the focus here is on the ideal types formed by the extremes.
28. For lengthy discussions of the shifting meaning of territory and the notions of sovereignty that attach to it, see Rosenau, "The Person, The Household, The Community, and The Globe: Notes for a Theory of Multilateralism in a Turbulent World," in Robert W. Cox (ed.), *The New Realism: Perspectives on Multilateralism and World Order* (Basingstoke: Macmillan, 1997), pp. 57–80; Rosenau, "Sovereignty in a Turbulent World," in Michael Mastanduno and Gene Lyons (eds), *Beyond Westphalia? State Sovereignty and International Intervention* (Baltimore: Johns Hopkins University Press, 1995), pp. 191–227; and John Agnew and Stuart Corbridge, *Mastering Space: Hegemony, Territory and International Political Economy* (New York: Routledge, 1995).
29. Self-centered citizenship is surely one explanation for the data amassed in Robert D. Putnam, "Bowling Alone: America's Declining Social Capital," *Journal of Democracy*, Vol. 6 (January 1995), pp. 65–78.
30. Cf. Rosenau, "Armed Force and Armed Forces in a Turbulent World," in James Burk (ed.), *The Military in New Times: Adapting Armed Forces*

to a Turbulent World (Boulder, Colo.: Westview Press, 1993), pp. 25–60.

31. For a discussion of other recent leaders who have resisted the lures of subgroupism, see Rosenau, "Notes on the Servicing of Triumphant Subgroupism," *International Sociology*, Vol. 8 (March 1993), pp. 77–90.

32. Quoted in Celestine Bohlen, "'What Country Do I live In?' Many Russians Are Asking," *New York Times*, June 14, 1992, p. 1.

33. Benjamin R. Barber, "Jihad Vs. McWorld," *Atlantic Monthly* (March 1992), pp. 54–5.

34. Donald Woutat, "Detroit in Rearview Mirror," *Los Angeles Times*, March 11, 1992, p. 1. Quoted is Gerald Hirshberg, former Buick design chief who is now Vice-president of Nissan Design International.

35. Woutat, "Detroit in Rearview Mirror," p. A7.

36. Ibid. Again the quoted words were expressed by Gerald Hirshberg.

37. A cogent analysis of the emerging global role of social movements can be found in R. B. J. Walker, One World, Many Worlds: Struggles for a Just World Peace (Boulder, Colo.: Lynne Rienner Publishers, 1988).

38. The conception of world politics as having bifurcated into two separate and distinctive (although interactive) worlds is presented in Rosenau, *Turbulence in World Politics*, ch. 10.

4 Praxiological Analysis of International Politics: between Systemism and Methodological Individualism

Jacques J. Herman

INTRODUCTION

Since political science is aiming at integrating the problem of the individual into its models of international relations, it has to face a formidable intellectual challenge. The epistemological analysis of the individual cannot be conducted without reflecting upon the classic notions of society, world, system and action. Modelling unprecedented situations that turn up in international relations involves redefining basic theoretical concepts such as power, sovereignty, network or citizen, together with classic notions such as Party, State, Nation or Empire.

As it belongs to the field of the sciences of man, political science has to face the wide variety and vast complexity of the subject matter it deals with. Without going as far as following the reductionist principles of methodological individualism, we none the less have to take into account the individual's reality made up of freedom and choice, of peculiarity and hazard. Key political actors undeniably play an important role in history. Gorbachev, John Paul II or Saddam Hussein are recent examples thereof. By aggregating a set of individuals according to an additive procedure, the political action becomes the resultant, predictable or unpredictable, simple or complex, ordinary or paradoxical of a 'collective' entity. Public opinion polls and democratic elections remind us constantly of this inevitable truth.

Furthermore, political science has to try to predict the behaviour of socio-political systems: parties, organizations, States. Socio-political systems show emergent behaviours when compared with the individuals in these systems. Several self-regulatory mechanisms contribute to the emergence and bring about unpredicted consequences: vicious effects or virtuous circles. The crisis in the systems of social protection, which is a feature of Welfare States, can be partly explained by the overdetermined nature of that systemic logic. In international politics, interference between different system logics in a real environment – see the conflict in former Yugoslavia – leads not only to global but also to local unpredictability. Political prediction of a macro-historical kind is almost speculation when it comes down to viewing global realities of an holistic kind such as Braudel's 'économies-mondes' or Spengler's and Huntington's 'civilizations'.

The present situation is unstable from a historical point of view and chaotic from a theoretical point of view. Thus the political scientist should have the opportunity to rebuild his ontology and evaluate the conditions of applicability. The richest source of inspiration for structuralism-functionalism has been the mathematical theory of communication as well as cybernetics. New 'meta-theoretical' fields have emerged ever since: dynamic systems theory, catastrophe theory, theory of self-organization (autopoiesis), chaos theory and fractal geometry. Political science has to give its methods and schemes of explanation new strength using new developments in formal and natural sciences.

PRAXIOLOGY AND METHODOLOGICAL INDIVIDUALISM

The paradigm of 'methodological individualism' has always found its place in social sciences, from Gabriel de Tarde and Max Weber to Mancur Olson and Raymond Boudon. It has recently been given full attention as it has aroused certain new interests in the field of political science.[1] Methodological individualism is a paradigm which aims at reducing the sociological explanation to the aggregation of individual behaviour. Can we rely on such micro-reductionism, heavily influenced by neo-utilitarian economics, in the field of international politics? Do we have to shift from ever more global explanations – for example, systemism – to methodological individualism? Asking the question like this means ignoring any realistic solution, which requires more than an ideological debate: rather, a thorough analysis on an epistemological, ontological and methodological basis.

In comparison with the other paradigms, praxiology displays a subjectivist tendency which is yet different from the approach of comprehension or understanding (*Verstehen*), in which the actor is essentially a 'Subject' determined by his conscience, in the phenomenological meaning of the word. The praxiological actor is directly defined by a situation, he is no contemplative subject who sees the world as his own representation. The subject is involved, willing or not, he acts, and in doing so moulds the resulting situation. There is interaction between a number of actors whose 'strategies' alter the situation. The praxiological approach involves traditionally the elaboration of what Herbert Simon called 'models of man'.

The 'homo economicus' is the cornerstone of the classic economic theory as the idealized concept according to which man is a rational individual who speculates, expresses preferences and makes choices. This model can be generalized to all human activities according to the reductionist principle of methodological individualism (George Homans). The 'homo sociologicus' is traditionally opposed to the homo economicus (R. Dahrendorf). He has a more complex behaviour, he is not free to make choices, but he unconsciously conforms to society-imposed standards. It is Durkheim's idea that human activity is socio-culturally conditioned. The 'homo psychologicus' is endowed with needs, desires and impulses of organic origin. His mental representations – conscience, memory, perception, attitudes – depend on this biological substratum. The psychological models have been of great variety, from Freud to Piaget and the 'cognitive sciences'. The 'homo politicus' can be distinguished by his will to power and his ability to manage conflicts. His political behaviour seems less rational because it is more undetermined. Politics is indeed 'the art of the possible'. Conflicts and the art of solving them are the typical aspects of purely political activity. Nevertheless, power can be rigorously conceptualized and axiomatized.[2]

Searching for a universal model is a useless undertaking because these different models have rules that contradict each other. Modelling the main types of human activity is more realistic. Some theories combine several of these models among each other. Pareto developed an economic as well as psycho-sociological conception of the actor in his concept of 'residue'. The residue or 'the instinct of combinations' refers to the calculating mind, the residue of the 'persistence of aggregates' refers to preserving the mental acquisitions. From there stems partly his typology of political elites which distinguishes cunning from force, the 'foxes' (e.g. Mitterrand) from the 'lions' (e.g. Churchill).

In praxiology, action is spatialized, i.e. it takes place in a socio-political space or field of action. The field of action does not correspond to the notion of system in structuralism-functionalism. In a system, the individual plays a role defined by the social structure and his activity is ultimately determined by the system. But the very notion of global society becomes a problem, Society as an autonomous and finalized entity seems an illusory myth.[3] Praxiology views action in a wider perspective, actually as a practice within a set of unlimited possibilities. In the system analysis, it is assumed that there are well-defined boundaries surrounding the system, that rules and functions do not change very much within the system, and that there exists an homeostatic equilibrium.

There is no accurate and stable border limiting a sphere of activity, which gives rise to a principle of indetermination. Any actor who enters the field of action modifies it automatically, and this generates an uncertainty principle. A relativity principle is related to the multi-subjective aspect in the sphere of activity. Each actor can proceed to a local and specific assessment of the sphere of activity and maintain his own representation. As far as praxiology is concerned, many epistemological problems bound to modelization must be solved. Indeed, is it possible to have an external 'objective' point of view regarding the sphere of activity, the limits of which are fuzzy and mobile? Can we recombine all the actors' positions, all stakes, all investments, and reach a global perspective? Can this perspective be synthetic and total or only syncretic and fractal?

This complexity can be seen among others in the praxiological analysis of international relations. If we take the example provided by the Gulf War or the Bosnian war, we can observe the different actors, each playing his own 'game' and making his investments in a sphere of activity where the rules change as the 'match' goes on. To make an objective science out of something subjective requires one to take into account all actors' strategies while avoiding any narrow-focus point of view. Moreover, the complexity of the praxiological analysis is greater because of the fact that the sphere of activity can include actors at different ontological levels:

systemic (national, transnational or interstate);
collective (public opinion);
individual (private persons).

This praxiological conception of international relations calls into question the very existence of the 'system of international relations'. A real system supposes constant and articulated connections, something quite different from a set of abstract relations of a juridical kind. The praxiological approach studies the actors who actually enter the sphere of activity at a certain time during the action. The UN as a specific organization is a socio-political system but the Nation-States do not form a system. From time to time, some States become involved in particular spheres of activity: agonistic, diplomatic, economic or even cultural.

The 'naturalist' conception holds that material conditions prevail over actors' strategies. These conditions still have to be perceived and assessed by the main actors. During the Gulf War, oil, for example, was an element in the definition of the situation given by the actors and was one among many stakes. The praxiological approach, while rejecting any naturalist point of view, cannot be reduced to a certain kind of voluntarism. Oil-related stakes, therefore, cannot offer a satisfactory explanation. However, analysing key actors' strategies only in terms of 'homo politicus' is not enough to give a full explanation of the dynamics of events. In the explanation, the assessment of the situation has to be combined with the appraisal of the strategic orientations.

LEVELS OF REDUCTION

For socio-biology, political phenomena such as aggression can be reduced to the infra-individual genetic level, whereas for monetarism, the dynamics of transnational money transactions subsume socio-political decisions. In international politics, taking into account the individual level can have disturbing consequences[4] because this heightens the epistemic tension between the micro level (the individual) and the macro level (Nation-State) which are usually dealt with in international politics. It can even challenge these levels as the ultimate relevant object of investigation. Methodologically speaking, the notion of the individual relates to the theory of measurement and the technique of observing that goes with it. However, the classic micro/macro distinction oversimplifies the case. The theory of measurement leads us to distinguish several effective levels of resolution, which are relevant for technico-practical reasons. (See Table 4.1.)

Table 4.1 Levels of analytic resolution

Resolution level	Objects of investigation
Macro	Nation-State
Meso	social class
Mini	group, party
Micro	individual, citizen
Nano	opinion, election

Everybody can see the arbitrariness of such a gradation. Its relevance will in fact depend on whether suitable investigation techniques are available and whether measuring units are efficiently defined. The notion of the individual points to an ideal object model which refers to the factual reality, subject of the scientific investigation. In a comparative analysis individual cases can be either Nation-States or individuals. The cases are endowed with a certain number of properties specific to their level of analysis, i.e. political regime or opinion, without specifying them any further concerning regions or roles.

The dualistic nature in the individual/society opposition all too often entails an artificial and illusory antinomy regarding the micro/macro levels. The micro/macro problem comes under mereology, which is the formal theory of the whole and its parts. Hence, whether an individual belongs to 'the system of international relations' will depend on a series of mereological prerequisites. The complexity of the micro/macro problem can be modelized in a finer typology where four ontological levels are distinguished: individual, collective, systemic and holistic.

The individual level includes simple elementary units, self-subsisting monads, the smallest possible units of certain actions (e.g. citizens). The collective level aggregates a set of individuals according to an additive procedure. The collective action is then the result, predictable or unpredictable, simple or complex, ordinary or paradoxical, of this aggregation (e.g. democratic election). The systemic level consists of the structured connection of certain specific elements, the organic structures have an emergent finality (e.g. political party). The holistic level refers to a set of elements, of groups or organizations viewed in their entirety (e.g. capitalism). (See Table 4.2.)

Logical connections can link different levels without necessarily complying with explanatory reductionism. The task is more to

Table 4.2 Typology of the micro/macro problem

Levels	Ontology	Effect	Articulation
Individual (i)	Atomism	Consequence	Interaction
Collective i	Collectivism	Resultant	Union
Systemic S(i)	Systemism	Emergence	Organization
Global <T>	Holism	Fusion	Totalization

articulate levels than reduce one level down to the other. Hence, Tocqueville's theory according to which revolution can be explained by earlier regime liberalization, can be analysed as an interconnection linking a micro level (elites' behaviour) to a macro level (revolution as a resultant). Let us call 'Liberalization' L, a macro set of institutional and cultural changes (e.g. the end of the *Ancien Régime*); 'Revolution' R, a macro set of political transformations (e.g. the events that took place in France between 1789 and 1815); 'Elites' Ei, the (micro) collection of actors belonging to political elites; 'Power' Pi, the (micro) number of cases when actors come to power. Tocqueville's theory will be spelled out as follows:

$$L \rightarrow \quad (Ei, Pi) \quad \rightarrow R$$

Macro   Micro   Macro

The formula is derived at the macro level. Designating a lower analytic level allows us to elucidate the law by combining global variables with index variables, that is to say a 'macro' level with a 'micro' level of description.

In addition to the ontological distinction between levels of reality, the political scientist faces a very different type of problems: the epistemic distinction between conceptual levels. Such an epistemic distinction involves various scientific disciplines like sociology, culture or economics. It is obvious that the ontological distinction does not correspond to the epistemic distinction. Different objects, micro or macro, can be taken into account at various epistemic levels. The individual (micro) will be in turn consumer, citizen, parent, speaker. The State (macro) can fulfil an economic, political, social and/or cultural function more or less developed in various historical contexts. Be that as it may, those levels are conceptual entities which point to series of events or objects, they cannot therefore influence each other concretely.

In particular, the expression 'micro-macro interaction' does not denote an interaction between micro and macro levels but an interaction between individual things belonging to a microlevel and things belonging to a macrolevel.[5]

Therefore 'psychologism' is the type of reductionism according to which a social fact is the result of individual actions generated by the actors' beliefs, values and intentions and where the environment only plays a secondary part. Talcott Parsons' classic typology with its four functional prerequisites (adaptation, goal attainment, integration, latency) and its four associated subsystems (Economic, Political, Social, Cultural) is a good example of the epistemic conception of analytical levels. The subsystem of personality in the Parsonian general action model corresponds to the political subsystem in the society model. In this model, politics is not reduced to power, which is only its means of exchange; it includes the fundamental function of goal attainment. The essence of politics can be located in the assertion of a will, the attainment of a goal, the definition of an orientation.

As we can see, the notion of the individual creates serious conceptual problems independently from historicist mythologies or philosophical reconstructions from Leibniz to Simondon. An individual *stricto sensu* is not a system in the sense that it represents a single atom, an indivisible and non-composed element which cannot be partitioned into subsystems. This atomistic convention has long shown its arbitrary nature, in physics as in psychology. When the individual is put into the dynamic perspective of its ontogenesis, the sharp distinction between the environment and the individual system fades away.[6]

The antinomy opposing the individual and Society is a classic matter in philosophical and sociological thinking.[7] It is, however, important not to be caught in the middle of the endless interplay between these antinomic categories so that we can understand correctly the socio-historical dimensions of individualism.[8] A concrete society cannot be conceived as a totally integrated system on an organicist basis. Herbert Spencer already made a clear distinction between biological and social organisms: societies have no specific external forms; social mass is discontinuously scattered in a geographic area; all members of society are endowed with a cognitive system while the community as a whole has no conscience of its own.[9] Mereologic relations, from the whole down to its parts, are therefore drastically different when in an individual organism or when in society.[10]

In anthropology, Louis Dumont understands the opposition between individualism, peculiar to the 'homo aequalis', and holism, peculiar to the 'homo hierarchicus', as being the fundamental axis which runs along the opposition between the western and the eastern world. The modern Nation-State is an essential factor in the emergence of an individualist culture, because of its emancipation processes which it promoted to counter religious authorities, economic interests and political groupings.[11] The Nation-State is the historical result of an individuation macro-process which means, as a consequence, the micro-individuation of its members. However, as can be seen from the persistence of anarchists and libertarians, there remains a tension between the societal system and its individual components.

Contrary to the individual conceived as a simple element within a system, the person is a socio-historical being, caught between roles and destiny. A person is an individual which is always already social. The question of the individual's integration into society is also the question of society's integration within the individual. This integration oscillates between three poles that each threaten the building of one's personality as well as that of society: anomia, alienation and plurinomia. Anomia is the absence of space to root one's identity. Its main features are the absence of normative and evaluative references. Alienation – or uninomia – enables one to root one's identity in an exclusive space. It is reductionist regarding the individual's identity-related plasticity. Plurinomia refers to a person's belonging to multiple fractal identity spaces. It carries with it normative and evaluative conflicts, 'logical duels' linked to identification. The present situation denotes sharp plurinomia, at a time when the post-modern individual rejects all rigid and unitarian memberships, wants to live several lives, when capitalism's global triumph distils schizophrenia into the masses while deterritorializing cultural identities.[12] Such an individual no longer finds the origins of his fantasies in his parental roots but indulges in transnational networks like the Internet. Plurinomia is a complex and ambiguous situation which gives rise to contradictory analyses even by theorists dealing with individualism![13]

In political sociology, 'elitist' theories from the Mosca–Pareto school presuppose methodological individualism where the concept of mass points to the simple unorganized aggregation of elementary individuals bound to follow elites which are specific interest groups. Even Marxism, in its critique of German idealism and British political economy, complies with methodological individualism. The gnoseological 'reflection theory' holds that class interest is a collective utility which aggregates individual utilities of members belonging to socio-economic groups. The so-called political 'awareness' reveals their real interest to the economically exploited and socially alienated, whereas the 'false conscience' prevents the wealthy upper classes from noticing. When applied to international political relations, these simplistic models remain far from harmless, despite their present apparent exhaustion. All-out percolation of political essentialism in post-modernist theories, e.g. in Michel Foucault's works, goes together with a breaking down of the individual's humanist figure. 'Everything is political!' implies 'We are all small groupings!', even 'We are all polities!' and, finally, 'We are all worlds!'. Absolute cosmopolitanism unites with radical individualism as globalism gives birth to solipsism.

Radical methodological individualism cannot keep its epistemological promises because its assumptions cannot overstep the formula: 'Individual i in a situation j completes an action k.' This paradigm's excessive pretensions can be explained by its willingness to reject any kind of holism in social sciences. Holism became dominant partly via Marxism. The ultra-liberal ideas of someone like Karl Popper assume perfectly rational actors whose choices would only be determined by their sole individual interests. An 'open' society is in correlation with this radical individualism. A 'closed' society, on the other hand, implies collective constraints which weigh heavily on individual wills. Though, whereas alienation and totalitarianism are typical of closed societies, anomia and the 'fear of freedom'[14] are likely to be typical of open societies.

THE INDIVIDUAL IN INTERNATIONAL POLITICS

The essential political question is that of the link between the individual, the State and democracy.[15] Democracy, whichever form it may take, direct, representative or participative, is the prototype political system which presupposes a rather large number of individuals, the *demos* from which the City's or the Nation's government originates. Democracy enables the individual–citizen–voter to impose himself as the ultimate source of legitimate power despite the usual disadvantages of voting systems.[16] Any challenge to individualism is a challenge to the modern State as exemplified by anarchist, socialist, fascist or fundamentalist ideologies. Any crisis in State models (Welfare State, democratic State) is a socio-cultural crisis upon the solution of which depends the future of individualism.

The individuals lost in the crowd show the chaotic face of democracy, just as anarchy is the kind of chaos that is purely political.[17] Ever since the nineteenth century, the masses have been a favoured topic for political thinking and psycho-sociological theories, from Le Bon to Freud. The crowd shows us what molecular chaos is, elements of which are a series of atomized individuals. At a certain threshold of receptivity ('suggestion'), the crowd can experience extreme feelings and attitudes; its behaviour then becomes unpredictable. The dynamics of a crowd can react very easily to slight changes in the environment, for example to the presence of security forces, to the number and stubbornness of certain leaders and so on. It also is irreversible, a wild or scattered crowd will not return to its initial state. The crowd is a fractal object, there is similarity between the whole and its parts, between the erratic crowd and disoriented individuals who are part of the crowd. Sometimes it represents itself through the charisma of its leader, who embodies its essence.

Modern Nation-States display the main features of individuality: self-representation, autonomy of government, sovereignty. They have enabled the individual's modern figure to arise, just as the Greek City enabled the ancient individuality to emerge. If a multi-ethnic State lets various individualized national feelings develop, that multinational State is likely to become a 'dividual', to quote Max Stirner. In such a plurinomic environment, where transnationality of neighbourhood (territorial), of parenthood (multi-ethnic) and of values (multi-religious) coexist, the post-modern individual is torn between local identity regression and global identity dissolution, between nationalist alienation and cosmopolitist anomia. The trick is to guess which system best enables the individual to survive. Ever since the dawn of humanity, this 'survival unit' has been in turn, the tribe, the clan, the city, the nation, or the empire. Is there an inescapable move towards globalization which would once and for all prove the individual's cosmopolitan nature?[18]

The notion of international political relations presupposes defined terms which refer to distinct objects: States, organizations, actors. Political analysis then deals with the type, intensity and structure of the relations between these entities. It is very important to distinguish international from transnational. International refers to a super-system and to relations between Nation-States, whereas transnational refers to a field in which elements such as relations are undetermined. While the expression 'the individual in international relations' may seem irrelevant, the expression 'the individual in transnational relations' seems quite natural. Indeed, 'international society' is not necessarily understood as opposed to the individuals who are its components.[19]

The emergence of the individual into international politics can seem untimely in many respects. Throughout modern political history, from the French Revolution to the Helsinki Agreements, under the Human Rights' juridical finery, the individual's figure has been the subversive light and the strange attractor of the Body Politic.[20] Meanwhile, the dialectic materialist ontology tried to sink bourgeois individualism into oblivion. Distinguished Western political scientists directed their Critique against 'the capitalist system', unavoidably condemned by Marxist Theory and the Praxis of global revolution.

'The social transformations of the twentieth century have resulted in two-thirds of the world rejecting the bourgeois order. The basic postulate of the old natural rights doctrine has thus been invalidated to that extent.'[21] At the end of our twentieth century, can Macpherson's assumption simply be overturned? While we witness the downfall of the Marxist-Leninist empire and the global expansion of liberalism, many think that individualist ontology has triumphed over holistic ontology. Possessive individualism has supposedly won the global match and the end of History supposedly honours the emergence of the individual.[22] This conception of ontology seems much more like theological-political speculation. It is a shame to see how so many enlightened critiques of the scientific approach in political science sacrifice Theory for the sake of Immediate History, even if it is yesterday's, that of decolonization, or today's, that of desovietization.

The breakdown of the USSR, the reappearance of different kinds of nationalism, the retribalization of societies, the pitfalls of European integration, invite more cautiousness. Besides, is it sensible to remember that civilizations can die and that empires eventually perish? The so-called 'democratic deficit' within European integration is more than an intellectual scandal when democratic revival occurs, it is the harbinger of a much more radical societal divide linked to delocalization in the economy and transnational migrations. The principle of subsidiarity anchored in the Maastricht Treaty may well imply that it has become important to locate the relevant systemic level that helps the individual secure his biological, psychic, economic and political survival.

SYSTEMISM AT THE BORDERS OF CHAOS

The systemic approach has very often been the target of ready-made and 'radical' challenges. In political and social sciences, the critique of theories is too often weakened by partisan prejudices, and the bad knowledge of methods leads to dubious analogies or groundless accusations. Current international politics needs more than ever an elaborate analysis of the systemic paradigm, which can still teach many more heuristic lessons. Invalidated by ideological prophecies and the media's hunger for fast news, most of the methodological schemes designed for systemism and praxiology have not been developed beyond the blueprint stage. However, the purpose is to avoid once and for all dogmas of established paradigms relying blindly on orthodoxies, in order to favour the middle ground, which combines theoretical thinking with factual research.[23]

In the field of international relations, the notion of system is omnipresent as well as polysemic. It legitimately comes under the structuralist-functionalist paradigm and systemism, but effectively it often belongs to a vulgar empiricism based on a simplistic distinction between what is inside and what is outside. Formally, a system Sy includes a set of elements, its composition C, the specific connections between the elements, its structure S, and its environment E. In the classic version of structuralist-functionalism, the open system is a real entity which maintains its borders, its differences from its environment, by means of an homeostatic mechanism resisting change.[24] The notion of a hierarchic system points to an interlocking of systems at different levels. Interlocking requires numerous pre-existing connection points, which is only exceptionally the case: for example, the UN represents a certain type of juridical and political connection between States, which does not qualify it as an integrative super-system.

The classic structural-functional conception of the system can hardly define with accuracy what the boundary of a societal system is.

Indeed, the notion of open system does not allow an understanding of the system's boundary as a limit for exchanges with the environment. From a static point of view, the boundary has its own reality: limit, membrane, fence; from a dynamic point of view, it is the result of symbolic or material fluxes. The openness of the system does not imply an absence of boundary at the local level, rather a kind of 'buffer', a specific interface. This explains why most socio-political systems – government, decision-making systems, social classes, administrative systems and so on – have no geometric limits.[25] Only the Nation-State, because of its territorial basis, is endowed with a clearly limited empirical boundary. Ever since Max Weber's time, the ideal-type of the Nation-State has been conceived as a closed system coinciding with a territory, a community, and a governing body which has the monopoly of legitimate violence. Even if economic and cultural subsystems do not generally fall within a closed territory, the Nation-State's mythical temptation is to pursue economic independence and achieve cultural identity.

At a time when empires break down and Nation-States stumble, socio-political systems' territorial dimensions and transnational fluxe management become crucial. The inadequacy between systemic openness and the Nation-State's enclosure, already mentioned by Fichte (1800), has been debated between the partisans of structuralism-functionalism and the 'statists'.[26] As the concept of State does not appear in the structuralist-functionalist checklist, the 'societal' dimension is assumed to have evacuated the 'State' dimension, and systemism is accused of having neglected the historical roots provided by the territorial State. The conceptual indeterminacy surrounding the notion of 'state system' can be solved by clarifying its ontological reference level. In a broader sense, the State corresponds to global society: the set of societal subsystems. In a more restricted sense, the State is reduced to the size of the political-administrative subsystem. Systemism's abstract categories, though, can induce the mistake of the 'misplaced concrete' if ever the researcher's methodological watchfulness (and intellectual honesty) were to fail. The fundamental scientific debate over the State is weakened by methodological haggling between historians and political scientists, and even avoided because of ideological prejudices between neo-Marxists and neo-Liberals.

A topological modelization of a system's boundary accounts more reliably for the blurred reality of the societal dynamic.[27] A concrete system is fuzzy when it has no precise boundary under the geometric form of continuous lines or surfaces (e.g. an information network, a political network, an atom of hydrogen). The systemic boundary can be defined by means of the topological notion of vicinity of its components. A component-boundary in a system is the component in the neighbourhood of which there are at least a component of the system and a component of the environment. The boundary of a system will simply be the total of its components-boundary. For each type of relations (political, economic, cultural, social) the system will have one dynamic boundary, legitimately precise and measurable. Such a topological model does not imply any particular geometric form.

On the other hand, fractal geometry makes it possible to modelize discontinuous boundaries and seemingly uneven although strictly delimitable surfaces.[28] The reality of the Nation-State combines the topological notion of boundary with the geographic notion of territory. The Nation-State is the geopolitical projection of a system of societal fluxes. This projection is almost bi-dimensional (there is a proper air space, though, but it is a thin film under the huge outer space where artificial satellites are orbiting out of sovereignty's reach), and it encourages social relations and maximizes random interactions (Brownoidal) between the elements.[29]

Systemism deals with new subjects which show much promise with regard to the conceptualization of the individual. In fact, the subject of autonomy is updated with the concepts of 'autopoiesis', used by F. J. Varela, and of self-organization, adopted by Edgar Morin. Self-organization is proper to all system categories, ranging from physics to politics.[30] The auto-poietical evolution in a system shows a high degree of plasticity. Traditionally, homeostasis points to the relative constancy of certain global, quantitative variables which are typical of a system, e.g. its entropy or degree of disorganization. By contrast, autopoiesis points to a form of organization which lasts through changes, a special type of qualitative invariant configuration among the system's elements. A system's structure is simply the synchronic connection between its elements, its organization is the set of diachronic rules of production and transformation of those connections; these rules guarantee the system's structural similarity in the long run. A system endowed with an auto-poietical device is open to its environment but its functioning does not respond to stimulus. It can respond to environmental challenges by internally reorganizing its configuration without producing specific outputs and without resorting to retroactive mechanisms. The system is thus capable, by endogenous regulation, of behaving like a proper individual.[31]

Applying the systemic paradigm has always been troublesome in social sciences because the concept of system can also be used in the formal sense of a set of abstract relations in a theoretical model, as is the case in game theory when we can talk of, for instance, a 'system' of oligarchic games featuring a European order. The concept of system can also connote a set of normative rules, as in the expression 'the European monetary system'. While the systemic paradigm has never been confined to objectivism, as we can see from the works of Talcott Parsons, Michel Crozier or Edgar Morin, classic praxiology also has to be revisited, it cannot be reduced to the kind of subjectivism suggested by 'comprehensive' actors, nor to the kind of idealism embodied by normative strategies from game theory.[32] The praxiological concept of the field of action refers to 'chaosmic' situations of determined uncertainties. There is no 'global' world-system, there is only a field of forces governed by rules of interference, there are only 'random meetings' according to Cournot's definition of chance.

The analysis of the evolutionary order in History has always been made difficult by formidable epistemological roadblocks, which in turn were overshadowed by dialectic voluntarism or haunted by nostalgia for a well-grounded Political Theory, making the intelligibility of the becoming of the world possible.[33] The scrambling of systemic logics in a concrete sphere of activity leads not only to global but also to local unpredictability. Models of disorder and of hypercomplexity as well as chaos theory seem to restore the rightful place of the undetermined individual, producer of bifurcations when subjected to irregular fluctuations. A dynamical system is said to be chaotic when it is very sensitive to very slight parametric modifications. A system's historical development is influenced by tiny changes in initial conditions. Historic causality is muddled with contingency.[34] In political and social sciences, however, it remains difficult to precisely study systems with chaotic dynamics because it would need the observation of long chronological series with sufficient accuracy.

The emergence of the individual into international relations cannot make the political scientist favour 'methodological individualism' at the micro-analytical level and give up the systemic paradigm at the macro-political level. There is not even a logical constraint which would impose the shift from systemism to praxiology, just as there is no historical fatality which could force the irreversible passage from civil society to transnational society, from uninomia to plurinomia, from order to chaos. Taking into account the individual in the field of international relations can but stimulate the careful and consequent use of an extended systemic paradigm in a praxiological framework. The renewal of socio-political systems' geometrization can benefit from the breakthroughs of systemic thinking, fractal geometries and new chaos theories. Various forms of reductionism are likely to affect the appropriate modelization of objects belonging to different reality levels – micro or macro; their articulation is an indispensable prerequisite for any analysis to be conducted regarding the complexity of individual–system relations in international politics. Likewise, the theoretical and empirical problem of the State system's boundaries deserves full attention. When applied to international politics, socio-political models, be they individualist, systemist or praxiological, seriously need to be elaborated from an epistemological and methodological point of view. This is the price to pay for providing political science with autonomy and protection against totalitarian and anarchy-linked ideologies.

NOTES

1. See Pierre Birnbaum and Jean Leca (eds), *Individualism: Theories and Methods* (Oxford: Clarendon, 1990).
2. See Ingmar Pörn, *Action Theory and Social Science* (Dordrecht: D. Reidel, 1977). See also Gottfried Seebass and Raimo Tuomela, *Social Action* (Dordrecht: D. Reidel, 1985).
3. Michel Crozier, *Etat modeste, Etat moderne* (Paris: Fayard, 1987), p. 302.
4. Michel Girard, 'Turbulence dans la politique internationale ou James Rosenau, inventeur', *Revue Française de Science Politique*, vol. 8 (1992), pp. 636–46.
5. Mario Bunge, 'The Power and Limits of Reduction' in Evandro Agazzi (ed.), *The Problem of Reductionism in Science* (Dordrecht: Kluwer, 1991), p. 37.
6. 'The living individual is an individuation system, individuating system and self-individuating system ... Psychosocial reality is transindividual reality: that reality the individuated system carries with him, this load of being for future individuations ... the name of individual is wrongly given to a more complex reality, that of the integral subject ... the

subjective being can be conceived as a more or less cohesive system of the three successive phases of being: pre-individual, individuated, transindividual, partly corresponding but not totally to the referents of the concepts of Nature, Individual, Spirituality.' Gilbert Simondon, *L'individuation psychique et collective* (Paris: Aubier, 1989), pp. 17, 193, 204.

7. Indeed, there is much inspiration to be found yet for methodological individualism in Leibnizian monadology. 'Each culture is a monad necessary for the cohesion of the whole (therefore to Mankind) and to the perfection that unfolds there gradually . . .' Alain Renaut, *L'ère de l'individu* (Paris: Gallimard, 1989), p. 199.

8. 'The relation of the multitude to the isolated human being that we call the individual and to the isolated human being to this multitude of human beings that we call the Society is not absolutely clear. But quite often people ignore that it is not clear, and they ignore in any case why.' Norbert Elias, *La société des individus* (Paris: Fayard, 1991), p. 31.

9. See W. H. Hudson, *An Introduction to the Philosophy of Herbert Spencer* (London: Watts, 1906), p. 69.

10. 'Society – from the couple to a possible planetary political system (politie) – is a system only by metaphor, because it distinguishes itself from system in the precise sense by this decisive feature that each constitutive element can function independently from that system . . . Briefly, the characteristic of human societies is to be composed of individual elements that can enter into conflict between one another and provoke new combinations.' Jean Baechler, *Démocraties* (Paris: Calmann-Lévy, 1985), p. 43.

11. 'Nation is precisely the kind of global society corresponding to the reign of individualism as value . . . Nation is a global society composed of people that consider themselves as individuals. The modern ideology is in this sense "individualistic".' Louis Dumont, *Essai sur l'individualisme* (Paris: Seuil, 1983), pp. 20, 21.

12. Gilles Deleuze and Félix Guattari, *L'anti-Oedipe: Capitalisme et schizophrénie* (Paris: Editions de Minuit, 1972).

13. 'The independence of the individual is directly related to the number of social circles to which he participates.' 'This social circle multiplicity that intersects in his person is not a true diversity. And it is not at all liberating for the individual. On the contrary.' Georges Palente, *Précis de sociologie* (Paris: Alcan, 1901), p. 170; and *Les antinomies entre l'individu et la société* (Paris: Alcan, 1913), p. 232.

14. E. R. Dodds, *Les grecs et l'irrationnel* (Paris: Flammarion, 1977).

15. 'The real question is to know: where does Sovereignty come from?' Herbert Spencer, *L'individu contre l'Etat* (Paris: Alcan, 1892), p. 121.

16. 'The Western State is this improbable and wonderful invention that guarantees the private autonomy and insures to all what can not be produced spontaneously by the civil society . . . it is the invention – in the etymological discovery sense of what exists already – of an order in accordance with the democratic nature of man and with the nature of democratic regime.' Baechler, op. cit., p. 523.

17. 'Until very recently, the picture we had of a behaviour so complex to

be unstable and recurring has been the picture of a crowd.' Stephen H. Kellert, *In the Wake of Chaos: Unpredictable Order in Dynamical Systems* (Chicago: University of Chicago Press, 1993), p. 5.

18. 'National units have already transmitted their function of guarantors of the physical security of their citizens and consequently their function of survival unit to supranational units... Social units of a more important size have resumed the main survival function of smaller units... the identification of the individual beyond its frontiers, the identity of "us" at the whole humanity level is starting to emerge. One of these indicators is the importance taken on gradually by the notion of human rights.' Elias, op. cit., pp. 283, 296, 300.

19. 'International systems... include units that have, one with the other, regular diplomatic relationships. Now, such relationships are accompanied normally by relationships between individuals that compose the various units. International systems are the interstate aspect of the society to which belong populations, submitted to distinct sovereignties.' Raymond Aron, *Paix et guerre entre les nations* (Paris: Calmann-Lévy, 1962), p. 113.

20. To quote Hobbes. As E. Faguet noted: 'Rightly speaking, every man having a human right and exerting it is a State within the State. Emile Faguet, *La politique comparée* (Paris: Lecène, 1902), p. 49.

21. C. B. Macpherson, *Democratic Theory: Essays in Retrieval* (Oxford: Clarendon Press, 1973), p. 236.

22. Francis Fukuyama, *The End of History and the Last Man* (New York: Free Press, 1992).

23. 'In political analysis the middle ground consists of a research strategy that gives priority to substantive problems (rather than to loyalty to an individual approach) and emphasizes the eclectic selection of an approach or mixture of approaches on the basis of the needs of a given piece of research.' Oran Young, *Systems of Political Science* (Englewood Cliffs, NJ: Prentice Hall, 1968), p. 106.

24. 'The definition of a system as boundary-maintaining is a way of saying that, *relative to its environment*, that is to fluctuations in the factors of the environment, it maintains certain constancies of pattern, whether this constancy be static or moving... we are operating on the level of theory which we have called "structural-functional",... for such theory to have relevance, it must apply to a boundary-maintaining type of system, because only in this way can the system to which a theory is applied be delimited.' Talcott Parsons, *The Social System* (New York: The Free Press, 1964), pp. 482, 483.

25. For the lack of a spatial dimension in theoretical sociology, see Anthony Giddens, *The Constitution of Society: Outline of the Theory of Structuration* (Cambridge: Polity Press, 1984).

26. Cf. Gabriel Almond, 'The Return to the State', *American Political Science Review*, 82–3 (9/1988), pp. 853–74.

27. Mario Bunge, 'System Boundary', *International Journal of General Systems*, 20 (1992), pp. 215–19.

28. Kenneth Falconer, *Fractal Geometry: Mathematical Foundations and Applications* (Chichester: Wiley, 1990).

29. 'In fact, for a Brownian motion in two dimensions . . . the probability of returning to the neighborhood of a given location, no matter how narrowly defined, is 1. By contrast, for Brownian motion in three dimensions, the embedding dimension 3 being larger than the Hausdorff dimension of the motion (DH = 2), the return probability is smaller than 1. This is believed to be an important reason why Mother Nature lets many crucial life-sustaining chemical reactions occur on *surfaces* rather than in three-dimensional space.' Manfred Schroeder, *Fractals, Chaos, Power Laws* (New York: Freeman, 1991), pp. 141, 143.

30. See the contribution of Edgar Morin in Jean-Pierre Dupuy and Paul Dumouchel (eds), *L'auto-organisation: De la physique au politique* (Paris: Seuil, 1983).

31. 'The autopoietic system is "autonomous" in the sense that it does not "care" about the environment. All it "cares" about is the preservation of its "identity". Its organization serves this purpose and no other.' Anatol Rapoport, *General System Theory* (Cambridge, Mass.: Abacus, 1986), p. 115.

32. See Jacques J. Herman, *Les langages de la sociologie* (Paris: PUF, 1988).

33. 'To us, the only problem of concern is about a scheme of becoming that would impose an order on the apparent chaos of relationships between political units.' Aron, op. cit., p. 320.

34. See. J. Briggs and F. D. Peat, *Un miroir turbulent: Guide illustré de la théorie du chaos* (Paris: InterEditions, 1991); and H.-O. Peitgen, H. Jürgens and D. Saupe, *Chaos and Fractals: New frontiers of Science* (New York: Springer-Verlag, 1992).

5 Non-individualist Rediscoveries of the Individual: Feminist Approaches to World Politics

Anna Leander

Feminism has played a central part in the resurgence of the individual in world politics. It is the explicit self-reference of many of the movements through which individuals engage in transnational politics. NGOs (non-governmental organizations) such as those demanding extended rights for women, the AWLUML (the Association of Women Living Under Muslim Law), the women's peace movement, or the movements demanding equal rights for homosexuals, are directly tied to feminist politics. Likewise, feminism has brought attention to the effects world politics has on individuals and in particular on women. The experiences of women are an integral part of reporting on issues as diverse as the Taliban take-over in Kabul, the war in Bosnia, transition in Russia or welfare cuts in Great Britain. Finally, feminism has contributed to making individuals a more central part of conventional inter-state relations. It has been directly active in bringing about the proclamation of the UN decade for Women, the integration of aid programmes and lending policies specifically directed at women, the adoption of the CEDAW, and the staging of the women's conferences which all undermine 'sovereignty' by making individuals, as opposed to sovereign states, the objects of international law and international relations (IR).

In spite of this direct link between feminism and the individualization of world politics, feminist approaches to the study of world politics are usually not individualist. In IR particularly, feminist approaches are squarely anti-individualist.[1] They oppose philosophical individualism, above all in the form of political liberalism, they attack

89

methodological individualism, and, most frequently, they do both.[2] This stark and seemingly paradoxical anti-individualism of feminist approaches in IR is the subject of this chapter. A first section shows that, in part, this anti-individualism has its origins in the overall development of feminist approaches in academia, which has tended to lead feminist scholars away from individualism. However, in IR the anti-individualism of feminism has gone further than in feminist academia in general and has led to the virtual exclusion of a variety of more or less individualist feminist approaches, which are certainly present and part of the debate elsewhere, even if they are not dominating. A second section proceeds to show that this disproportionate anti-individualism of feminism in IR is comprehensible only with reference to the development of IR theorizing. During the heyday of Realism there was little space for feminist thought. But with the epistemological turn during the eighties, feminism – and in particular its post-structuralist, that is, its most anti-individualist, version – was more easily plugged into the central theoretical debates. However, and this is the claim of the last section, the pendulum is on its way back. Current developments in IR as well as in feminist thought are beginning to widen the range of feminist approaches which are part of IR. Non-individualist rediscoveries of individuals by feminism are now complemented by a critically individualist rediscovery of women. Correspondingly, any simplistic view of the relationship between feminist approaches and individualism in the study of world politics is rapidly being undermined.

THE DISPROPORTIONATE ANTI-INDIVIDUALISM OF FEMINIST IR

An obvious explanation of the paradoxical anti-individualism of feminist approaches in IR is that feminism generally is anti-individualist and that the IR version of it merely reflects this overall attitude. Outside feminist circles, this claim may at first sight appear strange. Feminist academia is after all directly linked to the feminist movement. As feminist academics time and again point out, their roots are in feminist politics rather than in (male dominated) academic social sciences.[3] Feminist politics centres on the emancipation of women, i.e. a specific category of individuals. So what is the problem with individualism? What is at the origin of the apparently uneasy relationship between feminism and individualism? A main part of the answer, as the first part of this section shows, is that feminism generally has evolved in opposition to a predominantly liberal conception of politics, where formulations about individuals, individual rights, individual political participation and equal chances for individuals have masked partial conceptions that exclude women and their concerns, and have perpetuated this exclusion. Consequently, it has been very difficult for feminists not to engage in a criticism of the supposed universals of individualism, which are in fact socially, politically, economically or discursively constructed in a sexually biased way. This has left even the feminists favouring some form of liberalism very critical of any simplistic adoption of individualist formulas. However, as the second part of the section argues, feminist anti-individualism outside IR takes multiple forms, and a strong feminist tradition which is individualist, although critically so, continues to flourish. This makes the radical anti-individualism of feminist IR appear out of proportion and calls for an explanation referring to the specific situation in IR.

The Move Away from Individualism in Feminism

The history of feminist development in academia, in one of the more common versions, integrates the tension between feminism and individualism. It presents academic feminism as having developed in waves which removed it further and further from individualism.[4] Standpoint theories of the second wave followed the liberal/ empirical approaches of the first wave and were themselves followed by post-modern approaches; each wave representing a step away from liberalism. This self-representation of academic feminism clearly makes the distant – not to say overtly hostile – relationship between individualism and feminism in IR appear closely linked to the overall development of feminism. It is therefore worthwhile to look in some detail at the arguments implied in this self-representation, in particular with regard to individualism.

The first wave of 'liberal/empirical' feminism reflected demands for women's rights and increased recognition of women's specific problems and realities. Academically, this translated into what later-wave feminists have called an 'add women and stir the masculine soup' approach. In order to bring recognition to women, it was necessary to know about them, to study them empirically, to have statistics about things crucial to women's lives. Similarly, in order to demand equal rights or rights reflecting the specific needs of women, it was a precondition to show why the existing rights either were unequal or failed to adequately cover women. This meant studying the bias inherent either in the application or the design of rules. As later feminist chroniclers point out, the first-wave feminists did not demand radical reformulations. They accepted overall liberal political principles and the usually individualist social sciences. Their main concern was to give women equal weight and recognition in an existing social and political system. They hotly debated whether this meant to recognize and value women's difference from men or whether it meant to make them more equal to men. But whatever the position on this issue, they accepted the idea was that existing academic tools could bring adequate knowledge about women: 'the bias exists in the assumptions of the political theorists, but not in the techniques they employ'.[5] In other words, individualism (or other 'malestream' approaches) as such was not problematic. The malestream interpretation and application was the source of academic (and political) blindness to women and women's problems.

The second wave of 'standpoint' feminism was marked by two convictions which both moved feminists away from individualism. The first conviction – which is what has given the otherwise very heterogeneous group its illusion of homogeneity – was that looking at the world from the standpoint of women would give the observer a more adequate understanding of the mechanisms both of female oppression and of social relations in general. A variety of reasons have been given to support this claim. For some, the feminist standpoint should be privileged because it provides a new perspective which allows us to see formerly hidden truths. The feminist standpoint could be expected to have the same beneficial effect on academia as the child in the fable about the Emperor's New Clothes had on those watching the emperor parade.[6] For others it was essentially a political matter of taking the experience of the (most) oppressed as the basis for a study of social relations. Their experience and viewpoint, so runs the argument, are bound to be the most relevant to academia with the politically informed aim of understanding power relations (an explicit parallel to the role of the proletariat in Marx).[7] The second, and related, conviction shared by most standpoint feminists was that social structures (though not necessarily conceived in marxian, historical materialist terms) were of importance.[8] Understanding sexual discrimination required an understanding of the social structures through which it was reproduced. A study of female political participation and rights could only scratch at the surface of a deeper problem, as revealed by the inefficiency of measures eliminating sexism in formal laws and principles. In order to understand the issues at stake it was necessary to study social structures. This required a feminist standpoint, both to 'pierce ideological obfuscation' and to reveal the specifically gendered part of the social structure.[9] More generally, any explanation of the reproduction of social structures – and thus of relations of domination and oppression more broadly – required attention to the role of gender, the standpoint feminists claimed. That is, malestream theory was no longer deficient only because it did not pay attention to women, but also because it was inadequate to deal with what supposedly was its subject.

That both aspects of standpoint feminism distanced it from individualism is mostly treated as part and parcel of the story. Epistemologically, those who argued for a feminist standpoint claimed that there was not 'an individual' from which one could depart in doing social sciences but at best two groups of individuals; one male and the other female. 'Women's experience' became central in feminist theorizing. This can arguably be seen as merely another form of individualism, if the experience in question is seen in individualist terms, which it often was. However, the subdivision of individuals into two categories introduced a complication in individualist methodology which needed elaboration and explanation and precluded any easy generalization. Consequently, if the point of departure was to be the individual, it would have to be a rather more complicated version thereof. Secondly, and more centrally, most of the standpointers, although grounding their claims in the female experience or standpoint, gave priority to social structures in their explanations of social reality, something which evidently tended to place them in direct opposition to individualism.

The movement away from individualism was taken even further by the third wave of post-modern feminists. The third wave was partly triggered by a reaction against what was perceived as a reification of 'woman' and of 'the female experience' by empiricist and standpoint feminists alike. For a variety of reasons many feminists did not believe that their experience was adequately represented. The post-colonial, black-American and lesbian feminists resented the mainstream feminist project as being not only exclusionary, but in many ways totalitarian.[10] It used the experience of heterosexual, white, middle-class women as a basis for a general, unitary representation of sexual discrimination and for correspondingly unitary solutions to it, disregarding the very significant and perhaps essential differences among women. The third wave exposed the 'paradox at the heart of feminism: Any attempt to talk about all women in terms of something we have in common undermines attempts to talk about the differences among us and vice versa.'[11] In the name of feminist unity, differences had previously been discarded as less significant than what women shared, a solution third wavers found unacceptable.[12] In addition to this, they argued, the insistence on a feminist standpoint or on the unity of 'woman' had the paradoxical effect of simply reproducing the dichotomies (although usually reversing them) that any genuine emancipation required feminists to break out of.

This might have spelled a return to some form of individualism, but instead it fuelled interest in the discursive construction of gender and gender discrimination. With the growing awareness of the variety of sexual identities, and also in response to trends in the rest of the social sciences, the academic focus of feminism moved away from material and social structures into the realm where discourse is seen as constitutive of reality. Emancipation was no longer a matter of understanding material structures, even less of looking at women's political participation, it was increasingly a matter of doing 'epistemological politics', i.e. unmasking and showing the implications of discourses by which gender, and consequently gender discrimination, are reproduced. Ultimately, as argued by Judith Butler, discourse is what produces biological difference, 'gender performativity produces the effects that it names ... the regulatory norms of sex work in a performative fashion to constitute the materiality of bodies and more specifically, to materialize the body's sex, to materialize sexual difference in the service of the consolidation of the heterosexual imperative'.[13] Consequently, to deal with discrimination on the basis of gender, it is necessary to deal with gendered discourse more generally.

The third wave clearly moved the feminist approaches further away from individualism than ever, because it was critical of both philosophical and methodological individualism. The link to women and women's experience was lost. Feminism was interested in gender and discourse and widened to cover all studies of gendered discourses, including those dealing with the construction of male reality.[14] Feminism had so much lost touch with the *femmes* that some preferred to dub it 'post-feminism'.[15] This wave broke the weak, but possible, remaining link between the standpointers and individualism, inherent in the standpointers' focus on women's experience. With the focus on intersubjectively constituted discourses as the primary level of analysis, the sex, autonomy, interests, actions, ideas, statements, or political involvement of individuals must be understood as constructed intersubjectively. There was not one truth, but many discursive realities. And certainly the individual could hardly constitute the point of departure for understanding those realities.

The evolutionism lurking in this wave-presentation makes it clear why the methodologically and philosophically anti-individualist third wave position is often viewed as the dominant feminist position. There is an implicit, when not explicit, claim that each successive wave brought a somewhat irreversible advance of feminist approaches; it brought progress in that it resolved previously existing problems facing feminist theoreticians and brought them a step further on the road to theoretical sophistication and refinement.[16] Often enough the logical consequence is drawn as feminist theoreticians try to define feminist theory and underline that not everyone writing about women or proclaiming themselves feminist is truly feminist.[17] In view of this presentation it is no wonder that the pronounced anti-individualism of feminist approaches in IR is mostly seen as the mere reflection of the more general situation in feminist academia.

The Continuing Presence of Critical Individualism in Feminist Academia

The sweeping conclusion that contemporary feminism is anti-individualist and that, therefore, there is no need to think further about the strong anti-individualism of feminist IR, is none the less misleading. The evolutionist version of the wave story of feminist academia is not generally accepted and uncontroversial. Feminism generally is multifaceted, and many of the authors who define themselves as feminists, publish in feminist journals, and teach women/gender studies do not adhere to either this version of the development of academic feminism nor to any third-wave definition of what feminist theory is. As this section will show, taking this into account considerably complicates the picture of the relationship between individualism and feminism in academia and makes the strong anti-individualism of feminist IR stand out as needing to be explained with reference to something more than general feminist anti-individualism.

The inadequacy of the wave-presentation of the development of feminist academia becomes evident as soon as one pauses and tries to fit leading authors in feminist academia into the typology. Picture for example the difficulty of placing 'psychological' approaches such as that of Gilligan or that of Chodorow, both of whom have been central to feminist academia and academic debate over the past decades. The impression is reinforced when one tries to determine into which category any particular author fits. An author such as Fatima Mernissi could readily be placed into all three categories.[19] It is therefore hardly surprising that authors who use the wave-presentation to classify feminist approaches often manage to place the same author within several and in some cases *all* of the categories.[20] Much as with the 'paradigms' in IR, it seems that everyone agrees that the waves or their equivalent are inadequate representations of the ongoing debate, but they continue to be used, perhaps because they provide such a convenient shorthand for writing and teaching in contexts where things should preferably be neat and tidy.[21]

However, what is of more consequence for our discussion than the inadequacy of the categories – and what has provoked more reaction in feminist academic circles – is that the evolutionary message implied by the wave presentation is misleading, also with respect to the relation between feminism and individualism. In some sense it has acted as a self-fulfilling prophecy on feminist academia. Those who are not among the third wavers find themselves on the defensive. A fair number have slammed the door on women/gender studies in disgust and despair, complaining of the pressure from their supposed feminist colleagues. Perhaps the best-known case is that of Daphne Patai and Noretta Koertge, who not only left the circle, but published an extremely critical insider account of 'the strange world of women's studies'.[22] The authors accused feminist circles of exercising IDPOL in a double sense: as IDentity POLitics and as IDeological POLicing. Patai and Koertge argued that feminist IDPOL creates an environment of intolerance, directly hostile to rational argument, which is a threat to the process to learning and ultimately to the freedom of thought and expression. To underscore that their views and experience are not unique, the authors report a widespread sympathetic response to their book from former (and present) academics in women/gender studies.[23]

This said, the bulk of feminist academics who did not fit into the story and/or were outraged by it have not followed the path of Patai and Koertge. Many of the feminists placed in the categories of earlier waves understandably resent and resist being depicted as outmoded relics from the distant past of underdeveloped feminism. But they are also unwilling to give up the high ground of feminist thought to those who define them that way. They consequently not only continue to work and write, but also actively define and develop alternative views of what feminism is and should be about. Their continued, significant, presence in feminist academia is what ultimately exposes the evolutionary wave-presentation as simplistic and misleading.

Those commonly classified as standpoint feminists are explicit about their lack of sympathy for the post-modernists as well as about their position as feminists. In an early answer to the post-modernists, Nancy Hartsock argued that it is impossible to accept the death-verdict on the subject and the relativism of (political) arguments precisely when, for the first time, women and non-Western people are beginning to refer to themselves as subjects and to make political claims.[24] Similarly, in a recent and revealing debate, Nancy Hartsock, Dorothy Smith and Sandra Harding rather angrily reject an evidently well-intentioned attempt by Susan Heckman to argue that their standpoint theory has been 'written off' too rapidly by feminists. In fact, Heckman argues, standpoint theory does deal with some of the central issues of the debate today, namely the nature of truth and knowledge claims. The standpointers sourly reply that they don't consider standpoint theory to have been written off. Their theory is alive and well. Moreover, they refuse to be distorted by 'a kind of American pluralism that prefers to speak not about power or justice but, rather, about knowledge and epistemology'.[25] The standpointers may be no less anti-individualist than the post-modernists, but they are so for different reasons. Their key grievance has little to do with claims regarding the constitutive nature of discourses and the nature of knowledge claims. Their concern is with power relations as expressed in social and economic structures.

Likewise, feminists working roughly within a more or less liberal tradition of political theory resist the post-modernist definitions of feminism. A common argument is to down-play the differences by arguing that the supposed post-modern feminism is not really post-modern. Seyla Benhabib, for example, writes that the post-modern historical feminism of writers like Fraser and Nicholson, 'is less "postmodernist" but more "neo-pragmatist". By "postmodern feminist theory" they mean a theory that would be pragmatic and fallibilistic, that would tailor its method and categories to the specific task at hand, using multiple categories when appropriate and forswearing the metaphysical comfort of a single feminist method or feminist epistemology. Yet this even handed and commonsensical approach of tailoring theory to the tasks at hand is not postmodernist.'[26]

Liberal feminists have in different ways and contexts argued that the theoretical and methodological claims of their postmodern feminist colleagues are often overstated and could (should) have been phrased within a more classical tradition. O'Neill makes a strong argument against the claim that 'recognizing difference' must lead us to throw our intellectual heritage overboard. She argues that accounting for difference is already an integral part of our system of political and social thinking, for instance in judicial systems which consider circumstances, and tax systems which are differentiated.[27] Martin reacts against the 'compulsory historicism' and the 'methodological essentialism' implied by much of third-wave feminism. She argues that by rejecting essentialism (i.e. the idea that feminism is grounded on what women have in common), by demanding of everyone that they situate themselves historically and that they work with constructivist methods, feminists are stifling healthy and necessary methodological pluralism, losing crucial insights and committing logical mistakes at least as serious as those of the standpoint essentialism they react against.[28] Third, liberal feminists point out that the claims of the third wavers are theoretically naive if taken at face value, counter-productive for the cause of women and politically dangerous. Anne Phillips, for instance, stresses the crucial importance of making claims which go beyond the self in order to have any political movement.[29] Finally, the liberals react against the totalizing claims for a feminist theory. Elshtain protests that 'there is no single, overarching logic of explanation which can do everything for us ... psychoanalytic theory can no more account for the political economy of women under capitalism than Marxist economic theory can offer a coherent understanding of women's psychology and sense of self-identity'.[30]

The spectrum of feminist approaches which are alive and well in academia is clearly broader than the wave theory implies. Moreover, some of these approaches are directly concerned with central themes in individualism. They have dealt explicitly with many of the central assumptions of individualism as used in political theory. Starting with the notion and nature of the individual, feminists have worked extensively on both the constitution of the self and on the ways in which this individual self conceives its interests. Psychological feminism has among its central themes the construction and reproduction of gendered identities. Chodorow's studies of the 'reproduction of mothering' and Gilligan's study of women's moral development share one thing: they undermine the idea that social analysis can ground itself on individuals with self-interests defined independently of gender.[31] Drawing the implications of this for various individualist versions of political theory, authors have pointed to the extreme difficulty of using unified notions of self-interest. In a general study of the notion of self-interest, Jane Mansbridge – drawing on feminism among other things – discusses the general crisis of the notion of self-interest as a basis for explaining political behaviour. She argues that 'the claim that self-interest alone motivates political behaviour must be either vacuous, if self-interest can encompass any motive, or false, if self-interest means behaviour that consciously intends only the self as the beneficiary'.[32] In a more exclusively and explicitly feminist vein, Virginia Held argues that explanations resting on the idea that self-interest is the overruling motivation of behaviour rests on a specifically 'male' view of the world which ignores the fundamental importance (particularly for women) of emotions, empathy and care in motivating behaviour.[33]

The dialogue is further extended to deal explicitly with the problems in the view of politics that follow from individualist approaches. Benhabib criticizes Rawlsian contractarianism by arguing that, even as a thought experiment, the idea of the original position is utterly untenable, since it presupposes that the self could be disembedded and disembodied.[34] Carole Pateman takes a more radical line by showing that the 'social contract' of contractarianism is not social at all, but essentially sexual. It assumes and depends on the exclusion of women from the social contract.[35] Elshtain shows how the separation of public and private, crucial to all political theory, has to be rethought (not abandoned or fused as many more radical feminists would have it) if it is to be acceptable to both women and men.[36] And finally, Phillips spells out the consequences of what it means to make liberal democracy work in a gender neutral way, and in a way which would eventually eliminate the relevance of gender for political participation.[37]

As this indicates, feminist individualism is always critical. Indeed, the only plausible reason for which an author would label a work 'feminist' is that it expresses a concern with the fact that the gender and/or sex of the 'individual' makes a difference in the analysis. Otherwise the author would have no reason to refer to anything but individualism or the specific brand of it that was being dealt with. This concretely means that feminist individualism takes into account the role of the socially created/constructed either in the subjects studied (self, interests, actions, politics etc.) or in the ways that these subjects have been interpreted (if the approach concentrates on individualist interpretations of social reality). Thus, 'feminism as the daughter of individualism, carries the potential of bringing individualism back to its social moorings by insisting that the rights of individuals derive from society rather than from their innate nature.'[38]

In short, a reading of feminism which takes into account the wide variety of feminist approaches can certainly not come to the conclusion that feminism is post-modern and anti-individualist, as the general reception in international theory would have it. It is more than post-modern as shown by the vivid critique of post-modern feminism within the feminist camp. It is not necessarily anti-individualist but merely critical of simplistic uses of disembodied and disembedded individuals in much political theory.[39] Consequently, to understand the identification between feminism and anti-individualism in IR – which should now appear as clearly disproportionate in relation to the situation in feminist academia generally – we need to refer to a reality beyond that of feminist academia.

FEMINISTS TAKING THE 'EPISTEMOLOGICAL TURN' INTO IR

Feminism in IR has become largely identified with a post-modern version of feminism. This is the version that many, or most, of the leading feminist authors, such as Christine Sylvester, V. Spike Peterson or J. Anne Tickner, who are accepted as belonging to the field of IR represent.[40] It is also the version that most non-feminist IR scholars debate with and discuss in their overviews.[41] Of course all reckon that other versions of feminism do exist, but these other versions have remained amazingly silent in the IR debate itself. The following section will argue that this predominance of post-modern feminist approaches in IR – and the related view that feminist approaches to world politics is mainly anti-individualist – is only comprehensible as a consequence of the way feminist approaches have been integrated into IR. The argument is that while other feminist academics dealing with IR-related themes were relegated to subfields of IR and therefore failed to establish themselves within the core of the discipline, post-modern feminists became part of the debate at the centre of the discipline. They benefitted from 'the epistemological turn in IR', but more importantly they directly engaged in IR as defined by IR scholars. Thus, paradoxically, post-modern feminism – that is, the form of feminism most distant from the realist core of IR – managed what other feminist approaches had not: they made feminist approaches part of IR. This achievement, however, resulted in a situation where the feminism accepted in IR was the one the furthest removed from individualism.

Feminist Inroads in International Relations

Until recently there were little more than marginal inroads of feminism into subfields of IR. This is not due to a lack of feminist work on IR-related issues. On the contrary, there is a long-standing tradition of feminist scholarship on issues which are directly – at least if taken at face value – related to IR. Feminists have worked extensively on explaining war and peace, supposedly at the heart of the subject of IR.[42] However, as Murphy rightly points out, it makes little sense to consider this literature as a part of IR since it was totally ignored by IR scholars and since feminist authors did not consider themselves part of an IR debate.[43] Feminism only started to make inroads into IR with the 'third debate' which placed 'IR in disarray',[44] and even then feminism failed to become an accepted part of the discipline.

Fundamentally the reason for this is that IR has dismissed as irrelevant the concerns of feminist scholars: 'On the one hand it presumed that international relations as such are little if at all affected by issues pertaining to women. To put it in simplistic terms, the assumption is that one can study the course of relations between states without reference to questions of gender. On the other hand, by neglecting the dimension of gender, international relations implicitly supports the thesis that international processes themselves are gender neutral, that is, that they have no effect on the position and role of women in society, and on the relative placement of women and men.'[45] The basis for this judgement lies in the very wide gap which separated the interests of IR scholars and feminists at least until the 1980s.

IR not only focused on high politics between states interacting without an overarching authority, but saw this as the definition of the discipline. That is, IR was defined as the study of politics of a different kind than the politics involving individuals inside states. The lack of discussion around this definition of IR is well visible in the so-called 'debates' which have dominated the discipline. The first debate was a normative debate which opposed idealists and realists. The issue was how war was best avoided. The difference concerned the possibility of qualitative change in the anarchical international sphere. As pointed out by Waever, the main unifying theme of otherwise very diverse realists was 'the denial of the basic liberal argument that there is a possibility of progress'.[46] The 'second (Bull–Kaplan) debate' was a methodological discussion which opposed traditional diplomatic history approaches to behaviouralist ones. The issue was how to best study IR: according to scientific, behaviouralist methods or according to interpretative historical ones.

This definition of IR made feminist approaches seem irrelevant for two reasons. First, state-centrism made any concern with individuals (and consequently also with women) appear distant from the central preoccupations of the field. Individuals were not totally absent. Key statesmen and bureaucrats of course figured in the accounts to the extent that their actions and their decisions were the most concrete and immediate expression of 'the state'. Discussion of the role personalities such as Nikita Khrushchev, Henry Kissinger or Ho Chi Minh have played also is on the conventional IR agenda. Moreover, the 'international society' (of diplomats) – which constituted an important part of the practice of IR – figured prominently on the research agenda of at least the English school of IR. Finally, individuals appeared in the guise of abstract and anonymous citizens and soldiers on behalf of whom international politics was made, and who occasionally could become actors. Clearly, the individuals figuring in IR were individuals representing the state in its international functions, thus were rarely women, who, everyone agrees, have played marginal roles in these functions. To the extent that there were women, their significance was judged in the same terms as the significance of male political leaders. IR felt no need to refer to 'feminist approaches' to understand the significance of women such as Golda Meir or Indira Gandhi.

Secondly, and similarly, IR defined away feminist politics from its sphere. It located politics in an 'anarchical' international system/society with no government or overarching authority to rule over sovereign states, and by doing so it took a double step away from feminist approaches. The first step consisted in making an unproblematized and reified (often anthropomorphic) 'state' the key actor of international politics. This excluded discussion of the link between public and private central to feminism. The second step was to proclaim that international politics was separate and distinct from national politics. How it was distinct and what subjects were therefore relevant was defined by the IR scholars. They did not include feminist issues. If feminists generally tried to bring politics downward, to lift the curtain on the private sphere, IR scholars seemed tempted to do the opposite and to move it outward towards an increasingly abstract and abstruse level. Feminist approaches, almost by definition, required that the internal/external and state/society divides on which IR rested be abandoned.[47] IR scholars refused to see, and mostly even to discuss, the use of such a step.

The gap between IR and feminist approaches turned into an abyss as a result of the restrictive redefinition of IR by Kenneth Waltz and his 'neo-realist' followers.[48] The neo-realist turn made explicit the disinterest in feminism which had been implicit in the classical definition of IR. First, proclaiming that the only subject matter of IR was the international structure was the equivalent of canonizing the distance between the interest for individuals and personal politics of feminism, and the interstate politics of IR. It legitimized the exportation of the issues raised by feminist approaches to other fields. Further, the neo-realist move explicitly excluded the points of entrance which may have existed in more classical definitions of IR where, conceivably, women could appear in foreign policy-making or in the economic changes which underlay the altered power of any single country, and gender could play a role in the legitimation of colonial policies or in fomenting nationalism. But, according to neo-realism, all of this was not the subject of IR but of other fields (foreign policy analysis, political economy, and sociology). Thirdly, by proclaiming IR a field relying on an economic approach, neo-realism denied the legitimacy of other approaches in the field. This meant excluding the bulk of feminist work. Finally, by treating this method as a scientific and unproblematic given, neo-realism also tended to close the door even to the existing and extensive feminist discussion of economic methods from within economics.[49] This is what Elshtain refers to when she argues that the quest for parsimony and scientific method has been the greatest obstacle to the development of IR.[50]

However, at about the time of the neo-realist turn, the intellectual movements which had triggered the neo-realist defence of a narrow definition of IR and a unique 'scientific' method for studying it, also opened more favourable perspectives for feminist inroads in IR. Since the early 1970s, these movements had taken the lead in a serious debate about how to conceive of IR. The place of the state as the key actor, the focus on high politics, and issues of methodology were 'up for grabs'. They were at the heart of the critique which a rapidly growing 'international political economy' confronted IR with. Likewise, these issues separated authors later lumped together in the three camps of the 'inter-paradigm' debate. Alongside the realists appeared the 'pluralists' (those who wanted an extension of IR to non-state actors[51]) and the 'radicals' (essentially neo-marxists) who not only explosively increased the number of actors, but rejected the inside/outside and state/society binary oppositions of realism and neo-realism. Besides explaining what states do in relation to an international structure, explaining major events in the international economy, or inequality and poverty, became acceptable occupations for IR scholars. These developments seemed to create a natural space for feminist approaches within IR (as defined by the practitioners of the field themselves), and in certain ways it did. Through the widening definition of what was accepted as IR, feminist approaches began to penetrate the subfields of the discipline.[52]

But in most cases the feminists remained part of the subfields, rather than of IR proper. The fate of feminist writing on development and on political economy with a very direct bearing on International Political Economy (IPE) and on the neo-marxist approaches to IR is telling in this regard. Feminists had written on various issues of obvious relevance to both. There were both theoretical and applied works on the sexual division of labour and its significance and place in systems of economic accumulations.[53] Similarly, there were literally mountains of feminist literature on various aspects of development, including the way that international changes affected the role of women and the way that women were shaping foreign economic relations.[54] The spread and general acceptance of the message present in this literature is obvious in the influence it had already in the course of the 1970s on the development policies of international organizations (the UN, the World Bank or the regional development banks). However, in IR it remained largely invisible.

One reason may be the banal, and seemingly ever-present, personal and institutional resistance to change in academia, but there were also more tangible disciplinary reasons for the neglect. The aspects of IPE and neo-marxism which made them part and parcel of IR were those that were the most distant from feminist writings. They were the aspects that had a direct bearing on the power relations between states. The immense popularity of 'hegemonic stability theory' in its various incarnations and the central place of a strawman version of 'dependency theory' as the (mostly, only) reference to marxist IPE, are certainly intimately linked to their direct and obvious implications for 'power relations' among states which most IR scholars continued to see as the heart of their subject. One can even, as Stefano Guzzini suggests, consider the development of parts of IPE as an attempt to save an updated form of realism by an inclusion of the economic aspects of IR which were becoming too important to ignore.[55]

From this perspective it is not difficult to see why the feminist literature remained part of the subfields. This literature indeed dealt with the same subjects as the IPE scholars and the neo-marxists. It was certainly also read by many of these scholars. But more often than not the links between the feminist writing and these fields were precisely at the points where these were seen to leave IR. It was at the point where IPE touched comparative political economy and neo-marxism touched development studies. This was clearly not the part which could be used to rescue realism, or in other words the part which (explicitly or implicitly) reaffirmed internal/ external and state/society divides which made little sense to feminism. It was not the part which seemed most interesting to IR scholars. Consequently, in a 1988 article which is part of an attempt to integrate feminist approaches through the openness of the 'third debate',[56] Halliday could still marvel at the fact that 'twenty years after the emergence of feminism within the social sciences' feminism was still no more than an emerging concern in IR.[57]

Establishing a Feminist Voice from the Margin

When feminism finally did conquer a place in IR it was not as a part of the extended agenda which covered non-state actors, transnational phenomena and studies of inequality and wealth. Rather feminism made its entrance as part of the 'epistemological' turn in the late 1980s.

The 'epistemological turn' came in part as a response to (or a development of) the inter-paradigm debate of the early 1980s. This debate had legitimated research agendas and methods that had earlier been excluded, and in close relation to this it had increased the theoretical awareness and interest of practitioners within IR. This in turn had led to the realization that in many ways the boxes of the inter-paradigm debate were highly inadequate for capturing the significant differences between positions in the field, that the idea of paradigm was misused, and that there was a need to develop a better theoretical understanding. As a consequence, IR opened up to the theoretical debates and categorizations used in other parts of the social sciences. The discussion about the internal and external coherence and consistency of theories in IR was increasingly waged in terms of meta-theoretical arguments.[58] The 'agent–structure' debate found an entrance also into IR.[59] And Hollis and Smith eventually encouraged their colleagues to rethink the classification of IR theories and use a general meta-theoretical matrix developed for social sciences along the axis: naturalism/interpretivism and individualism/holism.[60]

Of particular significance for the later integration of feminism was the growing presence of 'reflectivist' approaches in IR in this context. The reflectivists included a wide mixture of approaches (critical hermeneutical, scientific realism, constructivism and post-structuralism) that did not share the mainstream convictions about how social sciences were best made. In various ways they questioned falsificationism, the search for single cause explanations, the attempts to establish general laws, and the way that empirical research was being done. In other words, the new 'reflectivist–rationalist' (sometimes dubbed fourth[61]) debate was about how good science in general and IR in particular was to be practised, and it was carried out at a highly theoretical level.

A central part in this new debate was played by what have interchangeably been called post-positivist, post-structuralist, and postmodern authors.[62] In what was a highly normative project, these authors tried to drive home the point that the realist conception of the world (and notably the strict and related inside/outside state/society divides) prevented IR, and political science more generally, from perceiving and dealing with crucial political issues; served to

legitimate and perpetuate given political orders and power relations, and effectively fended off the political and theoretical imagination which was needed for thinking out alternatives.[63] The
post-positivist did this by studying how discourses have shaped the
theory and practice of IR. Concretely, the bulk of their work consisted of critical studies of texts, something which earned them the
reputation of being abstruse and of lacking an 'empirical research
project', and therefore of not being worthy contenders for the theoretical leadership in the field of IR.[64] They were relegated to the
'margins' of the discipline.[65] However, even at the margin they were
part of IR. The 'reflectivists' published in the major journals, were
present on the disciplinary conferences, were part of the teaching
curricula, and were becoming standard reference in the debate.

This meant that the door was open for feminist approaches, and
particularly the feminist approaches of the third wave, to take part
in the IR debate. In accepting the post-structuralist critique, the
discipline became more sensitive also to the arguments of post-
modern feminists. Like the post-structuralists, the feminists concerned themselves with pointing out exclusions and marginalization.
They focused on recovering women (or gender more generally).
Another parallel was the interest in power relations and unspoken
biases. Feminists wanted to uncover gendered power relations and
their reproduction through the analysis of how specific discourses
embedded and shaped world views. Just as the post-structuralists,
the feminists were criticizing the construction of knowledge. The
affinity between post-structuralism and feminism in IR is very visible in the way feminist authors situate themselves in IR.[66] For
Sylvester, feminism is 'post-structuralist' along the lines defined by
Jane Flax.[67] For Tickner (whose own position is less clear), 'the
contemporary critique [that all knowledge is socially constructed
and is grounded in the time, place, and social context of the inves-
tigator] brings the IR discourse closer to the feminist perspectives'.[68]
Likewise, when Peterson situates feminist critiques and contributions, she sees them in terms of 'ongoing conversations' which concentrate on 'knowledge and its politics', that is, on fundamentally
'reflectivist' topics.[69] Another good indication of the many affini-
ties between feminism and post-structuralism in IR is the often
felt need of feminists to mark their distance from post-structuralists and hence to underline the usefulness and originality of their
approach. Thus, Peterson and Runyan point out that: 'Whereas
postmodernist critiques reveal domination relations as inscribed in

hierarchical dichotomies, feminist postmodernists expose the dichotomizing move itself as derived from masculinist experience.'[70]

The door was, however, not merely opened to third-wave feminists. It was also pushed open by them. Arguably, the emerging
feminist writings on IR were part of what forced the door open for
the other post-modern voices from the margins. Looking at the
exclusions and gender bias of the IR discourse and tackling its assumptions was an obvious way to bridge the earlier gap between
IR and feminism. Just as in other disciplines, feminists in IR were
increasingly impatient with having their 'relevance' measured in terms
of the dominant understanding.[71] 'Disciplining feminism to make it
acceptable to a particular discourse is not the goal of feminist IR
theorizing', as two key exponents of feminism in IR point out.[72]
Consequently, feminists were no longer content to be shoved off
to subdisciplines of the subdisciplines of IR. On the contrary, in
the late 1980s feminists began to pay direct attention to key issues
of IR proper, and they often did so from a post-positivist, if not
post-structuralist, perspective. One obvious reason for this is that
the post-structuralist focus on the way discourse is constitutive of
reality had more reason to debate with 'realism', in terms which
realists would acknowledge, than other brands of feminism which
were concerned with depicting some part of a gender discriminating reality.[73] Thus, Rebecca Grant developed a general argument
about the origins of gender bias in IR, which she found to lay in
the definition of the state and of security; and J. Anne Tickner
analyzed one of the central works in IR (that of Morgenthau) to
show the inherent gender bias.[74]

This frontal attack of feminists on IR made it increasingly difficult to ignore feminist writing. Clearly, the argument that they didn't
deal with IR was no longer tenable. They were explicitly directing
their critical efforts at the field of IR. They were writing about the
key figures in IR literature. And they were doing this in a way
which was parallel to and reinforcing the 'other critical voices from
the margins' that were increasingly part of the IR debate. Thus,
what Christine Sylvester hoped for in the mid-1990s was in many
ways a reality already in the late 1980s:

> It will no longer do to say that one is not adequately acquainted
> with feminist scholarship. The literature is there to be read like
> every other strand of international relations thinking, and it is
> unprofessional to think that one need not read it to do good

research. The time has come to recognize women and feminists by naming us rather than by winking at us as we walk by.[75]

This integration of feminism in IR through the 'epistemological turn' led to a very peculiar and restrictive view of feminism in IR. It led to an identification for all practical purposes of feminism with its post-structuralist (and consequently anti-individualist) variant. This was nowhere more visible than in the down-playing or even marginalization of other forms of feminism. Mainstream scholars were given a relatively convenient excuse for continuing to ignore feminists that were relegated to the subfields of the discipline and not to consider the enlargement that taking them into account would have required. After all, they were dealing with the feminist approaches directly relevant to IR, were they not? At the same time it justified keeping the feminism that was integrated into IR in the margins. Just as the other post-structuralist approaches, feminism was deemed excessively theoretical, abstract and in want of an empirical research project, at least one that would be relevant to IR. Finally, the focus on the gendered construction of various aspects of IR that many mainstreamers continued to treat and judge as essentially gender neutral, or at least as only marginally influenced by gender, buttressed an existing fear of a totalizing feminist position claiming that all gender is international, or inversely, that all international is gendered.[76] It is revealing both of the reception of feminism, and of the view of what feminism is in IR, that the reviewers of the work of Jean Bethke Elshtain (who identifies herself as a feminist, publishes in feminist journals, and who has worked extensively on feminist issues) refuse to deal with her as a feminist. The reasons given are, first, the uncertainty of 'her status as a feminist' (she is too 'conservative') and, second, the fact that treating her as a feminist would reduce her to one who 'speaks from the margins as feminist'.[77]

There has also been a tendency among the IR feminists themselves to down-play the role of other feminist approaches. The more benign version of this is when all feminist work is presented as belonging to one post-positivist category. Peterson is quite explicit on this when she writes that all feminist writing is inherently 'post-positivist' (by which she means critical of the way knowledge is constituted).[78] This may well be the case, but it is certainly not the light in which liberal and standpoint feminists like to think about their theories. A less comfortable version of feminist self-exclusion is when other approaches are either ignored or dismissed. The most obvious and well-known case in the literature is the widespread rejection of Keohane's proposal of an 'alliance' between standpoint feminism and his own version of neo-institutionalism.[79] His initiative was rather angrily rejected by the bulk of the feminists in IR on the grounds that it was based on standpoint theory; that he was asking 'David to ally with Goliath'; that he was foreclosing debate; and that he was trying to divide and rule by co-opting part of the opposition.[80] The tone and contents of this response is only comprehensible as the defensive reaction of a specific version of feminism. A view of feminism which gave more than nominal space to a standpoint or a liberal position would have had all reason to give the initiative a welcome, even if the welcome were a critical one.

To summarize, this section has argued that the long marginalization of feminist approaches in IR, and their eventual integration through the epistemological turn, have resulted in an accentuation of the general anti-individualist trend in feminist academia. It led to the integration first and foremost of post-modern feminism, which explicitly argues that the link between IR theory and individualism is one source of its gender bias.[81] It also left only a marginal place for feminist approaches which are either anti-individualist in a different way or simply critical of individualism abused. The liberal and standpoint feminist literature – which might have been integrated alongside neo-marxism, pluralism or various strands of IPE in the mid-1970s to mid-1980s – never managed to bridge the gap between feminism and IR. They remained confined to the subfields. Consequently, as a leading exponent of feminist IR writes, the stress of feminist IR has been on the dual project of 'deconstructing gender bias' and 'reconstructing gender sensitive theory'. That is, women and gender were introduced in IR as socially and intersubjectively constituted meaning and identities, not through a focus on individuals.

THE EMERGING CRITICALLY INDIVIDUALIST CONCERN WITH WOMEN IN WORLD POLITICS

Since feminism conquered a place in IR, its position has been consolidated and is continuously widening. This section will show how the presence of post-modern feminism in IR is currently being complemented by a far wider range of feminist approaches. The main reason for this is changing and widening agendas both in IR and in feminism. In feminism, the many voices critical of the third wave's exclusive claims are making themselves heard and, in addition to this, post-structuralism is losing its dominant grip as in other social sciences. In IR the end of the Cold War is pushing the tension between two trends (back[82]) on the agenda: namely the tension between the increasing globalization of politics and political power and the continuing, accentuated, nationalization of politics.[83] This tension is leading to renewed interest in a variety of subjects, such as the nature of sovereignty, important international actors (e.g. international businesses, individuals, organized crime, transnational movements), and political phenomena intimately linked to the tension (e.g. regionalism, nationalism, social contracts and international ethics). One thing these otherwise very diverse subjects have in common is that they lead IR scholars to move away both from narrowly defined neo-realist frameworks and from highly theoretical argumentations. This in turn, creates space for, and interest in, a wider range of feminists in IR, as this section will show by linking up three central themes on the IR research agenda (identity, economic globalization, ethics) with existing feminist work which is already partly integrated into IR. These trends are encouraging for those who favour a broad and diversified feminist presence (and general debate) in IR, as I do; they none the less sap the easy conclusion that feminism and individualism are basically antagonistic in the study of world politics.

Feminism Applied to the Construction of Identities and the Return of Culture and Identity in IR

IR is experiencing an upsurge in studies about identity.[84] There are a variety of reasons for this. Part of these are directly linked to international developments. The members of the growing number of transnational political movements (catholic, orthodox, muslim, green, and ... feminist) claim that their political identity and their political struggles have no reason to accept the borders of the nation state. Also, sub-national political groups (the East Timorese, Bosnian Serbs, Kurds, or the members of la Lega Nord, for instance) affirm that their political identity is at another level than the nation state. Clearly a large share of the post Cold War conflicts have been triggered by precisely this kind of claim, and there is a corresponding sense of necessity in IR to develop ways of dealing with the problems raised by 'identity'.[85]

The more theoretical move towards the issue of identity initially had a post-structuralist point of departure, but it has now become clearly constructivist. It focuses on different ways in which identities, nationalism and political movements are constructed. The underlying assumption is that the constitution of meaning gives or creates actors' identities and the meaning that is given to 'reality' and 'action'. The systems of meaning are logically prior to individual action. Indeed, constructivists singled out the analysis of identity as a critique of 'rationalist' approaches: even if we accept that actors are interest-driven, constructivists argue that interest is itself determined by identity. As a result any action theory must include ('endogenize') identity as part of the actors' formation of interests.[86] Feminists were part and parcel of the initial post-structuralist movement and of the later constructivist one.[87] Moreover, the theory-driven interest in identity formation has drawn attention to parts of psychoanalytical feminism dealing with how identity is reproduced, and how identity makes people more likely to share specific forms of behaviour.[88]

However, the widening of the IR and the feminist agenda is presently bringing a wide range of less theoretical, more practice-driven approaches into the centre of the picture. This is where a place seems to be emerging for a feminist agenda which goes beyond the third wave. Part of this practice-driven feminist literature is a (not very sophisticated form of) critical individualism. This is the case with the already old and well-established feminist practice-driven interest in identity and peace politics. Thus, much of the extensive feminist work on transnational feminist movements posits (rather than explains) the specific nature of women, usually perceived to be more peaceful than that of men, and then explains the solidarity, peace efforts and interactions of these (individual) women on this basis.[89] More interestingly, and perhaps also more centrally, an applied feminist literature on identity construction is being discovered and integrated into IR. This literature does not need to rely on any assumptions about the inherently peaceful and nurturing nature of women but concentrates on explaining how images of women have been constituted and instrumental in the construction of identities. There are a great number of studies that focus on how the images of women have been instrumental in fostering militarism or nationalist projects. Just to mention two examples:

Kandiyoti's work clarifies how the cause of women has been used in the colonial and post-colonial context to create varying political identities with enormous political impact. She argues that reference to the situation of women has been politically used to justify colonialism, to demand national self-determination, to create modernizing national identities, or of late to legitimize religious fundamentalism (but rarely for the emancipation of women themselves).[90] Similarly, Elshtain explores the ambiguous role of women in fostering militarism. While she points to the role of women as peacemakers, and the image of women as peaceful and anti-militaristic, she also insists on the importance of women in fuelling militarism. Women not only need protection, but value and encourage the sacrifice of their men and sons in war.[91]

This second type of practice-driven feminist interest in identity is not individualist in any simple way. It is more a literature which adds an applied dimension to the non-individualist approaches to identity and culture. Thus, it is widening the place of feminism in IR not so much by fundamentally altering the approach as by adding an applied dimension.

Non-post-modern Anti-individualist Feminism in the Study of Economic Globalization

The second central theme on the present IR agenda – economic globalization and changing social contracts – is also paving the way for a wider range of feminist approaches. It is bringing in another type of usually applied feminism which has so far had little place in IR.

The growing attention in IR to phenomena commonly grouped under the heading economic globalization is fuelled by an awareness of the increasingly impossible task of thinking about 'national' political economies without accounting for their interaction with the global.[92] In political debates, globalization and competitive pressures have become common currency. Likewise, comparative political economy seems to (belatedly) have become aware of the importance of the interaction between global and local, as reflected in the stress put on this in recent work.[93] This development has led to a considerable increase in the weight given to IPE within the overall framework of IR. In fact, Susan Strange argues that it should be given absolute priority.[94] Even if not all go so far, few would deny the general importance of including the issues which arise

from the discrepancy between global economies and (largely) local-
ized politics, on the agenda of the study of world politics.

The focus on economic globalization and changing social contracts opens a second potential meeting point with feminism, but
of a different kind than that focusing on identity construction.
Expectedly, because of the topic, feminist writing on globalization
and changing social contracts lacks the theoretical ambitions of the
third-wave feminists. In fact, most of it implicitly or explicitly shares
the assumptions, and takes sides in the disagreements, of malestream
theory (regarding truth, measures, valid arguments, writing style).
The work tends to be based on similar arguments, where the collection of qualitative and/or statistical evidence plays a crucial role
in supporting the claims made. The questions also tend to focus
on similar issues to those raised in political economy generally,
with the difference that the gendered aspect receives attention. It
focuses on how globalization affects gender relations in society (for
example, how the gendered patterns of social policies, employment,
or the family are altered through globalization) and how gender
relations in turn influence the patterns of globalization (for example,
how the gendered aspects of work, of media, or of states shape the
uneven globalization and the reactions against it).

Feminists tend to tackle these issues from a prevailingly non-
individualist perspective. As with a large part of the work in IPE,
a very widely shared assumption is that structures (however defined) play a fundamental role in shaping outcomes. Their role is
considered so important that they should constitute the point of
departure, be it for understanding how a political economy works,
be it for understanding the options, choices and actions of individuals within it. For feminists this is fundamental. Much of the
feminist work on national political economies has aimed precisely
to show how patterns in markets, in state intervention, in social
benefit entitlements, etc. have functioned (in combination or each
taken alone) in a way which is far from being gender neutral.[95]
Consequently, it seems only logical that the bulk of feminist work
related to IPE should share this assumption and deal with different aspects of the social, economic and political construction of
gender and how it changes.

Some examples from recent literature may be useful to illustrate
the argument. Discussing the impact of globalization in the context of Western welfare states, Griffin Cohen, studying the engagement taken through NAFTA, points to ways in which globalization

undermines the grip of the state on the economy. She goes on to argue that this correspondingly diminishes possibilities women have to influence their own fate.[96] Similarly, Cresy Cannan develops the argument that the 'culture of enterprise' (itself placed in a wider context of international neo-liberalism) in the UK is penalizing women, who are the main dependants on state provision of social services and welfare benefits.[97] Discussing the impact of globalization in the context of central and eastern Europe, Molyneux convincingly shows how the combined and mutually reinforcing effects of a communist heritage and an international liberal order are producing a rather catastrophic situation for women.[98] Finally, in a very informative and interesting work on the changing position of women in the Middle East, Moghadam connects (local and global) economic, social and cultural factors in her explanation.[99]

There are, also many feminists who work on issues pertaining to changing social contracts and globalization, but who do not fit into the above presentation of feminist work as rather mainstream, and anti-individualist. On the one hand, 'radical' feminists, such as Catherine MacKinnon, are definitely not mainstream, nor do they subscribe to mainstream assumptions about truth, method and argument.[100] MacKinnon sees little point in placing any hope in a masculine state which is bound to perpetuate the oppression of women endlessly. Consequently, she does not see much point in asking the typical mainstream questions about the future of social policy and state intervention in favour of women. On the other hand, 'liberal' (in the economic sense) feminists are arguably not anti-individualist since they rest on the individualist foundations of liberal economics.[101] However, the individualism of liberal feminists is not altogether clear cut: they take a liberal stance because they think about the market as a liberating force undermining the (social, economic or political) structures that perpetuate gender discrimination.[102] That is, they tend to think about the economy in terms of how one system, the market, changes another one, social, economic or political structure.

These exceptions underline that there is a wider range of feminist writing on globalization and changing social contracts than the anti-individualist mainstream presentation makes room for, and which will hopefully receive wider attention in IR circles. However, this does not alter the fundamental point that an extensive anti-individualist, structuralist feminist literature overlaps with an increasingly central part of IR, is being integrated there, and is thereby broadening the range of feminist approaches which are part of the IR debate.

A Place for Critically Individualist Feminism: the Debate around International Ethics

A third and last central theme on the changing IR agenda, that of the possibility of international ethical norms, is also widening the scope of feminist approaches. It is argued here that this is so, because of the increasing relevance of the work of the critically individualist feminist scholars also to IR.

There are pressing political reasons why this theme has been (re)discovered. An individual who engages in international politics, the UN when it formulates private international law, the security council when it decides upon humanitarian intervention, or those who seek to formulate international rules of business conduct or CO_2 emissions, all make implicit or explicit moral judgements. When IR scholars try to clarify these, their validity and their implications, they head straight into the thorny debate about whether it is possible to formulate universal ethical norms or whether these norms are always context bound. And with the individualization of world politics – which is but another expression for the increased significance of (or attention paid to) the category of phenomena mentioned above – IR scholars are increasingly called on to take position in this debate.

The ethical positions which have conventionally received attention in IR are particularly ill-suited to deal with these questions. The 'decisionism' of the classical realists focuses on the ethics of responsibility of the statesman. It thereby makes individuals (except the statesmen, members of an 'international society') disappear, and by the same token it also steers clear of issues regarding conflicting individual judgements.[103] Neo-realists bypass ethical concerns altogether. But the tide is turning. IR scholars have begun to rediscover the debate on ethics which has long existed in the margins of the mainstream. The communitarian–cosmopolitan debate is again at the centre of the agenda,[104] and there is growing interest in deontological approaches to ethics.[105] There is a new openness to and interest in ethics more generally, which is paving the way for an increased presence of feminist approaches.

The debate about how to deal with 'difference' (i.e. that women have different experiences and values) in feminism has pushed feminists to deal with questions which inevitably arise when one tries to formulate ethical norms at the international level. It has produced a wide range of feminist writing on the thorny issue of how to ensure that values and norms on which judgements are founded do not reflect merely the ideas and interests of a dominant group, but can indeed be justified on more general grounds. To make the link with IR even more evident, it should be noted that a great deal of this debate has been conducted with practical, international examples in mind.[106] The extension of international women's rights has increasingly forced feminists to take a stance on how far change can be required in the name of universally just principles and how far it is necessary to respect varieties in culture, customs and traditions. They confront the question of whether to be for or against the reservations many states place on the international women/human rights conventions where these purportedly offend their cultural heritage.[107] Similarly, they are pushed to take a position on issues such as whether the exclusion of muslim women in India from certain rights granted other Indian women through family law is an issue of minority protection or a matter of unjustified oppression. And, finally, they increasingly have to ask themselves what parts of any one national feminist movement they want to work with and for what reasons. The result is a lively and interesting debate about the nature of moral judgements at the international level.

There are two reasons why the feminist literature tends to be richer and more informative than much of what else is written. The first is theoretical. Feminists are pushed by their combined political and theoretical ambitions to look for ways in which they can both respect difference and maintain an attachment to universality. As Phillips writes:

> as we turn from this [from a view of 'the individual' in political discourse as a man] towards a greater emphasis on sexual and other kinds of difference, we do not thereby abandon all the universal pretensions of political thought. We can do well enough without an abstract, degendered, 'neutered' individual as the basis for our aspirations and goals. We cannot, however, do without some notion of stretching outside of ourselves, some capacity for self-reflection and self-distance, some imaginative – and more importantly some practical – movement towards linking up with those who have seemed different.[108]

The second reason is institutional. Feminists of diverse strands continue to consider themselves as largely engaged in a common academic endeavour. Unlike most of their mainstream colleagues, they continue to read and argue also with the positions with which they disagree. To borrow from Phillips again, feminism is an experience in participatory democracy.[109] This makes for more sensitivity to the position of those with whom one disagrees. An increasing presence of the normative feminist debate in IR is consequently to be expected and is in fact already visible. For instance, a recent article by Jabri (drawing heavily on the work of Benhabib) 'rejects the dichotomous representations of cosmopolitanism and communitarianism in favour of an intersubjective conception of the just and the good which recognizes difference and dissent as the formative elements of a shared individuality'.[110]

In terms of the relationship between feminism and individualism in IR, the integration of this normative debate brings into the picture the critically individualist approaches of feminists working in political theory. They can clearly not claim to be the only feminist writers on normative issues. On the contrary, it may be recalled that the project of post-modern feminists is a highly normative one as well, often centring on the very same issues as those treated by critically individualist feminists. Even so, critically individualist feminists certainly have a central position in the debate, as the above references indicate. Through their integration, feminist approaches to World Politics are consequently widened to include roughly the same range of relations to individualism that marks feminism generally.

CONCLUSION

Although feminism was born of a movement that puts the rights of (particular) individuals on the forefront, in IR only the most anti-individualist feminism is integrated in the theoretical mainstream debates. The reason lies not in the non-existence of alternative feminist approaches, but in the coincidence of the 'third wave' of feminism, critical both of philosophical and methodological individualism, and the epistemological turn in IR. The present chapter further wanted to show that even other feminist writing, in IR as elsewhere, is rarely individualist in an uncomplicated way. Methodologically marxist, post-modern and most standpoint feminists are directly anti-individualist. They emphasize different aspects of how gender and gender discrimination are constructed. At the normative level much of feminism is critically individualist. Feminists emphasize the dangers of using a 'disembedded and disembodied' individual as the basis for thinking about political and social reality, without necessarily abandoning the individual as the point of departure for their analysis. The integration of feminism in IR, which initially favoured the decisively anti-individualist post-modern approaches, now gives scope to a more representative range of feminist approaches.

The present widening of feminist presence in IR is undermining any attempt to establish a neat, clear and general conclusion about the relationship between feminism and individualism in world politics. It leaves this chapter, and all other attempts to discuss 'the' feminist position, with the rather unsatisfactory conclusion that there is not one feminist position but a whole gamut. This leads to a second point about the presence of feminism in IR, which runs through the essay and deserves to be made explicit. The plurality of feminist approaches has been stressed. Feminist approaches have been presented in terms of their interaction with other approaches in IR and in social sciences more generally. This implies a view of feminist academia and what it can hope to achieve which is rather 'modest'. It reflects the belief that feminist approaches share the same problems and build on the same traditions as the rest of social and political sciences. It also reflects a fundamental disbelief in the usefulness of throwing our intellectual heritage overboard because it is gendered and biased (which it no doubt is) with the aim of constructing a unitary feminist science resting on a feminist epistemology, as distinct from masculine epistemology. The role attributed to feminist approaches here is not that of replacing existing approaches. Nor do I claim that there is, or should be, one feminist approach to World Politics. Rather, feminist approaches are seen as an important part of the responsible methodological pluralism that IR has been striving towards for some time already, and needs to develop further. The neatness of a clear conclusion about the feminist position on individualism in world politics must be abandoned following the encouraging development incorporating a more complete reading of feminist theories in an enriched IR debate.

NOTES

1. IR will be the focus of this essay since it is the academic discipline devoted to the study of world politics. The claim that feminism in IR is identifiable with anti-individualism is substantiated in the second section of the paper.
2. Philosophical individualism here indicates philosophical traditions which take individuals as their point of departure; and similarly methodological individualism refers to the position that any explanation must, in the last instance, depart from individual action. This differentiates individualism from hermeneutic and holistic approaches which rest on system, structure, discourse or an intersubjective reality. As Michel Girard points out, it is, however, often difficult to separate holism and individualism neatly, since individualist explanations often rely heavily on elements of structure or system (see his introductory essay in this volume). This is reflected below, in the many references to the problematic nature of feminist individualism.
3. For instance, Dorothy Smith makes it her first objection to a treatment of standpoint theory which claims that this theory has its 'roots in marxism'. See her 'Comment on Heckman's "Truth and Method: Feminist Standpoint Theory Revisited"', *Signs* (Winter 1997), p. 392.
4. The categorization has been extensively adopted and stems from Sandra Harding's study *The Science Question in Feminism* (Ithaca: Cornell University Press, 1986). This said, there are many alternatives available. One equally common classification distinguishes between liberal, marxist, radical and post-structuralist (or psychoanalytical) feminist approaches following, among others, Jean Bethke Elshtain, *Public Man, Private Woman: Women in Social and Political Thought* (Princeton: Princeton University Press, 1981). The idea that there is a steady move away from liberalism is, however, present in most of the stories told about feminism.
5. Judith Evans, quoted in Anne Phillips, *Engendering Democracy* (Oxford: Polity Press, 1991), p. 4.
6. Marcia Millman and Rosabeth Moss Kanter, 'Introduction to Another Voice: Feminist Perspectives on Social Life and Social Science', in Sandra Harding (ed.), *Feminism and Methodology: Social Science Issues* (Bloomington: Indiana University Press, 1987), pp. 29–36.
7. Nancy Hartsock, 'The Feminist Standpoint: Developing the Ground for a Specifically Feminist Historical Materialism', in Harding (ed.), *Feminism and Methodology*, pp. 157–80.
8. In fact, standpoint feminism is often wrongly equated with feminism of marxist inspiration, an objection made by the commentators to Susan Heckman's treatment of standpoint feminism. See Susan Heckman, 'Truth and Method: Feminist Standpoint Theory Revisited', and the comments by Nancy Hartsock, Patricia Hill Collins, Sandra Harding and Dorothy Smith, all published in *Signs* (Winter 1997).
9. Mary E. Hawksworth, 'Knowers, Knowing, Known: Feminist Theory and Claims of Truth,' *Signs*, 14 (Spring 1989), p. 536.
10. For excellent statements of this position see bell hooks, 'Feminism:

A Transformational Politic', in Deborah L. Rhode (ed.), *Theoretical Perspectives on Sexual Difference* (Yale: Yale University Press, 1990), pp. 185–93; Judith Butler, *Gender Trouble: Feminism and the Subversion of Identity* (New York: Routledge, 1990); Elizabeth Spelman, *Inessential Woman: Problems of Exclusion in Feminist Thought* (Boston: Beacon Press, 1988). Gayatri Chakravorty Spivak, 'The Politics of Translation', in Michèle Barrett and Anne Phillips (eds), *Destabilizing Theory: Contemporary Feminist Debates* (Stanford: Stanford University Press, 1992), pp. 177–200.

11. Spelman, op. cit., p. 3.
12. There is an obvious parallel there to the paradox of individualism Girard points to in the Introduction: namely that there can be general thinking about individuality only at the risk of ignoring the uniqueness of the individual.
13. Judith Butler, *Bodies that Matter: On the Discursive Limits of 'Sex'* (New York: Routledge, 1993), p. 2.
14. Terrell Carver, 'Public Man and the Critique of Masculinities', *Political Theory*, 24, no. 4 (November 1996), pp. 673–86.
15. Butler, *Gender Trouble*, p. 5.
16. See for instance Hawksworth, op. cit., *passim*; and Anne Sisson Runyan and V. Spike Peterson, 'The Radical Future of Realism: Feminist Subversions of IR Theory', *Alternatives*, 16 (1991), pp. 73–4.
17. Elizabeth Gross defines what feminism is, and what it is not, in clearly post-modern manner. See Elizabeth Gross, 'Conclusion: What is Feminist Theory?', in Carole Pateman and Elizabeth Gross (eds), *Feminist Challenges: Social and Political Theory* (Boston: Northeastern University Press, 1986), pp. 200–3. See also Jane Flax, *Thinking Fragments: Psychoanalysis, Feminism and Postmodernism* (Berkeley: University of California Press, 1990); Nancy Fraser and Linda Nicholson, 'Social Criticism without Philosophy: an Encounter between Feminism and Postmodernism', in Nicholson and Fraser (eds), *Feminism/Postmodernism* (London: Routledge, 1990) and, as I will return to later, most of the approaches and definitions provided within feminist IR.
18. Nancy Chodorow, *The Reproduction of Mothering* (Berkeley: University of California Press, 1978); Carol Gilligan, *In a Different Voice: Psychological Theory and Women's Development* (Cambridge, Mass.: Harvard University Press, 1982).
19. I develop this point in Anna Leander, 'Le féminisme dans les relations internationales: entre relativisme culturel et impérialisme', in Klaus-Gerd Giesen (ed.), *L'éthique de l'espace politique mondial: métissages disciplinaires* (Bruxelles: Bruylant, forthcoming), pp. 304–33.
20. Consider the parallel, but unrelated, treatment of Enloe's work by Krell and Murphy. Craig N. Murphy, 'Seeing Women, Recognizing Gender, Recasting IR', *International Organization*, 50, no. 3 (Summer 1996), pp. 517–19, and Gert Krell, 'Feminismus und Internationale Beziehungen', *Zeitschrift für Internationale Beziehungen*, 3, no. 1 (June 1996), pp. 149–82.

21. Ole Waever, 'Figures of International Thought: Introducing Persons instead of Paradigms', in Iver B. Neumann and Ole Waever (eds), *The Future of International Relations: Masters in the Making?* (London and New York: Routledge, 1997), p. 16.
22. Daphne Patai and Noretta Koertge, *Professing Feminism: Cautionary Tales from the Strange World of Women's Studies* (New York: Basic Books, 1994).
23. Daphne Patai, 'What's Wrong with Women's Studies?', *Academe* (July–August 1995).
24. Nancy Hartsock, 'Rethinking Modernism', *Cultural Critique*, 7 (Fall 1987), pp. 187–206.
25. Nancy Hartsock, 'Comment on Heckman's "Truth and Method: Feminist Standpoint Theory Revisited": Truth of Justice?', *Signs* (Winter 1997), p. 367.
26. Seyla Benhabib, 'Feminism and the Question of Postmodernism', in Seyla Benhabib, *Situating the Self: Gender, Community and Postmodernism in Contemporary Ethics* (New York: Routledge, 1992), p. 221.
27. Onora O'Neill, 'Friends of Difference', *London Review of Books*, 11, no. 17 (1989).
28. Jane Roland Martin, 'Methodological Essentialism, False Difference, and Other Dangerous Traps', *Signs*, 19, no. 31, pp. 641–3.
29. Anne Phillips, 'Universal Pretensions in Political Thought', in Michèle Barrett and Anne Phillips (eds), *Destabilizing Theory: Contemporary Feminist Debates* (Stanford: Stanford University Press, 1992), pp. 10–30. For similar arguments see also Elshtain, op. cit, pp. 298–9 and *passim*; Susan Moller Okin, 'Thinking Like a Woman', in Deborah L. Rhode (ed.), *Theoretical Perspectives on Sexual è Difference* (Yale: Yale University Press, 1990), pp. 145–59.
30. Elshtain, op. cit., pp. 302–3.
31. Chodorow, *The Reproduction of Mothering*; Gilligan, *In a Different Voice*.
32. Jane Mansbridge, 'The Rise and Fall of Self-interest in the Explanation of Political Life', in Mansbridge (ed.), *Beyond Self-interest* (Chicago and London: University of Chicago Press, 1990), p. 20.
33. Virginia Held, 'Mother versus Contract', in Jane Mansbridge (ed.), *Beyond Self-interest* (Chicago and London: University of Chicago Press, 1990), pp. 287–304.
34. Seyla Benhabib, 'The Generalized and the Concrete Other', in Benhabib, *Situating the Self: Gender, Community and Postmodernism in Contemporary Ethics* (New York: Routledge, 1992), pp. 148–78.
35. Carole Pateman, *The Sexual Contract* (Stanford: Stanford University Press, 1988).
36. Elshtain, op. cit., ch. 6.
37. Phillips, *Engendering Democracy*.
38. Elizabeth Fox-Genovese, *Feminism Without Illusions: A Critique of Individualism* (Chapel Hill and London: The University of North Carolina Press, 1991), p. 241.
39. I consequently find that feminists go to considerable lengths to chal-

lenge individualism, although they do not do this in a unified way, and find it hard to agree with Fox-Genovese, who thinks that: 'Feminism's reluctance to challenge individualism has left feminists torn between small patchwork gains on the margins of individualism and utopian negations of everything male. Yet it increasingly appears that to realize its own promise feminism must, in the spirit of "radical obedience", undertake that critique of individualism which men, of both the left and the right, seem to be avoiding.' Ibid., p. 233.

40. V. Spike Peterson, 'Introduction', in V. Spike Peterson (ed.), *Gendered States: Feminist (Re)visions of International Relations* (Boulder and London: Lynne Rienner, 1992), pp. 7–9; Sylvester Christine, *Feminist Theory and International Relations in a Postmodern Era* (Cambridge: Cambridge University Press, 1994), pp. 150–5. Anne J. Tickner, *Gender in International Relations: Feminist Perspectives on Achieving Global Security* (New York: Columbia University Press, 1992), p. 21.
41. Adam Jones, 'Does "Gender" Make the World Go Round? Feminist Critiques of International Relations', *Review of International Studies*, 22, no. 4 (October 1996), pp. 405–29. Murphy, op. cit.; Krell, op. cit.
42. Rebecca Grant, 'The Quagmire of Gender and International Security', in V. Spike Peterson (ed.), *Gendered States: Feminist (Re)visions of International Relations* (Boulder and London: Lynne Rienner, 1992), p. 86.
43. Murphy, op. cit., p. 515.
44. Stefano Guzzini, *Realism in International Relations and International Political Economy: The Continuing Story of a Death Foretold* (London and New York: Routledge, forthcoming), ch. 8.
45. Fred Halliday, 'Hidden from International Relations: Women and the International Arena', in Rebecca Grant and Kathleen Newland (eds), *Gender and International Relations* (London: Open University Press, 1991), p. 159.
46. Waever, op. cit., p. 10.
47. Birgit Lorcher, 'Feminismus ist mehr als "political correctness"', *Zeitschrift für Internationale Beziehungen*, 3, no. 1 (June 1996), p. 385.
48. For more detailed accounts of the neo-realist turn, see Guzzini, op. cit., ch. 9 and Hans Mauritzen, 'Kenneth Waltz: a Critical Rationalist between International Politics and Foreign Policy', in Iver B. Neumann and Ole Waever (eds), *The Future of International Relations: Masters in the Making?* (Routledge: London and New York, 1997), pp. 66–89.
49. For an introduction and overview to this critique see Janice Peterson and Doug Brown (eds), *The Economic Status of Women Under Capitalism: Institutional Economics and Feminist Theory* (Aldershot: Edward Elgar, 1994).
50. Jean Bethke Elshtain, 'International Politics and Political Theory', in Kenneth Booth and Steve Smith (eds), *International Relations Theory Today* (Oxford: Polity Press, 1995), pp. 274–8 in particular.
51. As persuasively argued by Guzzini they were often defenders rather than opponents of realism, but became seen as opponents. Guzzini, op. cit., ch. 8.

52. Runyan and Peterson, op. cit., p. 77.
53. Maria Mies, *Patriarchy and Accumulation on a World Scale: Women in the International Division of Labour* (London: Zed Books, 1986). Betty Reardon, *Sexism and the War System* (New York: Teachers College, Columbia University Press, 1985).
54. For a good overview and introduction see Anne-Marie Goetz, 'Feminism and the Claim to Know: Contradiction in Feminist Approaches to Women in Development', in Rebecca Grant and Kathleen Newland (eds), *Gender and International Relations* (London: Open University Press, 1991), pp. 133–57.
55. Guzzini, op. cit., ch. 10.
56. *Millennium* published a special issue (Winter 1988) on feminist approaches where the bulk of the articles used the enlarged International Relations agenda (covering non-state actors, the economy and transnational phenomena) to argue for a greater place for feminist approaches. A collection including a large part of the essays and some new ones was then published by the Open University Press in 1991.
57. Halliday develops what he sees as the emerging concerns, op. cit., pp. 160ff.
58. For an illustration see Friedrich Kratochwil and John G. Ruggie, 'A State of the Art on an Art of the State', *International Organization*, 40, no. 4 (Autumn 1986), pp. 753–75.
59. Alexander Wendt, 'The Agent–Structure Problem in International Relations', *International Organization*, 41, no. 3 (Summer 1987), pp. 337–70. Walter Carlsnaes, 'The Agency–Structure Problem in Foreign Policy Analysis', *International Studies Quarterly*, 36 (September 1992), pp. 245–70.
60. Martin Hollis and Steve Smith, *Explaining and Understanding in International Relations* (Oxford: Clarendon Press, 1990).
61. Waever, op. cit.
62. This is not the place to discuss what an adequate denomination would be. It may just be observed that Walker, for instance, defines his own approach as Kantian. See Robert J. Walker, 'Gender and Critique in the Theory of International Relations', in V. Spike Peterson (ed.), *Gendered States: Feminist (Re)visions of International Relations* (Boulder and London: Lynne Rienner, 1992), p. 199 n. 1.
63. For an overview of these approaches see Stefano Guzzini, 'Maintenir les dilemmes de la modernité en suspens: Analyse et éthique poststructuralistes en relations internationales', in Klaus-Gerd Giesen (ed.), *L'éthique de l'espace politique mondial: métissages disciplinaires* (Bruxelles: Bruylant, 1997), pp. 247–85.
64. Robert Keohane, 'International Institutions: Two Approaches', in Keohane, *International Institutions and State Power: Essays in International Relations Theory* (Boulder: Westview, 1989), p. 173.
65. See the self-description of the authors in 'Speaking the Language of Exile: Dissidence in International Studies', *International Studies Quarterly*, Special Issue, 34, no. 3. (September 1990).
66. Consider also the inverse parallel: that the post-structuralists tend to identify with part of the feminist project. Walker, op. cit.

67. Sylvester, op. cit., pp. 150–3.
68. Tickner, *Gender in International Relations*, p. 21.
69. Peterson, 'Introduction', pp. 11–13.
70. Runyan and Peterson, op. cit., p. 76.
71. Jean Bethke Elshtain, *Women and War* (2nd edn with new epilogue, Chicago: University of Chicago Press, 1995; 1st edn 1987), pp. 87–8.
72. Runyan and Peterson, op. cit., p. 97.
73. There are some obvious exceptions (such as Enloe or Elshtain) who were trying to provide alternative accounts of the same reality realism deals with, but not primarily by showing the biases of the realist discourse and knowledge production.
74. Both articles were published in the *Millennium* 1988 special issue on International Relations and Gender.
75. Sylvester, op. cit., p. 211.
76. Halliday, op. cit., p. 168.
77. Jenny Edkins and Véronique Pin-Fat, 'Jean Bethke Elshtain: Traversing the Terrain Between', in Iver B. Neumann and Ole Waever (eds), *The Future of International Relations: Masters in the Making?* (Routledge: London and New York, 1997), p. 291.
78. V. Spike Peterson, 'Transgressing Boundaries: Theories of Knowledge, Gender and International Relations', *Millennium*, 21, no. 2, pp. 183–208.
79. Robert Keohane, 'International Relations Theory: Contributions of a Feminist Standpoint', *Millennium*, 18, no. 2, pp. 245–53.
80. See Murphy, op. cit., p. 529; Sylvester, op. cit., pp. 210ff. Runyan and Peterson, op. cit., p. 96. Marysia Zalewski, 'Feminist Standpoint Theory Meets International Relations Theory: A Feminist Version of David and Goliath?', *Fletcher Forum*, 17 (1993), pp. 13–32.
81. Sylvester, op. cit, p. 155.
82. 'Back', since the tension is in many ways similar to that discussed and at the heart of IR debate in the 1970s.
83. See for example Susan Strange, *The Retreat of the State: The Diffusion of Power in the World Economy* (Cambridge: Cambridge University Press, 1996); Bertrand Badie, *La fin des territoires* (Paris: Fayard, 1995); Michael Zürn, 'The Challenge of Globalization and Individualization: a View from Europe', in Hans-Henrik Holm and Georg Sorensen (eds), *Whose World Order? Uneven Globalization and the End of the Cold War* (Boulder, San Francisco and Oxford: Westview Press, 1995), pp. 137–63; and Rogers Brubaker, 'National Minorities, Nationalizing States, and External National Homelands in the New Europe', *Daedalus*, 124, no. 2 (Spring 1995), pp. 107–32.
84. Yosef Lapid and Friedrich Kratochwil (eds), *The Return of Culture and Identity in IR Theory* (Boulder and London: Lynne Rienner, 1996), and Peter Katzenstein (ed.), *The Culture of National Security: Norms and Identity in World Politics* (New York: Routledge, 1996).
85. Yosef Lapid and Friedrich Kratochwil, 'Revisiting the "National": Toward an Identity Agenda in Neorealism?', in Lapid and Friedrich Kratochwil (eds), *The Return of Culture and Identity in IR Theory* (Boulder and London: Lynne Rienner, 1996), pp. 105–26.

86. Alexander Wendt, 'Anarchy is What States Make Out of It: the Social Construction of Power Politics', *International Organization*, 46, no. 2 (Spring 1992), pp. 391–425; and Wendt in Kratochwil and Lapid.
87. See references in previous section.
88. Chodorow, *The Reproduction of Mothering*.
89. Sarah Ruddick, *Maternal Thinking: Towards a Politics of Peace* (Boston: Beacon Press, 1989). Adrienne Harris and Ynestra King (eds), *Rocking the Ship of the State: Toward a Feminist Peace Politics* (Boulder: Westview Press, 1989). Simona Sharoni, 'Middle East Politics through Feminist Lenses: Toward Theorizing International Relations from Women's Struggles', *Alternatives*, 18 (1993), pp. 5–28.
90. Deniz Kandiyoti, 'Identity and its Discontents: Women and the Nation', *Millennium*, 20, no. 3 (1991), pp. 429–43.
91. Elshtain, *Women and War*; Deniz Kandiyoti (ed.), *Women, Islam and the State* (London: Macmillan, 1991); K. Jayawardena, *Feminism and Nationalism in the Third World* (London: Zed Press, 1988); Nira Yuval-Davies and F. Antias (eds), *Woman–Nation–State* (London: Macmillan, 1989).
92. This view is of course not entirely uncontested. For counter-arguments see D. Gordon, 'The Global Economy: New Edifice or Crumbling Foundations', *New Left Review*, 168 (1988), pp. 24–64; Paul Krugman, 'Competitiveness: A Dangerous Obsession', *Foreign Affairs*, 73, no. 2 (1994), pp. 28–44.
93. Gosta Esping Andersen (ed.), *Welfare States in Transition: National Adaptations in Global Economies* (London: Sage, 1996); Robert Boyer and Daniel Drache (eds), *States Against Markets: The Limits of Globalization* (London and New York: Routledge, 1996); J. Rogers Hollingsworth, Phillipe Schmitter and Wolfgang Streeck (eds), *Governing Capitalist Economies* (New York: Oxford University Press, 1994).
94. Susan Strange, 'Traîtres, agents doubles ou chevaliers secourables? Les dirigeants des entreprises transnationales', in Michel Girard (ed.), *Les individus dans la politique internationale* (Paris: Economica, 1994), p. 227; Susan Strange, 'ISA as a Microcosm. 1995 Presidential Address', *International Studies Quarterly*, 39, no. 3 (1995), pp. 289–97.
95. Jane Lewis,'Introduction: Women, Work, Family and Social Policies in Europe', in Lewis (ed.), *Women and Social Policies in Europe: Work, Family and the State* (Aldershot: Edward Elgar, 1993), pp. 1–24; Lena Dominelli, *Women Across Continents: Feminist Comparative Social Policy* (New York: Harvester Wheatsheaf, 1991).
96. Marjorie Griffin Cohen, 'Democracy and the Future of Nations: Challenges for Disadvantaged Women and Minorities', in Robert Boyer and Daniel Drache (eds), *States Against Markets: The Limits of Globalization* (London and New York: Routledge, 1996), pp. 399–414.
97. Crescy Cannan, 'From Dependence to Enterprise? Women and Western Welfare States', in Barbara Einhorn and Eileen Janes Yeo (eds), *Women and Market Societies* (Aldershot: Edward Elgar, 1995), pp. 160–79.
98. Maxine Molyneux, 'Women's Rights and the International Context: Some Reflections on the Post-communist States', *Millennium*, 23, no.

2 (1994), pp. 287–313. See also Valentine M. Moghadam (ed.), *Democratic Reform and the Position of Women in Transitional Economies* (Oxford: Clarendon Press, 1993).

99. Valentine M. Moghadam, *Modernizing Women: Gender and Social Change in the Middle East* (Boulder: Lynne Rienner, 1993).
100. Catherine A. MacKinnon, *Toward a Feminist Theory of the State* (Cambridge and London: Harvard University Press, 1989).
101. I have never come across any, but reportedly they exist. See for instance Molyneux, op.cit., p. 295 fn. 27.
102. This is incidentally the position taken by Susan Strange in this volume when she points to the liberating effects of the extension of the market on Kenyan and Malaysian women. See Chapter 7 below.
103. Klaus-Gerd Giesen, 'Entre décisionnnisme et structuralisme. La précarité de l'éthique individuelle dans les théories des relations internationales', in Michel Girard (ed.), *Les individus dans la politique internationale* (Paris: Economica, 1994), pp. 25–38.
104. Chris Brown, *International Relations Theory: New Normative Approaches* (New York: Harvester Wheatsheaf, 1992).
105. Klaus-Gerd Giesen, 'Corporatisme paradigmatique, théories déontologiques et nouvel ordre mondial', *Etudes internationales*, 24, no. 2 (June 1993), pp. 315–29. Deontology refers to the ethics of judging an act to be just if it follows from norms that are just in themselves, and not by reference to its consequences (the latter underlies many Realist approaches).
106. For a detailed discussion of this see Anna Leander, op. cit., *passim*.
107. The CEDAW is the international convention with the largest number of reservations placed on it. For a discussion of the issues involved, see Ann Elizabeth Mayer, 'Cultural Particularism as a Bar to Women's Rights: Reflections on the Middle Eastern Experience', in Julie Peters and Andrea Wolper (eds), *Women's Rights, Human Rights: International Feminist Perspectives* (New York and London: Routledge, 1995), pp. 176–88; and Arati Rao, 'The Politics of Gender and Culture in International Human Rights Discourse', in the same volume, pp. 167–75.
108. Phillips, 'Universal Pretensions in Feminist Thought', p. 27.
109. Phillips, *Engendering Democracy*, ch 5.
110. Vivienne Jabri, 'Textualizing the Self: Moral Agency in Inter-cultural Discourse', *Global Society*, 10, no. 1 (January 1996), pp. 57–69.

6 Disarmed Prophets
Marcel Merle

We owe the term 'disarmed prophets' to Machiavelli. Traditionally, it used to describe, with just the slightest hint of condescension and commiseration, the particular kind of characters who believe they can change the course of history without disposing of the necessary means of coercion to do it. The simple fact that Mussolini felt the need to highlight this sentence in his preface to the French edition of *The Prince* is proof enough that this assertion should be classified in the arsenal of arguments belonging to the realm of *realpolitik*.

However, the scope of the expression 'disarmed prophets' is not limited to the debate between idealists and realists. By definition prophets are not groups or communities but individuals who mean to declare their convictions in public and uphold their beliefs in the face of, if not against, groups. This is why prophets regardless of their domain always are referred to by name.

In order to explore this category of agents one must therefore begin by finding those individuals who can claim the gift of prophecy while at the same time lacking all means of coercion against their opponents, and these must be found in an international setting. The importance of adopting this approach is in direct relation to the fact that the authors who recognize the role played by individual agents in international relations appear in dispersed battle order.

TYPOLOGY

Among these authors there are first of all those who merely line up in an imaginary gallery the portraits of celebrities whose names have been handed down to us by history, such as Plutarch in search of 'illustrious men'. Moreover, the aim of this undertaking is not so much to lay down historic truth as to edify the reader-spectator through paintings showing vice in order to make the merits of virtue stand out. This kind of hagiography, the Plutarch way, is all the more useless in that it encompasses half-legendary characters and that the only criterion of selection seems to be the fame bestowed upon them by their author.

Closer to our concerns is the cult of the hero. In the preface to Thomas Carlyle's classic, Jean Izoulet declares: 'society goes through perpetual metamorphoses; the heroes are the agents of this transformation'.[1] This is clearly about establishing the relations between this or that character and the course of history. However, the concept of 'hero' also puts the criterion of fame first. Moreover, Carlyle opens up his gallery to a typology which is as eclectic as it is confusing, since he distinguishes six different models of heroes:

the hero-divinity: Odin (paganism, Scandinavian mythology)
the hero-prophet: Muhammad (Islam)
the hero-poet: Dante, Shakespeare
the hero-priest: Luther (Reformation)
the hero-writer: Rousseau, etc.
the hero-king: Cromwell, Napoleon

Compared to Machiavelli's distinction, the list contains 'heroes' who remained disarmed next to others who were fearful warriors. There is no guiding line to tie these fates together, nor compare their respective influences on international relations. The 'hero' is a variable character whose contour is too blurred to be used as a target for rigorous investigation. On the contrary, J.-B. Duroselle's 'Statesman' has perfectly well-defined features.[2] This is one of the few attempts to grasp the different characteristics which allow an analysis of the variations in behaviour by individuals faced with similar or comparable situations. The works of Duroselle highlight the influence that these seemingly secondary details can have on the decision-making process and thereby on the course of international relations.

However interesting this research may be, the case of 'Statesmen' cannot help us shed light on the relevance of the distinction established by Machiavelli. Firstly, Statesmen are mainly managers and more rarely prophets brandishing a message announcing great changes. Furthermore, Statesmen are 'armed', if not literally, then at least potentially; the position they hold enables them to summon the armed forces to defend their cause or their interests.

For want of 'illustrious men', 'heroes' or 'Statesmen', does one however have to go looking for the telling signs of the individuals' capability to influence the course of international relations in the

anonymity of the crowds? History has no lack of anecdotes highlighting the importance of the part played by individual characters
in particular circumstances (for instance Grouchy and Blücher on
the battlefield of Waterloo). However, those are haphazard events
(fruits of fate or necessity), weaving the fabric of history day by
day; their effects cannot be ascribed to the prophetic and the revolutionary vision of one individual considered separately, no matter
how considerable they may be. Indeed this is the very lesson of the
works on methodological individualism.[3] From this point of view it
is by no means a question of substituting the individual for the
group, but 'in order to explain a phenomenon ... [one must] re-
construct the motivations of the individuals concerned by the phenomenon in question and appreciate this phenomenon as the result
of the aggregation of individual behaviours dictated by these
motivations'.[4]

Avoiding the pitfall of holism, this dialectical conception restores
the rightful place of the community of individuals. However, it does
not manage to account for the role (action and influence) of such
individuality, selected at random from within a group whose units
should be considered to be interchangeable. Despite its attractive
label then, methodological individualism does not help us encircle
this strange character whom Machiavelli refers to as a 'disarmed
prophet'.

There can only be prophets where there is prophecy, i.e. the
delivery of a message. This message must show several characteristics; most importantly, it must hold an element of accusation, such
as a condemnation of the established order or at the very least a
break with the current state of things. Next, the message must herald
change and thereafter be followed by results to the effect of the
announcement. Thus it is not sufficient to be a great theorist (e.g.
a philosopher honoured by posterity) to become a prophet; the
message must be embodied in proposals likely to alter reality. Finally,
the message must have a far-reaching scope, if not universal then
at least international. This is to say that the message should address the masses even if its object is limited. Becoming a prophet
by trade is therefore not an option for everybody, including those
who practise the prophecy of doom on a daily basis.

Moreover, the prophets that Machiavelli has in mind have the
peculiarity of being disarmed. In other words they cannot lean on,
at least at the outset, any kind of organized force to help them
make their ideas prevail. Besides, this is the inevitable situation of

those whose ideas are far removed from the mainstream. The disarmed prophet may be able to gather a small troop of followers around him; later he will be able to look for a stronghold in the public and thereby attempt to offset the power of the incumbent authorities. But at the outset the prophet is an empty-handed character armed only with his words or his pen, standing up alone to those who hold the power and who have the right to impose silence upon him.

Obviously this kind of composite picture is not just the fruit of imagination; it has been made from figures whose identity and features can be revealed at present. Still, the characteristics given to the above model have at the same time provided the criteria used to make up the sample. For basically this is an unprecedented challenge: how can one prove that an individual, an ordinary private person at the outset, can end up bending the course of history against the will of those who have received a public mandate to act and the force to compel? In order for our test to be convincing, we have had first of all to distinguish the 'disarmed prophets' not only from armed prophets, but also from 'illustrious men' or 'heroes' or even from anonymous individuals without the gift of prophecy.

Now to finish this adjustment of our definition – one is almost tempted to talk about accommodation in the optical sense of the word – there is a final sorting to do amongst the candidates for the title of disarmed prophets. Allowing for exceptions (Muhammad) this encompasses the founders of the big religions. Each of them meets the stated requirements. But if it is true that their messages have indeed contributed to 'changing the world', this is because their impact was felt in all fields of individual and social activity. To avoid getting lost in a disproportionately huge field of investigation, it seems legitimate to limit the sample to characters whose actions have manifestly and irrefutably influenced the course of international relations.

PORTRAITS

Count Saint-Simon, Karl Marx, Henri Dunant, Theodore Herzl and John Paul II have been selected amongst the personalities who deserve to be present in the Portrait Gallery of History. The respective merits which have determined their selection are obviously very different, but we will see that each of these prophets has a corresponding statement of a message related to the subsequent evolution of events.

Saint-Simon was one of those brilliant self-taught men who have been gifted with a remarkable capacity for intuition and anticipation.[5] Rigour was not exactly the dominating feature of his thought, which often proceeded by analogy, and was given to a certain mixing of styles. His philosophy was inconsistent, if one takes philosophy to mean a methodical exposition of a system of thought. Nevertheless his work developed a decisive change: the abolition of the secular distinction between reflection and observation, ethics and science, nature and society, politics and physics.

As such Saint-Simon can be considered the founder of scientism, which dominated the evolution of thought at the end of the nineteenth century. Still, he was also a eulogist of industrialism. He was no doubt one of the first social reformers to recognize, beyond the immediate free-trade-versus-protectionism controversy, the phenomenal potential for human ingenuity to transform the world embedded in mechanization and its applications. Hence the 'grands projets' to exploit the globe undertaken by his followers (Michel Chevallier, Ferdinand de Lesseps), but also the renovation of society's hierarchy, e.g. in politics by favouring the representatives of producers, experts or 'organizers' (if one is to use the terminology subsequently employed by James Burnham). At the same time, Saint-Simon (author of *Le Catéchisme industriel*) was also aware of the negative aspects of ever-expanding progress, and once again he was one of the first to understand the importance of having a 'social organization', later called 'socialism'. Finally, Saint-Simon made light of borders by suggesting a 'reorganization of The European Society'. Although the idea was not new at the time, the contents certainly were, firstly because the author advocated a form of federative union which went far beyond previous projects towards integration and, secondly because the idea behind reorganization was for it to spur on European mobilization and expansion worldwide.

The master's followers made the mistake of wanting to extract a doctrine out of this ideological do-it-yourself kit. Indeed, Saint-Simon, who never took part in current affairs, public or private, laid the foundation for a School and even a 'religion' which outlived him. Still, it is not in the wild imaginings of the small flock of zealots that one can measure Saint-Simon's gift of prophecy. The true filiation is both more abounding and more complex: it is embodied in the system of Auguste Comte (transfixing certain brilliantly inspired intuitions) and the system of thought later associated with it, but also in the large-scale civil engineering projects carried out in the field (the Suez Canal, the colonization of Algeria) by faraway followers. Apart from this legacy, one must credit Saint-Simon with an amazing visionary talent: he detected far better than most of his contemporaries the changes that had started to take root in society and he indicated the direction of coming developments with exceptional perceptiveness. Is this sufficient to call him a prophet? Yes, if one considers the outstanding quality of his intuitions and his predictions. No, if one tries to establish a direct and immediate link between Saint-Simon's thinking and the subsequent behaviour of the agents *in situ*. There is nothing to maintain that the era of organizers, the triumph of industrialism, the reorganization of the European society would not have taken place if Saint-Simon had not announced it a century to a century and a half previously. The case of Saint-Simon must therefore be put aside for the time being.

In this respect, the case of Marx is much less controversial. Whether or not one agrees with his vision of the world, no one can question its scope nor, especially, its influence on the course of events. For a long time the only weapon available to the founder of communism was his pen. Even when he did find followers they were neither warriors nor professional street fighters, but came from the social classes oppressed by the owners of the means of production. Right away Marx's vision of history was internationalist, and foundation of the First Workers' Internationale in London in 1864 represented a significant challenge not only to the capitalist system but also to the states system of international relations. Despite the failure of Marx's enterprise in his lifetime, Marxism gave impetus to the revolutionary movement which triumphed in Russia in 1917, and influenced the course of history for three-quarters of a century.

Even if the legitimacy of the link between Marx's thought and the politics of the Soviet leaders is debatable, the leitmotif of the latter is sufficient in itself to establish a presumption of paternity. Although it is true that the followers have not hesitated to take up arms, the fact remains that the international social movement known as communism was founded to begin with on the thought and action of one man rather than on the exercise of violence.

Although of an altogether different kind, the part played by Henri Dunant nevertheless takes its rightful place in the realm of the disarmed prophets. It was on the battlefield of Solférino, where he was by accident, that this 31-year-old Swiss had the horrors of war brutally revealed to him. Immediately he drew the conclusion that it was necessary to create widespread 'relief associations with the aim of giving medical assistance to the wounded in wartime by devoted and zealous volunteers; well-qualified for such work'.[6] This project, which initially had a limited scope, could seem utopian. However, Dunant's sheer zeal, sustained by the determination and the clairvoyance of his Genevan partner Gustave Moynier, worked wonders. They managed to mobilize public opinion and especially succeed in winning over a certain number of princes and other leaders in Europe. As early as 1863 a committee of five private personalities was formed in Geneva. It rapidly took the initiative to convene an International conference which met unofficially at expert level to begin with, then from 1864 onwards officially, uniting the plenipotentiaries. The first Geneva Convention signed on 22 August 1864 by the representatives of twelve countries laid down the legal foundations which allowed Red Cross, a private organization, to take on an international function which has been growing ever since.

Thus one of the oldest and most famous international organizations really was founded on a private initiative sparked off by a sort of individual revelation. The original mechanism used the states in order to recognize this initiative and perpetuate the role of a network of non-governmental organizations is the best possible illustration of the capacity of some disarmed prophets. No constraint whatsoever was imposed on the creation of Red Cross. The sheer force of the convictions of a few men was enough to make the rulers sign up. The same strength of conviction founded a human relief organization which has defied time.

'In Basle I founded the Jewish State.' This statement by Theodore Herzl followed immediately after the first Zionist Congress in Basle in August 1897, and the publishing of a book titled *The Jewish State* in 1896.[7] Once again we can witness the undeniable personal responsibility of a single man. Of course, the 'Jewish question' had been asked for a long time, at least in Europe. But so far no political project had sprung from the agitation maintained by the periodical waves of anti-Semitism. By putting forward the idea of the creation of a 'Jewish national Residence in Palestine' (a forerunner of the Jewish state), Herzl set a target for the Zionist movement which was soon to become an absolute priority. Herzl, who died in 1904, never saw his ideas come true. But his successors carried on and in 1917 they obtained the famous 'Declaration' from Balfour, which authorized and indeed encouraged Jewish settlement on the territories of Palestine (future British mandate). Thus the road lay open, in accordance with Herzl's predictions, to the creation of an independent sovereign Jewish state which saw the light in 1948.

Not surprisingly, the birth of the Jewish state was both lengthier and more painful than the one of Red Cross. One cannot dispose of a people and a territory without undermining acquired rights. If the initial idea was indisputably Herzl's, the onus of implementation relied on several generations of Zionist activists. Circumstances, notably the trauma left over from the Second World War, in the form of survivors of the 'final solution', also played a part which Theodor Herzl did not and could not have foreseen. Besides, one might ask whether the creation of a Jewish state would not have been imposed anyway one day. The relation between the commitment of Herzl and the creation of the state of Israel in its present shape is both indirect and uncertain. It remains nevertheless a fact that Herzl's statement heralded a change in the face of the world, and mobilized the energy and the forces which soon were to take over from him. Nobody can mention the birth of Israel without referring to Herzl.

The most recent example of the action of a disarmed prophet is also one where the link of causality between the impulse of the individual and the communitarian aspect of the result obtained is the strongest: the example is the intervention of the Pope John Paul II in the Polish crisis in the early 1980s. Admittedly, John Paul II is both a spiritual leader and a secular sovereign since he reigns over the minute territory of the Vatican. As such he could be put in the category of statesmen rather than prophets. However, this worldly sovereignty is purely symbolic and the material forces at his disposal to face up to the world powers are in the proper sense of the word insignificant ('the Pope? How many divisions?', Stalin is supposed to have asked in 1945). Therefore it would be more appropriate to attribute John Paul II's challenge to the Polish authorities to his intuition and his personal charisma rather than to his power. His success is for a large part due to his perfect knowledge of the terrain and the strategy he deployed, which cunningly combined firmness with the quest for reconciliation. Usually though, these skills are attributed to great politicians and experienced diplomats rather than to prophets. If John Paul II can nevertheless be considered a prophet it is partly due to the fact that his intervention had been preceded by an announcement and partly because it constitutes a particular case of the application of a message intended to be universal.

Without entering into details, one can just mention John Paul II's speech at UNESCO in 1980 when he talked about 'the fundamental sovereignty possessed by every Nation by virtue of its own culture'. On the same occasion, he also opposed the inalienable rights of history and culture to those exerted momentarily in the name of the state by those in power. The entire thrust of the papal thinking is aimed at separating legality and legitimacy, formal state structure and genuine, sovereign nationhood.[8] The statement can rapidly turn subversive. In the case of Poland it served the purpose of disclosing the nakedness of authorities lacking any popular backing and forced to lean on a foreign power in order to remain in place.[9] The rescue operation carried out in the name of the defence of the Polish identity was a perfect success in so far as it allowed successively to neutralization of the capacity for repression of the communist authority; restoration of the dialogue between the rulers and the opposition, and finally facilitation of the peaceful transition to a democratic regime.

Looking at the example of Poland one might be tempted to qualify John Paul II as a demiurge. Indeed some authors have not hesitated to interpret the Pope's action as the main instrument of the disintegration of communism. The is being too hasty. Even if it is true that the downfall of the Polish stronghold did hasten the collapse of the other bastions and eventually the Soviet citadel, numerous other factors apart from the frontal collision between religion and politics explain the crisis and the collapse of the system. Actually, it is not bad at all to be able to attribute a decisive role in the first stage of the process to one specific person. Besides, the Pope's repeated appeals for peace, notably at the time of the Gulf War, have not always been heeded, and the subversive character of his support for the right of Peoples and Nations against those of States might have spurred on crises that can no longer be checked peacefully, notably in the Balkans. The appraisal on the diplomatic level of this not yet terminated pontificate will no doubt contain both bright and dark sides and should not be treated in advance as just one more piece of Golden Legend. None the less, the resolution of the Polish conflict represents a typical example of the triumph of individual will-power over the accumulation of arms. Few prophets can flatter themselves with having neutralized their opponents through the sheer strength of their word and their presence.

Saint-Simon, Marx, Dunant, Herzl, John Paul II: the choice of the sample is no doubt arbitrary. It would have been possible to continue and extend the list by adding, for instance, apostles of non-violence (Gandhi, Martin Luther King), theorists of colonization (Lugard, Lyautey) or the Founding Fathers of Europe (Coudenhove-Calergi, Jean Monnet, Robert Schuman, Alcide de Gasperi, etc.). But the first ones unfortunately failed their enterprise, the second ones only managed to impose their model for a limited time in a limited space, and the third ones are so numerous that they defy the search for paternity.

Based on these examples, it is possible to establish the existence of a relation (more or less direct, depending, but at any rate certain) between the thought and the action of one isolated individual, on one hand, and on the other hand the subsequent course of events which can be catalogued as 'international relations'. The disarmed prophets are therefore not as lame and powerless as Machiavelli wrote and Mussolini thought. It is not necessary to have a popular mandate or to command means of coercion in order to impose one's ideas and turn the established order upside-down. Without any doubt such a phenomenon is both exceptional and marginal. But as it exists, one must try to explain it: is it a matter of isolated and unrelated cases, that are but the fruits of freak incidents or fruits of circumstance? Or, while still admitting the part of irreducible specificity attached to every situation of this kind, is it possible to discern constants which would enable us to understand the complex game of interaction between the individual and the group?

ATTEMPT AT EXPLANATION

There are very few useful references to help us answer these questions. Max Weber did try to establish a 'sociology of the prophet',[10] but only as an element of his 'sociology of religion'. Outside this context, Max Weber's arguments can hardly be applied to the 'secular' prophets, for they find their oracles within themselves without pretending to herald the triumph of supernatural forces. Being unable to draw on Max Weber then, it is possible to go back as far as Hegel, even though the latter mentions 'heroes' rather than 'prophets' in the parts of his writings he devoted to the role of the 'great men in history'.[11]

Keeping this in mind, Hegel's contribution to the debate can be considered from a dual perspective: 1) do individuals have a real capacity for innovation or are they merely a product of necessity and the interpreters of collective forces? 2) assuming the gift of prophecy is recognized for certain individuals, does the way their message is received depend on a specific interpretation induced by the course of history?

1) In search of the course of history, Hegel only grants a limited albeit essential role to individuals, even if they are 'great men'. On one side he denies that the individual genius can bend the course of events to his liking. Events are dictated by Reason, whose instrument is the spirit of the People. Hence Hegel's repeated warnings: 'only those who have grasped the Spirit of their People and conform to it are intelligent . . . Individuals disappear from our sight and they only have value insofar as they have implemented what the Spirit of the People wanted . . . Individuals disappear before the substantiality of the whole which is the creator of the individuals that it will need. Individuals cannot prevent what must happen from happening'.[12] Or elsewhere: 'Every individual is the son of his people at a certain stage of the evolution of this people. Nobody can vault the spirit of his people, much as nobody can vault the earth.'[13] In other words, the voluntarist claim to be able to shape the world as one wished is refuted by a determinist vision of evolution: 'Historic individuals are those who wanted and accomplished not something imaginary and presumed, but something just and necessary, and something which they understood because it was revealed to them from the inside what was necessary and what really belonged to the possibilities of time.'[14] Having taken these precautions against the intrusion of imagination, Hegel nevertheless recognizes the great men's merit of having brought to light the Spirit of the People, itself a fragment of the World spirit, by showing their contemporaries the course of their destinies: 'The great men of history are those whose particular ends contain the substantiality which the will of the world spirit confers upon them. Indeed this content is what constitutes their actual force. The content is also present in the collective subconscious instinct of man and it controls their deepest forces. This is why they do not show any substantial resistance towards the great man who has identified his personal interest with the accomplishment of his goal. People

will gather beneath his banner: he reveals and accomplishes their own immanent disposition.'[15]

On this last point, Hegel's argument certainly ought to be taken into account. As a matter of fact there is only 'prophecy' where the message has been heard by an audience large enough to spread it and thereby contribute to its coming true. This is actually a useful criterion for discriminating: among all the prophecies professed simultaneously, the dominant opinion will instinctively choose between those which belong to the realm of abstraction and Utopia, and those which can be considered operational. Thus Fourier never achieved an influence comparable to Saint-Simon's despite his cleverness; and Cabet's ideas never inspired the same interest as Marx's. A prophecy is only recognized as such if it corresponds to a need felt more or less intensely by the 'People', and the merit of the 'great men' consists mainly of having revealed, beyond appearances and common sense, the course of the current evolution in society.

The way the prophecies are spread also shows the dialectic relation between the individual and the social milieu. The true prophets, unlike Cassandra and Antigone, never remain solitary. They immediately collect a following, and among their followers are activists determined to see their ideas triumph eventually. The Saint-Simonian religion, the Communist Party, the Geneva Committee, the Zionist movement, Solidarnosc; they all seem to be so many vital staging posts between the initial impulse and its insertion into the social fabric. In that sense there is nothing mysterious in the appearance and the accomplishment of a prophecy. So without giving in to determinism, it is sufficient to note that the 'revelations' stand a much better chance of coming true if they arrive at the right moment and if they are based on a correct assessment of reality. Ten years earlier, John Paul II, were he already the Pope, would not have been able to prevent a Soviet intervention in Poland.

Admitting this much, Hegel's interpretation nevertheless leaves out several problems. We will assess this by looking at the second aspect of his evaluation of the social role of individuals.

2) Even if one admits that the thoughts of 'great men' are largely a result of the milieu and the surrounding circumstances, one can still ask whether all the initiatives which are ascribed to them belong to the same value scale. Hegel studies the question in the name of a postulate: namely the cumulative character of Progress which strives towards the universal triumph of Reason. Bearing in mind that observing reality usually reveals in detail quite a few

contradictions and some incoherence, Hegel has invented two concepts which allow him to sustain his optimism. The 'trick of Reason' permits him to explain that the encounter of individual passions benefits the general interest as a whole: 'In the universal history, something different results from the actions of men than what they projected and reached for, what they know and want immediately . . . the immediate action can likewise hold something vaster than what is apparent in the will and the science of the author.'[16] If one admits that an immanent force, in the shape of Reason, organizes all behaviour, all possibility of major incoherence has been eliminated right away.

The dialectic of the particular and the universal effectively cancels out all other contradictions. To Hegel, the different moments of History are but stages on the road to unity and universality. 'The interest may be entirely particular, but it is not necessarily opposed to the universal. The universal must be achieved by the particular.'[17] This goes for the actions of men as well as for states taken collectively: 'the great men seem to obey only their passion, their whim. But what they want is the universal.'[18] Or still: 'The particular has its own interest in history; it is a finite being and as such it must perish. It is the particular which is used in the battle and it is partly destroyed. It is from this combat and this disappearance that the universal results.'[19]

Whether one adopts a mechanicist conception according to which the piling up of stones eventually will form a mountain, or a more subtle interpretation according to which every initiative has a positive and redeemable part, Hegel's postulate nevertheless seems rather optimistic as far as the studied examples are concerned. The Saint-Simonian industrialism is a relatively neutral anticipation whose effects have been so diluted in time and so contrasted in space that one cannot attribute a universal value to it. The combat initiated by Marx, on the other hand, does have a universal aspiration and intention; but experience has shown, first that this universalism (of class) has not succeeded in eliminating its competitors – whether it be the capitalist system or the system of states; and next that it is that former universalism which has succeeded in triumphing over the new one. The progress of history is not linear. The other cases we looked at invite different comments: the creation of the Red Cross can be considered a (small) victory of the universal over the particularism embodied in the sovereignty of states. However, it is a triumph limited to a specific sector of humanitarian activity. The decisive breakthrough towards the establishment of a model for universal organization is yet to come. In the creation of the state of Israel, one can see but the triumph, at least provisionally, of the particular, without the counterpart of a subsequent advance towards the universal. As far as the liberation of Polish society by John Paul II is concerned, it has an ambivalent meaning, in so far as it constitutes the revenge of a national identity on a pseudo-universalism, as well as a universal model offered to all oppressed countries. In the papal vision the triumph of the universal does not go via a negation of the particular, unlike the Hegelian vision, on the contrary it goes via the spontaneous harmonization between authentic particularisms.

The Hegelian perspective then does not offer a key to a unique interpretation of the cases we have studied. It is true that the sample used was of small dimensions and of heterogeneous character. However it is not certain that the conclusion would have been different with another sample. One can show that individuals can, in certain limited cases and in specific conditions, exert a direct influence on international relations. But there is no ascending curb onto which these experiences could be plotted in order to calibrate the progress of universal conscience. Individuals are not, no more than communities, subject to the pseudo iron law of Linear and Indefinite Progress.

CONCLUSION

For a long time, too long, international relations theory made the mistake of ignoring the impact of individual personalities on the international sphere. Today, at the excuse of wanting to mend past evils, we are running the risk of going to the other extreme.

Taking everybody, one could have extended the list of these personalities indefinitely. To keep to the contemporary era, the inventors of penicillin and the atomic bomb most certainly contributed more to changing the face of the world than many professional politicians or diplomats. Apart from scientists, one could mention numerous other active parties in the international debate: from spiritual leaders to broadsheet leader writers via the leading manufacturers, explorers, financial key figures, etc. But what is true for the present, is also true for the past: the inventor of gun powder and the inventor of vaccine ought to be mentioned in the same way as Einstein or Sir Alexander Fleming, Christopher Columbus ought to have his portrait in the same gallery as Savorgnan de Brazza and Commander Cousteau, and so forth.

In this permanent and universal kaleidoscope, the concept of agent would unfortunately be diluted to the point of utter uselessness. One would discover many characters, well-known or more obscure, who never had the intention of playing an international role and who might not even have been aware of it, but whose discoveries or ideas were retrieved and used for their own ends by other operators. The latter are the only political agents to be identified as such, even if they did not initiate the changes or the reforms that are attributed to them.

Still, we must not overuse the argument founded on the specificity of the politicians. For the limits of our discipline are fragile; they are as fluid in space as in time (what is political here is not political there, and inversely). Other and better-founded reasons justify a restrictive approach to the role of individual characters. The first is to do with the difficulty of making a census of a heterogeneous population and of identifying all its members (some characters only leave the shadows for a while and then are reabsorbed into the darkness after a brief burst of energy). The task of tracing these characters and measuring the influence they exerted on decision-makers would be even more delicate. Countless monographs would not suffice, for the most diverse influences meet, reinforce one another or neutralize one another depending on the object in question and the temperaments present. A political analysis wishing to take the totality of interpersonal relations into account – even only between those characters deemed to have a capacity for influence – would get stranded on thousands of anecdotes, and history exposed to the same ordeal would not survive unscathed.

None the less it remains to be seen if the recent transformation of international relations (retreat of the nation-state, rise of infranational and transnational forces) will not eventually favour the emergence of new types of individual agents. It is a probability which must nevertheless be treated with care. It is yet too early to say whether characters with genuine charisma will manage to free themselves of the organizational networks which enabled them to ascend to a certain level of responsibility in the first place. Were they to show durability (which must still be proven), the multiplication and the differentiation of centres of power could produce contrasting effects: favour the emergence of a new species of prophets, while at the same time limit the scope of influence for each of them.

For the time being, the historical retrospective provides us with a most useful testing ground for models which can be applied to the study of non-state actors. By adapting these models to the study of contemporary reality, it would be wise though not to forget the lesson inherited from the Ancients: Hercules was strong enough to lift the world, provided he could find a fulcrum for leverage. There are still numerous applicants to Hercules' succession, but it has not been established whether the number of fulcra have increased.

NOTES

1. Thomas Carlyle, *Les héros – Le culte des héros et l'héroïque dans l'histoire* (Paris: A. Colin, 1902).
2. Pierre Renouvin and Jean-Baptiste Duroselle, *Introduction à l'histoire des relations internationales* (Paris: A. Colin, 1964), part II.
3. See Pierre Birnbaum and Jean Leca (eds), *Individualism: Theories and Methods* (Oxford: Clarendon, 1990).
4. Raymond Boudon, 'Individualism and Holism in Social Sciences', in Birnbaum and Leca, op. cit.
5. Henri de Saint-Simon, *Oeuvres complètes*, 6 vols (Paris: Anthropos, 1966). See also Sébastien Charléty, *Histoire du Saint-Simonisme* (Paris: Aubier, 1931) and *Saint-Simon: La pensée politique*, preface by G. Ionescu (Paris: Aubier-Montaigne, 1979).
6. Henri Dunant, *Un souvenir de Solférino* (Lausanne: L'Age è d'homme, 1986), p. 101. The first edition is from 1862. Reading this book is compulsory to shed light on Dunant's personality, who over time voiced increasingly pacifist and anti-military opinions.
7. Theodor Herzl, *L'Etat juif* (Paris: Stock, 1981). This edition includes highlights from the author's diary in which he recounts the different overtures he made towards various governments in order to disseminate his ideas.
8. See Marcel Merle, 'Le Saint-Siège et les acteurs internationaux', in Merle, *Les acteurs dans les relations internationales* (Paris: Economica, 1986).
9. Patrick Michel, *La société retrouvée – Politique et religion dans l'Europe soviétisée* (Paris: Fayard, 1988).
10. See Max Weber, *Economie et société* (Paris: Plon, 1971), p. 464; and H. H. Gerth and C. Wright Mills (eds), *From Max Weber: Essays in Sociology* (London: Routledge & Kegan Paul, 1970), pp. 267–301.
11. G. W. F. Hegel, *La raison dans l'histoire. Introduction à la philosophie de l'histoire* (Paris: Plon, 1965), ch. 2 section 2. For selections see

Hegel, *Reason in History: A General Introduction to the Philosophy of History* (Indianapolis: Bobbs-Merrill, 1978). All the following quotations are translated from the French version.

12. Ibid., p. 81.
13. Ibid., p. 119.
14. Ibid.
15. Ibid., p. 113.
16. Ibid., pp. 111–12.
17. Ibid., pp. 107–8.
18. Ibid., p. 125.
19. Ibid., p. 129.

7 Corporate Managers in World Politics
Susan Strange

That individual men and women can play crucial roles in the evolution of the world system or international political economy is a proposition hardly worth discussing. The most desultory newspaper reader, or the most indolent schoolchild in a history class, has no doubt of it. Who can deny that world politics would have taken a different course in the absence of, say, Bismarck or De Gaulle, or even Mrs Thatcher? Or that the course of development in Africa or Asia has been affected by the characters of, for example, Lee Kuan Yew,[1] Idi Amin, Gaddafi or Saddam Hussein? Or that national economies and indirectly the world economy was not affected by the decisions of J. P. Morgan, the partnership of Benjamin Strong and Montagu Norman in opposition to Etienne Moreau,[2] the ingenuity of Schacht or the technical and managerial innovations of the Fords, the Rockefellers, Carnegies and Agnellis of international business?

If realist writers in Europe or from Europe have given a different impression by writing of states as the actors in the international system, that false analogy with the theatre is partly the fault of the international lawyers.[3] For in international law, such rules as there are, are only observed by preserving the fiction that states alone are subjects of international law, while individuals are mere objects of that law.

That fiction is now under attack, as are some other fundamental principles sustained until recently by international courts, and written into documents like the Charter of the United Nations.[4] But my point is simply that it always was just that – a fiction – and that active participants and ordinary observers of world affairs were never taken in by it.

If we can agree about the past, there are, in my view, three important questions about the present and the future that are still open to debate. The first is whether the kind of individual who plays a crucial role in the evolution of the world system has changed

145

at all in recent decades. The second question follows and is causal – how and why, if indeed a new category of decision-makers has come to play a significant part in world politics, this has come about. In other words, what has brought about the change in which heads of state and their military commanders on land, at sea and in the air have become less significant players, while bankers, business-men, scientists, media tycoons and so on have become more significant?

The third question is consequential: whether the fate – or as Dahrendorf would say, the 'life chances' – of various categories of individuals have been significantly changed by the change in the relative importance and power of different kinds of decision-makers. I shall argue that they have, some for the worse, some for the better. And that these changes substantially put in doubt certain popular interpretations of the world economy. Indeed, that they require some basic rethinking of the nature of politics and of some of the fundamental concepts used in political theory, and espe-cially in theories of international relations.

Since I shall also argue that these consequences for individuals are the result of structural changes, my answers to all three ques-tions requires some brief explanation of what is meant by struc-tural change in the world system. It includes changes not only in the security structure, but also in what I have called the produc-tion structure, the financial structure and the knowledge structure.[5] In international political economy, it has come to be accepted that no one of these basic structures of power can be treated in isola-tion from the other three; and that changes in each are apt to reverberate in and upon the other three.

STRUCTURAL CHANGE

The argument that the kind of individuals capable of influencing the course of politics and economics in the world system has changed requires, first, a definition, then an explanation, of what is meant by structural change. 'Structure' is a word too often loosely used, and one which is given significantly different meanings by different writers. In my definition, a structure in political economy is the system by which power is exercised in the distribution of basic social values, not directly but through the way things are customarily done, the way in which the system works to provide those basic values of security, wealth and social order without which no economy can function. Thus structures have value-laden consequences as well as distributional ones.

Sociologists and political philosophers differ in how they label and describe these values. But I think most would agree that one essential value necessary to, and prized in, all economic systems, whether state-directed or market-oriented, primitive or developed, is the provision of a measure of security of person and property. Another essential value is wealth – the provision of those goods and services thought necessary to sustain what Braudel calls 'material life'. To these values, all human societies have added two more necessary requirements for social cohesion: some measure of justice, and some degree of freedom or autonomy for the individual and for social groups. At different times and in different places, societies have differed very widely in their interpretation of what constitutes justice or equity, and in the nature and degree of autonomy to be accorded to individuals and subgroups within society. But neither of these two basic values has ever been totally absent from systems of political economy.

Structures of power also – as sociologists have long argued – have important distributional consequences. Who gets how much security, who acquires how much wealth, who enjoys how much freedom to choose, and who is treated with what kind and degree of justice – all these are, and always have been, the very stuff of politics. Nor are we as political economists concerned only with the who-gets-what-where-when-and-how distributional consequences as between nations or states. As shown by contemporary debates, there are other categories in world society that matter just as much. There are distributional consequences of structural power as between genders. There are still distributional consequences as between classes of society, as the marxists always argued. And now environmental debates raise new inter-generational questions about the distribution of security, wealth, freedom and justice as between those alive today and future generations as yet unborn.

The distribution of structural power is the sum of arrangements in the four major, or primary, structures of a modern industrialized, market-based political economy. These four interact and interlock with each other. They are (1) the security structure through which political authority supplies the political and legal order necessary to all production and exchange; (2) the production structure through which economic actors, individually and collectively, produce the kind of wealth, by such a mix of factors of production (land, labour, capital and technology) and on such terms for each; (3) the financial structure through which credit is created and allocated for consumption or production; and (4)the knowledge structure though which ideas, beliefs and information are developed and communicated.

Each of the four basic structures is a source of a different kind of power. Each is the creation of essentially political decisions taken by individuals or collectivities (such as states) in the past, and difficult to change in the present. How structural power is exercised in the world system requires an essentially transnational approach. 'Who gets what, where, when and how' is therefore a question that must now be answered in terms of class, gender and generation just as much as in terms of states or national societies. So is the value-mix question. If there has been structural change shifting power to non-state authorities, how has this affected the relative weight given in the global political economy to security, wealth, justice and freedom? This said, let me add a few words of explanation concerning each of the four main structures.

THE FOUR STRUCTURES

In international relations, scholars have customarily concentrated on what I call the security structure, for the very good reason that their concern – the problematic which distinguished their field of inquiry from other social sciences – was the phenomenon of inter-state war and conflicts, and sometimes too, of inter-state cooperation and collective action. The term they commonly used to describe the structure within which issues of inter-state war and peace were decided was the 'international political system'. But in my opinion, this was far too broad and imprecise a term. Security structure, by contrast, emphasizes the dual nature of the system and its social implications. These are, that in the global security structure prevailing for the last 200 or 300 years, the state has been both a threat to personal security and its guarantor. For a major characteristic of the Westphalian system of inter-state relations, after all, has been that each state in that system claimed for itself the monopoly of the legitimate use of violence within the state, while at the same time – and as part of the implicit bargain with society – assuming responsibility for the defence of the realm against threats to its security coming from outside its frontiers.

For most of the second half of this century, this implicit bargain was reproduced at a transnational level. That is to say, instead of the implicit bargain being between the government of each state and the national society, it became an implicit bargain between the government of each of the two superpowers, the United States and the USSR, and the societies of a group of states allied to each. The protection offered by the Soviet and American nuclear umbrellas against the risk of attack by neighbours (and to some extent against the threat to security arising from revolution within these states) was given in exchange for acceptance of Soviet or American domination over economic and social issues hitherto pertaining to the national governments of their respective allies. Described as a balance of power system, it was not so much a balance between states, as in earlier centuries, as a balance between two military blocs in which decisive power in security matters lay with each superpower. This balance came to an end as a result, not of developments in foreign policy, but because of the internal disintegration of the economy and society of one of the superpowers, the Soviet Union, and consequently of the bloc it had protected.

That evident truth has been obscured as a result of using a general term like political system to describe a more specific power structure relating only to the security concerns of states and individuals. For it has served to exclude from the discourses of international relations all those kinds of structural power affecting social and economic relations in world society that lay outside the realm of national 'foreign policies'. In recent discussions of world affairs since the end of the Cold War, the underlying social, economic, technological and financial changes, within national societies and in transnational economic affairs, which so largely contributed to this major political change, have therefore been given far too little attention. Overlooking the role of corporate managers in structural changes in world politics has been one aspect of this professional myopia.

The second structure affected by great change in recent decades has been the Financial Structure – the system in which money and especially credit is created and allocated for the furtherance of economic exchange and the promotion of productive investment as well as for the support of state authority. A capitalist or market economy cannot exist without money as a medium of exchange, nor without markets for credit as a system for allocating resources and translating savings into investments – that is, markets in which those wanting money today can effect transactions with those who prefer money tomorrow. Change in this structure has become the driving force behind growth in the world economy. Peter Drucker described it as the 'flywheel' of the world economy, meaning that the creation of credit and its ability to move across national frontiers had been the engine of social and economic change throughout the planet.[6] The structural changes that brought about the easier creation of credit – capital for investment – have been a necessary condition for the remarkable and unforeseen economic growth not only of America and Europe but also of Asia and Latin America. The other necessary condition – also brought about by structural change in the Financial Structure – was the increased mobility of capital, greatly enhancing the power and influence of transnational corporations and, of course, those in charge of them.

This has been the major change in the third basic power structure, the Production Structure. Instead of a collection of national systems of production – capitals, as the marxists call them – in which most production was destined for the local consumers, and most exchange was within the national economy, the Production Structure has changed to a global one. Where, in earlier times, foreign trade, foreign investment and foreign-owned firms affected only a very small and marginal part of the production structure of each national economy, today all three permeate and influence life-chances of people in all walks of life and in most national societies. Only in the largest national economies, like those of the United States, China or India, do national markets still occupy a larger space than the global market. For the rest, the number of firms and kinds of business still untouched by change in the global production structure shrinks year by year; while the number of firms and kinds of business affected by global changes in technology, in managerial strategies, in marketing and design of products, processes and services correspondingly increases.

For this to happen, there has had to be change in the fourth power structure, that relating to Knowledge and Information. It too has affected the relations between government and business, the state and the market economy. How it has done so, I can best explain by briefly referring to conclusions drawn from some recent research done in collaboration with John Stopford. But before doing that, I should emphasize that the role of corporate managers in world politics can only be fully appreciated, in my view, through an understanding of change in each of the four basic power structures in the global political economy, and a recognition that no one of these four structures can be treated in isolation from the other three. Change in each one reverberates in and upon the other three, so that change in the security structure cannot be understood in isolation from change in the Production Structure, nor the latter in isolation from the Knowledge Structure and the Financial Structure.

Competing for world market shares, such was the sub-title of *Rival States, Rival Firms,* the book co-authored with John Stopford, Professor of International Business at the London Business School.[7] Its argument, drawing on the concept of structural power and change in structural power, is highly relevant to any discussion of the role of corporate managers in world politics.

Briefly summarized, our purpose was to study the negotiations conducted in the late 1980s between national governments and foreign-owned firms. To simplify the task, we looked at bargaining over more than 100 plants and projects in just three contrasted developing countries – Brazil, Malaysia and Kenya. We interviewed government officials in each country and the corporate executives of over 50 firms, seeking to understand how and why their relationship with each other had changed over the previous 15 or 20 years. What became steadily clearer to us as the research data accumulated was that, while the responses of different governments and different enterprises varied rather widely – more widely than most development experts would have predicted; the forces driving them, the forces to which they were responding, more or less adequately, were fundamentally the same. These forces were those of structural change in the international political economy. We came by this means to see common forces of structural change behind a whole series of apparently unrelated events on the world stage. The liberation of Central Europe, the disintegration of the former Soviet Union, the imbalance of payments between Japan and the United States, the mounting US fiscal deficit, the rapid economic growth of the East Asian 'tigers', and the U-turns of so many governments away from protectionism, import-substitution and state ownership and towards liberalization, privatization and competition – all these we saw as the product of certain driving forces of structural change in the global political economy.

Most significant among these common forces of change was, first, the accelerating rate and escalating cost of technological change in the production structure. In a fashion not at all anticipated in the 1970s, this has speeded up the internationalization of production –

that is, the change from production for local or national markets to production for a world market. Because states are still gate-keepers to the national economies which make up this world market, firms who wish to sell in state X often have to agree to produce in state X. In this way, the technological imperative speeded up the dispersion of industrial manufacturing from the OECD 'core' economies to the rest of the world. The 'new reality', as Peter Drucker has observed, was that only those firms who became transnational could survive the competition of others.[8]

In short, it is not that international business is a new phenomenon – on the contrary, as business historians remind us, it is a very old one. Rather, it is that it has grown and spread and has become a dominant instead of a subsidiary or minor phenomenon.

Second among the driving forces of structural change has been the increased mobility of capital, creating out of a series of more or less separate national credit-creating financial structures, one loosely integrated global credit-creating financial structure. Political scientists who fail to understand the steps and the modalities by which this change has occurred have missed a vital clue to problems of the world economy. They should take the trouble to read some recent international monetary and financial history and to follow developments in the financial press. Without this change, there can be no doubt that the transition of enterprises from national to transnational would have been much slower and more difficult.

Third, the same observation applies to the global systems of transport and communication. Without the improvement in reliability and frequency and the lower real costs, the management problems of firms producing goods or services in a dozen different locations worldwide would have been wellnigh impossible. Without this improved, speeded-up communication system reaching into the farthest corners of the world, the popular awareness of economic and social change elsewhere – an awareness on which most of the political changes in ex-socialist and developing countries have depended – would have been missing. This is one aspect of change in the knowledge structure that has been crucial. No less important is what Lukes calls the third level of power – the ability to win others over to your own fundamental beliefs and value judgements. One of the most striking examples of this structural power has been the American use of the IMF to convert a whole generation of other countries, central bankers and finance ministry officials to accept the desirability and inevitability of an open, deregulated world economy.

Fourth and last, I claim that there has been profound change in the security structure. Despite continued violence, much of it civil or internecine rather than inter-state, I believe that the above, mainly economic, changes have fundamentally altered the nature of competition between states.[9]

The economically advanced states in particular are competing for shares of the world market, for exports, licensing and franchising fees and other forms of invisible earnings. Only so can the national economy support the material expectations of new classes and, through rising GNP, can manage to moderate the social conflicts between classes, ethnic communities and regions which continually jeopardize national unity and political stability. What has caused so many LDC and ex-socialist governments to make radical changes in their economic policies is their perceived need to succeed in this competition for market shares.

THE ROLE OF FIRMS

But none can do so alone. Like it or not, they need the cooperation of the enterprises that successfully supply goods and services to the world market, whose distribution systems open the door to it and whose command of technology and of access to international capital can be shared with, or denied to, a national government.

One more recent example of this symbiosis between host-state and foreign-owned firm (FOF) comes from Malaysia. In February 1997, prime minister Dr Mahathir Mohamad went personally to Silicon Valley in California to solicit business interest in the information technology (IT) field in his proposed 'multimedia super corridor' near his capital, Kuala Lumpur. To induce large American, Japanese and European IT firms to invest in it, Mahathir offered them a 10-year tax holiday, freedom to employ foreign nationals and to operate without Malaysian partners,and preferential terms for their investments. The government for its part was planning to spend some $12 billion on the development.[10]

An important insight of the Stopford/Strange book, therefore, was that TNCs had come to play a formative role in world economic development, so that the concept of diplomacy could no longer be confined to what professional diplomats do, but must include the bargaining functions of firms. This corporate diplomacy is conducted in part with foreign states, and sometimes indeed with their home state. But it is also increasingly conducted with other firms. Strategic alliances with other firms have been forced on transnational enterprises by structural change in the system, just as they have been forced to bargain with governments. The high costs of research and development and the accelerating pace of technological change mean that few firms can afford to keep up with new technology in all the fields that they may need to know about to stay in business. To take advantage of steeply falling unit cost curves in production, firms need both to operate in several countries at once, and to forge alliances with other firms whose expertise and market access are complementary to their own. As any day's newspaper columns will show, these two kinds of corporate diplomacy – the second and third dimensions, in our perception, of contemporary transnational diplomacy – may affect national interests and the fortunes of the state every bit as much as the outcome of a negotiation between governments.

The point for our present debate is that these two new dimensions of diplomacy impose decision-making roles on corporate managers that are essentially political rather than economic. Which country to choose for the location of a new plant to supply its market and possibly that of its neighbours obviously depends on political judgement more than on economic calculations of relative costs and benefits. The economic future of the chosen country thus depends increasingly on the political decisions of individual corporate executives. This, rather than dependence on the political decisions of people in other governments, is the true nature of that much-abused concept of 'interdependence'.

Let me give some more particular examples. In many European countries, governments in the postwar years have come to play a key role in mediating between managers and workers over pay and conditions. Neo-corporatist solutions to the commodification of labour involved government in a triangular bargaining situation. This is fast being eroded by the structural changes I have briefly described. As car manufacturers like Fiat or Volkswagen or General Motors start production in Brazil, for example, a political problem for the managers of these firms is how to reconcile the interests of the workers 'at home' and the new workers of their plants in Brazil. The old solutions do not work; the political process is internalized within the firm. It may even involve a clash with the home government, as when General Motors annoyed the Office of the US Trade Representative by accepting subsidies from the Brazilian government for agreeing to produce auto parts in Brazil for export to the United States. For Washington, GM's managers were betraying the national interest of the USA as interpreted by the US Trade Representative.

Another example is to be found in the launching of the Single European Market in the mid-1980s. It is by now fairly generally acknowledged that although a British Commissioner in Brussels, Lord Cockfield, drafted the proposal, much of the steam behind it came from a group of European industrialists led by Wisse Dekker, the CEO of Phillips, the Dutch electronics firm. Dekker, in particular, had been highly vocal for some years previously in his criticism of the member governments of the European Community for being so slow to do away with the remaining barriers to intra-European trade and investment. If they did not hasten to pull them down, he warned, firms like Phillips would increasingly build their businesses elsewhere than in Europe. Politicians paid heed.

Another well-known instance of corporate diplomacy in Europe was the support given by the major steel manufacturers to the restructuring plans proposed by the commissioner, Etienne Davignon, back in the 1970s. Without the established links between these firms, reflected as they were in the effectiveness of their Eurofer association, the EC's diplomacy over the management of international trade in steel with the United States and with Japan would have been seriously weakened.

Some of the dilemmas facing governments as a result of strategies chosen by corporate managers are not easy to resolve. One recent example of rival firms posing difficult choices for governments was the negotiations between the Mexican government on one side and Volkswagen and BMW on the other. In return for its offer to modernize the design of the famous Beetle and produce it for home sales and export in Mexico, Volkswagen was to be allowed to import some of its more up market cars into the country. This brought immediate objections of discrimination from BMW, who objected that they too were promising new production units in Mexico and expected equally favourable concessions for their imported cars.

These structural shifts in the locus of decision-making power in the world market economy, I suggest, are significantly altering the fate of many individuals. Let me give just two examples of cases where women's life chances may actually have been improved through the internationalization of production and the decisions of the managers of foreign-owned firms. One is from Malaysia, where such firms took advantage of the government's invitation to conduct the assembly of electronic products like integrated circuits with cheap Malaysian labour in export-processing zones. These EPZs have been much criticized for allowing the exploitation of Malaysian girls, unprotected by labour unions. But research for the OECD's Development Centre on the spot found that the girls themselves saw it differently. 'True,' they said in effect, 'we ruin our eyes with this work and we are not paid much money. But,' they added, 'after two years we can save enough for a dowry which will get us better husbands. That is more than we could hope for by working for father for nothing back home in the village.'

Similarly, in Kenya, one of the few really successful export industries, unhampered by a lot of government controls, produces cut flowers and pot plants. African women more often than men work in the fields – but the foreign firms pay them, while husbands and fathers expected them to work for nothing – and to do the cooking at the end of the day.

Of course, there are other stories of foreign firms taking decisions that harm individual life chances. Everyone remembers Bhopal, and Nestlé's indiscriminate sales of baby milk. There are Chilean farmers growing olives whose livelihood was ruined by a Swiss-owned iron smelter poisoning their trees. The point is only that some of the winners as well as some of the losers are to be found in developing countries, just as some of the losers, as well as some winners are to be found in the rich, industrialized countries. But the internationalization of production has offered opportunities as well as risks to individuals that their own governments just had no power to offer. Many poor people stay poor, but some poor people become rich, or moderately better off, as a result of structural changes and a new allocation of power from governments to firms. Against the deaths and the damage must be set the new job opportunities and the rise of new owners and managers of third-world multinationals.

THEORETICAL CONCLUSIONS

Neither the old divisions between special branches of social science, nor the old conceptual tools, nor the conventional categories of society seem appropriate for future inquiry into either the kinds of individuals influential in the international political economy or into the consequences of structural change for individuals. Such questions are not unique in demanding a wholly new perspective on the political issues for the international political economy. Whether researchers are interested in optimal development strategies for a region or a country, whether it is the United States or Italy or Nigeria, or whether they are interested in the sociological implications of changing family relationships, or indeed any other topic that has exercised the minds of social scientists, it is necessary to start from a global perspective, and from one that does not separate politics from economics. I do not think it necessary to labour this point because I believe a growing number of political scientists, sociologists, geographers and even economists have come to the same conclusion. But the implications for university administrations, for the programme of courses offered to students, and the kind of reading they are asked to undertake have not yet been thought through.

In truth, our notions of the 'genealogy', as it were, of the social sciences has to be turned upside-down. Let me explain what this means for political science. In the old, established perspectives reflected in the organization charts of many universities, at least in Britain, the 'grandfather' field of study is politics – or as it is sometimes labelled, 'government', or 'political science'. That is subdivided – the next generation, so to speak – into comparative politics, political philosophy or the history of political thought, national political systems and their institutions, and international relations. The latter is again subdivided into strategic studies, foreign policy analysis, international relations theory and – as an afterthought – the politics of international economic relations, or international political economy.

The conclusion of the argument I have made here about the effect of global structural change on the kind of individual role that is significant politically, and the consequences for different groups of individuals, is that this 'genealogy' should be reversed, as should the comparable 'genealogy' of the way in which economics is studied and subdivided, with international political economy figuring as the 'grandchild' of economic science. In other words, the 'grandparent' – not to discriminate between the sexes – of social science ought to be international political economy. It is the context, the framework, within which other relationships, institutions, rules and behaviour exist. To study it, we may need to include political and economic philosophy and theory; the great thinkers from Plato and Thucydides to Marx and Keynes have much to say that is directly relevant to the analysis of the global political economy and the problems and policy issues it presents. As subsidiary, or second-generation, studies, we can specialize on international history, political and economic, or for that matter on environmental political economy, market regulation, financial systems, or trade relations. And as a third generation, we can study the 'domestic' politics of particular countries, or groups of countries, or the sociology of particular social groups, generations or occupations. Of course, no hierarchy of intellectual pursuits is perfect. But since for practical purposes it is necessary to have one, the IPE 'upside-down' one seems to me rather more logical than the conventional IR-centred one.

But even if such a change is too revolutionary for vested interests in the existing intellectual hierarchy to swallow, there is still a strong case for much more collaboration and mutual comprehension between political scientists, economists, sociologists and people in management studies than there is at present. And international political economy still has a long way to go to challenge the stultifying intellectual domination of neo-classical economics. Inter-disciplinary research and inter-disciplinary teaching must be positively encouraged. This should come more easily to European universities than to American ones if only because the separation of the social sciences has never been as extreme as in the United States.

Secondly, political scientists must be prepared to rethink quite fundamentally some of the concepts on which their analysis of policy issues has been based. As my car manufacturers example suggests, the concept of 'class' as a unifying category in society becomes less and less clear and less and less useful. The interests of workers conflict with those of other workers. The dividing line between workers and capitalists, between managers and wage-earners becomes more and more blurred.

The concept of 'Nation' so central to the study of international relations, is also becoming less and less useful – at least as a way of describing one of the characteristics of economic enterprise. What nationality is a Canadian firm like National Telecom if most of its profits, most of its employees are to be found outside Canada and inside the US? As the authority of national institutions is diminished by the integration of economies and economic enterprises into a global market economy, and as the loyalty of individuals once more becomes a shifting complex of attachments to profession, family, firm, political party, city, region or religion, it is clear to me that a big question-mark hangs over the future study of international relations. To respond to it, a reconsideration of the role of individuals, in politics, business and academic life is surely a good place to start.

NOTES

1. Prime Minister of Singapore from 1959 to 1990.
2. These last three persons played a key role in building the international monetary system of the 1920s. They were respectively President of the Fededal Reserve Board, Governor of the Bank of England, and Governor of the Banque de France.
3. It is no coincidence that in Europe most of the early pre-1939 professors of international relations were nearly all trained in continental university faculties of law, as international lawyers – Georg Schwarzenberger, William Rappard, Hans Morgenthau, Frederick Schuman, for example.
4. See, for instance, article 2, paragraph 7.
5. Susan Strange, *States and Markets* (London: Pinter, 1988).
6. Peter Drucker, *The New Realities: in Government and Politics, in Economy and Business, in Society and in World View* (New York: Harper & Row, 1989).
7. John Stopford and Susan Strange, *Rival States, Rival Firms: Competition for World Market Shares* (Cambridge: Cambridge University Press, 1991).
8. Drucker, op. cit.
9. For a further elaboration of this argument see my contribution, 'The Name of the Game', in N. Rizopoulos (ed.), *Sea Change* (New York: Council on Foreign Relations, 1990).
10. *Financial Times*, 27 February 1997.

8 Atomic Scientists and Disarmament – the Pugwash Movement
Jean Klein

The role of public opinion in the promotion of peace and disarmament has often been asserted, and movements opposed to the deployment of Pershing rockets and cruise missiles in Europe made front-page news all through the 1980s. However, only limited attention has been paid to the activities of a transnational organization – the Pugwash movement – which has devoted itself since the end of the 1950s to the problems caused by the invention of the nuclear weapon, and which has consistently acted with the intention of warding off the threat which consequently weighs on humanity. Only when president of the movement Joseph Rotblat was given the Nobel Peace Prize in the autumn of 1995 did the media turn their attention to an organization which had mostly acted behind the scenes and which had been suspected of having at some point been too accommodating towards Soviet positions on disarmament.

Indeed, some people believed that Pugwash, by referring to nuclear pacifism, had objectively served the interests of the Soviet Union during East–West antagonism, and had contributed to discrediting the security policies of Western states.[1] Others also did not fail to point out the connection, established by President of the Nobel prize committee Francis Sejersted, between the award received by the Pugwash movement and the condemnation of the resumption of French nuclear testing in the Pacific. According to him, France had set the wrong example by breaking the moratorium which it had accepted in 1992, only a few months after the decision taken in New York to extend the Non-proliferation Treaty for an unlimited time. Moreover, by experimenting with nuclear weapons in defiance of the obligation of 'utmost restraint' which it had endorsed while waiting for the conclusion of a comprehensive nuclear test ban treaty, France had risked jeopardizing the success of disarmament negotiations. Since Nobel prize-winner Joseph

Rotblat multiplied similar declarations, it seemed clear that the choice made by the Oslo jury contained an anti-French jab. Nevertheless, in its preamble, the Norwegian committee had also expressed the wish for the decision to 'encourage all leaders of the world to intensify their efforts in order to get rid of nuclear weapons'. Based on the universal aims of the decision, the French government congratulated the prize-winners and reaffirmed its position in favour of disarmament, including nuclear disarmament, as long as the state's right to security was secured.[2]

This was not an opening shot for the Pugwash movement: the four members of its executive council, among whom was Joseph Rotblat, had already remonstrated with the French government. They had indeed sent a letter on 20 June 1995 to President Jacques Chirac in order to ask him to reconsider his decision to initiate nuclear tests in the South Pacific.[3] In their views, the tests could only be motivated by the intention of 'developing new nuclear weapons'. But France had subscribed to 'the principles and objectives of nuclear non-proliferation and disarmament' adopted at the end of the conference prolonging the NPT, and had particularly committed itself to putting a stop to the nuclear arms race. Moreover, the signatories of the letter did not understand why France should persist in improving its nuclear equipment when the military threat had faded with the end of East–West antagonism, and since the country was situated in a region of the world where conflicts had disappeared. They were therefore urging the French President to abandon his project and proclaim that France would subscribe without delay to a comprehensive nuclear test ban treaty.[4]

Such an untoward measure aroused a critical reaction from three former officials of the French association of the Pugwash movement. In a letter sent to the Secretary General of the movement, they regretted the tone of the plea addressed to the head of state, as well as the absence of preliminary coordination. This letter was published in the movement's bulletin with a comment which only partially complied with the intervening parties' concerns, and which left open the question of the advisability of adopting positions in public on controversial topics.[5]

Even if they were not frequent, similar incidents had happened in the past, but they were not subject to publicity since Pugwash members make it a rule to observe a certain reserve, and consider that their disagreements should not be displayed publicly. But the fact remains that the positions taken in public by council members have often been attributed by external observers to the whole movement, which can generate misunderstandings as to its philosophy and functioning method – especially since the association cultivates discretion and cannot even take advantage of written statutes.[6] Moreover, its leaders consider that only the guarantee of 'confidentiality' can prompt the renowned scientists who meet regularly under its patronage to express themselves freely about the technical aspects of defence policies and disarmament. Therefore special precautions have been taken so that opinions expressed at annual conferences or within working groups or symposia are not attributed to this or that individual. Finally, it is agreed that those taking part in the 'conferences on science and world matters' will be considered as 'private persons' whose remarks do not in any way commit the scientific institution to which they belong, nor reflect the point of view of the government of the country of which they are nationals.

According to the code of conduct defined in 1962 at the London Conference, Pugwash is a transnational organization which includes scientists from all continents with the aim of examining social problems raised by the applications of science. But the sudden awareness in the Anglo-Saxon world of dangers arising from nuclear weapons was what the movement originated from. In this respect, philosopher Bertrand Russell played a decisive role, and among the founding members are several atomic scientists who were involved in the Manhattan project.

By agreeing to help finalize the American nuclear weapon, they had wanted to equip democracies with means to defeat Nazi Germany and to outrun Hitler, who was suspected of wanting to follow the same nuclear route. This hypothesis was plausible, since Otto Hahn had carried out laboratory experiments at the Kaiser Wilhelm Institute of Berlin in 1938 on the chain reaction caused by the neutronic bombing of a uranium nucleus; and the Germans had a plentiful supply of this matter since they controlled the uranium mines of Bohemia following the splitting up of Czechoslovakia. Albert Einstein, Edward Teller and Leo Szilard had shared their concern about this with President Roosevelt as early as 1940, and their warnings probably influenced his decision to embark in 1942 on the path of a military nuclear force, and to channel considerable resources into the development of the new weapon as part of the Manhattan project, placed under the supervision of General Leslie Groves.[7]

But when the first atomic device was tested in the desert of New Mexico on 16 July 1945 (operation Trinity), Germany was already defeated, and it was known by then that the Third Reich had decided not to go down the nuclear road in its armament programmes and had finally given up the idea of having the bomb.[8] On the other hand, the nuclear weapon was perceived as an efficient means of speeding up the end of hostilities in the Pacific and reducing the losses of human lives which would result from the conquest of Japanese islands. However, the American scientific community did not agree on this point, and the bombing of Hiroshima and Nagasaki is known to have raised objections from those who could not conceive of the use of a mass-destruction weapon against the urban centres of the enemy.[9] Thus they felt the need to sound a warning about the dangers of a nuclear arms race and to mobilize in order to ward off the threat it represented for the survival of the human race. The Russell–Einstein manifesto, first made public in London on 9 July 1955, and the communiqué of the first Pugwash conference of 10 July 1957, both eloquently testify to this preoccupation. Subsequently, the 'Pugwashites' broadened the scope of their activities and also tackled the problems of under-development, the demographic explosion and the protection of the environment.[10] However, they never ceased to assert that 'disarmament and the prevention of conflicts' should be a priority and that Third World problems should be handled primarily from the angle of security, although also taking into account its economic and social dimensions.

It is therefore quite legitimate to wonder about the nature of the commitment of the Pugwash movement, and to check whether some scientists have thereby been able to contribute, as individuals, to solving disarmament problems and to organizing regional or world security. From 11 to 17 September 1992, the 42nd Annual Conference of the movement was held on the theme 'Shaping Our Common Future: Dangers and Opportunities', and the debates which took place on this occasion displayed the continuity of Pugwash concerns. The communiqué drafted by the Council on 18 September 1992, for instance, summarizes the work of the conference and recognizes that the collapse of the bipolar system and the dissolution of the USSR both call for a new approach to security problems. But it also insists on the necessity of pushing on with nuclear disarmament and reinforcing rules for the non-proliferation of mass-destruction weapons. The communiqué points out with satisfaction that significant progress has been achieved in the elimination of tactical nuclear weapons, the reduction of strategic armaments (START), and the suspension of nuclear testing. These diplomatic successes are seen as so many incitements to go further down the road of a 'Nuclear Weapons Free World' (NWFW). But the achievements of disarmament fall short of such an objective, it notes; and there is still a long way to go before it will be possible to reach the shores of a pacified world where defence would be based on 'sufficient' means. There can thus be no question of Pugwash scientists demobilizing, and it is up to them to make a technical contribution, as they have done in the past, to solving problems which disarmament negotiators have to face, while keeping alive the hope of an ultimate total elimination of nuclear weapons.

This profession of faith was intended to dispute the validity of the argument which stated that the Pugwash movement had lost all meaning after the changes which occurred in the international system at the end of the 1980s. Indeed, professional diplomats played from then on a decisive, if not exclusive, role in the negotiations of arms regulation, and the mediation of Pugwash was no longer as essential as at times when communication between the two protagonists was not yet institutionalized. In addition, Russian and American scientists were mostly concerned with solving problems raised by the organization of the strategic balance between the United States and the Soviet Union, while arms control required new approaches following the collapse of communism and the dissolution of the Warsaw Pact organization. 'Cooperative security' in a bipolar world would not be achieved by referring to a tradition inherited from the Cold War, and without reform Pugwash would be condemned to insignificance or decline.

Such a clear-cut judgement not only neglects the vitality of an institution which has proven capable of adapting to new geostrategic realities, but also imperfectly accounts for its past action. Of course Soviet and American scientists played a decisive role in the definition of Pugwash positions and they may have tipped the balance in favour of bilateral arms control, but it would be an exaggeration to maintain that this was the vision of all its members. The analysis of Council communiqués and study group recommendations alone shows that the Pugwashites always defended a general arms limitation, and only grudgingly subscribed to the selective approach imposed by the two Great Powers in the 1960s. According to them, partial measures such as the Moscow treaty of 1963 on the halting of nuclear testing, the Non-proliferation Treaty of 1968, or the SALT agreements of 1972 and 1979 were only the beginning of a process which was meant to lead to 'general and complete disarmament under strict international control' and to the establishment of a universal collective security system. Today conditions for a general limitation of nuclear as well as conventional armaments seem to be fulfilled, and Pugwashites can only be pleased with an evolution which satisfies their desires.[11]

However, they are aware of the scope and complexity of the task still to be accomplished, and they remain convinced that the success of the project depends to a large extent on their expertise.[12] In the past they have contributed to solving technical problems caused by inspection in line with the ban on nuclear testing and chemical armaments. In the future, the scope of their activities will remain very open, and areas where science could serve disarmament are easy to find. Pugwash has served since 1960 as a framework to discussions on the terms and conditions of a 'minimum deterrent', which has been a topical question ever since the Americans and Russians decided to relinquish redundant nuclear capacities and broke out of the game of stabilization of the strategic balance at a high level of weaponry. In addition, the convention on chemical weapons, signed in January 1993, has only just come into force (April 1997), and it is worth noting that experts who have gathered under the patronage of Pugwash in the last two decades have contributed significantly to the success of this project, particularly concerning verification of the non-production of chemical weapons by industrial firms. Finally, the model of a purely 'defensive' defence based on high-performance conventional means drew the attention of experts in the 1980s,[13] and it was sometimes seen as an efficient way of guaranteeing security on the European continent in the absence of progress towards an agreement on 'mutual and balanced forces reduction' (MBFR). On several occasions, the Pugwash movement organized workshops which brought together specialists who examined the ways and means of reducing 'military confrontation' between East and West. Their recommendations, however, were never taken into account by the governments, and the treaty on conventional forces reduction signed in November 1990 can hardly be said to bear the stamp of Pugwash.

One can therefore easily understand why the Pugwash movement arouses such contrasted reactions. Some consider its role to be overrated, and its contribution to solving disarmament to be limited, if not non-existent. Others believe that its interventions allowed the ideological peak of the debate on disarmament to be smoothed out, and facilitated the search for compromise solutions. Finally, others see in the movement a channel for communication between adversary-partners and the vehicle for a parallel diplomacy in favour of pacifism and Soviet ideology. We will restrict ourselves in the following observations to clarifying the premises of the problem by referring to the philosophy from which the Pugwash movement claims its origins and by pointing out some of the initiatives taken by scientists in order to contribute to solving disarmament problems. We will then try to assess the impact of the positions they take on the conduct of negotiations and on the implementation of the concluded agreements. Finally, we will ponder on the specific role of 'individuals' in an NGO (non-governmental organization) which was at the time of East–West confrontation the vehicle for governmental policies or a framework for parallel diplomatic communication, but which seems less useful now that dialogue between the adversary-partners has gone back to normal.

ORIGIN AND PHILOSOPHY OF THE PUGWASH MOVEMENT

Soon after the Second World War, problems raised by scientists' responsibility in the invention of the nuclear weapon were discussed in the United States and Great Britain, respectively in the Federation of American Scientists and the Atomic Scientists Association. A monthly publication directed by Eugene Rabinowitch, *The Bulletin of Atomic Scientists*, ensured the spreading of opinions on the subject, and the Soviets were invited to get involved too in order to broaden the debate. Up to 1954, exchanges remained confined to the Anglo-Americans, but in August 1955 the Association of Members of Parliament for a World Government, whose headquarters were in London, organized a conference in which four Soviet scientists took part. Among them, Alexander Topchiev clearly favoured regular cooperation between scientists from East and West, and he later became one of the major actors in the creation of the Pugwash movement on the Soviet side. At the end of the London conference the Russell–Einstein manifesto was adopted and three commissions were created for the study of questions to be examined in further meetings. These questions included civil and military applications of nuclear energy, problems caused by disarmament, and the social responsibility of the scientist. This programme was never applied on an international level, and the study workshops became dormant.

This was when Bertrand Russell decided to take advantage of the media coverage around the manifesto which he had written in 1955, and which had received Albert Einstein's backing a few days before his death. Russell had very early displayed his concern about the effects of nuclear weapons. In a speech delivered on 28 November 1945 in front of the House of Lords, he had sensed how big a risk weapons even more powerful than the Hiroshima bomb would be for civilization if an international control system was not introduced in cooperation with Soviet scientists. In 1954, when a new step was taken in the arms race with the access of the two protagonists to the thermonuclear weapon, Russell considered that the time was ripe for action and he used a broadcast on 23 December to draw attention to the danger which threatened the human race (*Man's Peril*). Later on, he clarified his thoughts in a manifesto which was made public on 5 July 1955 in London. In addition to the two initial signatories – Bertrand Russell and Albert Einstein – nine other scientists, most of whom were Nobel prize-winners, joined in this initiative which underlined the dangers of a nuclear war and called on the scientific community to ward off this peril. A conference was to be organized in order to discuss the ways and means of preventing a war and promoting a peaceful settlement of disputes between states.

The first meeting was to be held in New Delhi in January 1957 in connection with the Indian Science Congress, and to be organized by the World Science Workers Federation. But Bertrand Russell did not wish to be dependent on an organization whose political ties were too visible, because independence was what counted for him above all, and independence alone could guarantee success for the project. Finally, the deterioration of the international situation in the autumn of 1956 (Anglo-French intervention in Suez and repression of the Hungarian uprising), as well as financial difficulties, led the project to be abandoned. None the less, the idea of a conference took shape in July 1957 thanks to the support of Cyrus Eaton, a very rich American manufacturer who offered 22 scientists hospitality in his property at Pugwash in Nova Scotia (Canada), where he left them all latitude to organize the debates as they wished. The designation which was later given to the 'Conferences on Science and World Affairs' (COSWA) comes from the name of the place where the first of these conferences was held.

This first meeting was fundamental for the pursuit of the process, since some of the participants, among them Leo Szilard, had taken part in the Manhattan project and were able to give first-hand information about the relations established with the American government and the action undertaken to control atomic energy. The work continued in three commissions devoted respectively to the pacific and military use of nuclear energy, to the regulation of nuclear weapons, and to the social responsibility of scientists. While the scientists had no difficulty agreeing on technical problems such as the evaluation of the risks of nuclear testing, they were more circumspect when it came to giving an opinion about nuclear arms regulation given the complexity of the problem and its political nature. They therefore limited themselves to general declarations about abolishing war and stopping the arms race, leaving it to experts to study the question of disarmament and to make practical suggestions on how to contribute to a solution. Finally, a consensus emerged about the role of scientists in the promotion of peace, and the final communiqué of the conference stated eleven 'articles of faith' which were reaffirmed the following year in the Vienna declaration of 19 September 1958.

Once scientists who came from countries which had been in conflict during the Cold War managed to agree on fundamental questions about the prevention of a nuclear war and the end of the arms race, some drew the conclusion that they were qualified to contribute to solving the complicated problems created by military applications of science, and that their meetings had to be institutionalized. Since the conclusions of the Pugwash conference were on the whole welcomed by scientific and political circles, the organizers were encouraged to pursue their effort, and a five-person Continuing Committee was put in charge of defining the programme of future activities.

This committee met in December 1957 in London to define the shape of future meetings and took into account the answers to a questionnaire that had been sent by Messrs Rotblat and Rabinowitch to their colleagues in order to get their opinion on the subject. Most of those who answered the survey showed a preference for restricted meetings of two kinds. Some of the meetings would deal with current issues and would allot themselves the objective of influencing governmental policy, while others would analyse the social implications of the progress made by science and attempt to draft a code of conduct for scientists. Finally, some scientists considered organizing larger meetings in order to examine general problems and adopt resolutions which would receive the greatest publicity possible. After two days of intense discussions, the committee decided to pursue a triple objective – influence governmental policy, establish a channel of communication between scientists, and influence public opinion. But the programme was clearly not feasible in one go, and had to be carried out in stages. In the immediate future, priority had to be given to facing the crisis triggered by the breaking off of negotiations in the London subcommittee on disarmament. The Continuing Committee once again appealed to Cyrus Eaton, who agreed to fund a second Pugwash conference in Lake Beauport, Canada, from 31 March to 11 April 1958. Simultaneously the organization of an enlarged conference was decided for the following year in Europe, taking advantage of the participation of many scientists at the Geneva conference on the peaceful use of atomic energy.

The Lake Beauport conference foreshadowed future conferences in the 1960s since there was a majority of Anglo-Americans and Soviets, and since the participants were chosen according to their knowledge on the question of disarmament. Of the 22 scientists who took part in the conference, 8 originated from the United States, and 4 came respectively from the United Kingdom and the USSR. The three nuclear powers of the time were thought to have a decisive role to play in the establishment of a long-lasting peace, and frank discussions between scientific advisers of each government were seen as contributing to solving pending problems. As it happened, the main focus of attention was on problems related to the ceasing of nuclear testing as well as the resumption of talks on disarmament. At the end of the conference, the communications presented were transmitted to the heads of state of 15 countries, to the Secretary General of the UN and to the Pope. Some of these people reacted positively, welcoming the scientists' action in favour of peace. Of course Soviet and Anglo-American approaches were so different that converging conclusions were highly unlikely. But the exercise was considered useful since it had made possible a clarification of Eastern and Western positions on problems of security, and had initiated a dialogue which everyone was determined to pursue according to methods which were to be specified later on and laid down in the Continuing Committee's report of the 17th Pugwash Conference which was held in Ronneby, Sweden from 3 to 8 September 1967.

Whereas the first two conferences resembled expert meetings, the third had a more ambitious purpose since it was aimed at debating the social implications of science and defining a long-term programme, while continuing the reflection already begun on the dangers of the nuclear Age and the ways of warding them off. Owing to the support of the Theodor Körner Foundation, run by Bruno Kreisky, who was then Foreign Affairs Minister of Austria, 70 scientists and 14 observers gathered in Kitzbühel in Austrian Tyrol (14–20 September 1958) and discussed a particularly busy agenda. Among the issues raised figured notably the consequences of a nuclear war, technical and political aspects of disarmament, international cooperation and the scientist's role in taking up these challenges. Furthermore, an *ad hoc* committee made recommendations on the way in which future meetings would be organized.

While some wished for the creation of a formal organization with paying members, a central office and a newsletter, a large majority favoured light structures because what mattered was to give scientists the possibility of freely exchanging views on world issues. The choice of topics for discussion was to be left to the discretion of the Continuing Committee, but the *ad hoc* Committee believed that the effort should be concentrated on 'topics . . . directly related to the easing of international tension, the establishment of mutual security systems, the elimination of war as an instrument of national policy, nuclear control and disarmament, and the role of scientist in creating a peaceful and abundant world'. It also advised tackling the questions of the 'contribution of science and technology to the development of under-developed countries' and of 'international exchange of scientists'. Finally, the wish was expressed for future conferences to open up more widely to social science representatives, who would thus reinforce the founding group in which so-called 'natural' science representatives were in the majority.

These recommendations were unanimously approved, and the Continuing Committee which was in charge of their implementation was enlarged by the addition of 5 new members. Moreover, the conference adopted a doctrinal text which was in line with the Russell–Einstein manifesto of 1955 and which may be considered as the credo of the Pugwash movement. It was made public during the closing session of the Vienna conference at the headquarters of the Austrian Science Academy on 20 September and aroused

wide interest. Furthermore, the Pugwash movement obtained unofficial recognition since the conference ended with a reception
offered by President of the Republic Adolf Schärf, while a huge
event at the Wiener Stadthalle allowed the movement to spread its
message to an audience of 10,000.

Thus, as the years went by, the Pugwash movement asserted itself as one of the most visible transnational organizations in the
field of studies and action in favour of nuclear disarmament and
banning the resort to force in the settlement of international disputes. None the less, scientists who met within Pugwash did not all
subscribe to the philosophy of the Russell–Einstein manifesto and
the Vienna declaration. After all, the latter had not won unanimous approval, and Leo Szilard had abstained during the final vote
of the Kitzbühel conference. This did not prevent him, however,
from actively taking part in the work of Pugwash and throwing in
original ideas such as that of 'minimum deterrence' during the
Moscow conference of 1960.

Beyond the differences of opinion on the ways and means of
maintaining peace in a nuclear Age, the founding members of the
Pugwash movement were convinced that the resort to nuclear weapons would be inevitable in another world conflict, and that it would
have disastrous consequences for all the belligerents. From then
on the issue was to ensure that East–West antagonism would not
be solved by violent means, the only alternative to war being peaceful
coexistence. The Russell–Einstein manifesto also starts from the
fact that a general war would be a major disaster, but it draws
attention to the long-term effects of massive use of thermonuclear
weapons, and mentions the hypothesis of the extinction of the human
race as a result of spreading radioactive particles over the whole
surface of the Earth. From then on, the choice was clear – either
renounce war, or run the risk of the 'human race' disappearing.

The call of Einstein and Russell rests on assumptions which are
not unanimously accepted, and the positions taken by Pugwash do
not necessarily comply with the logic of this founding text. Firstly,
nuclear weapons are thought to have devalued the political function of war, in the Clausewitzian sense of the term. And states
which have nuclear weapons have displayed caution, if not wisdom
in their handling. On the other hand, armed confrontation has not
ceased since the end of the Second World War, and after Hiroshima the fact of war has undoubtedly persisted in its conventional
form. Now if war and peace are divisible, and if precautions are

taken to avoid thoughtless use of nuclear firepower, the fears expressed by Bertrand Russell and Albert Einstein fade, and the alternative is no longer between everlasting peace and nuclear Armageddon. Thus strategies of nuclear deterrence implemented within NATO and the Warsaw Pact Organization have contributed to preventing a major conflict in the Northern hemisphere while limited conflicts run with conventional means multiplied in peripheral zones. The war phenomenon thus persisted in the Nuclear Age, but it did not necessarily lead to an unlimited outburst of violence.

Moreover, the Russell–Einstein manifesto implies that banning the use of modern weapons or even eliminating them by means of an agreement could have only a limited influence on the prevention of war. Indeed, international law would hardly restrain the belligerents, who would not hesitate to use nuclear or thermonuclear weapons if their vital interests were at stake. And in the case of the breaching of a disarmament agreement, the first of the adversaries to reconstitute a stock of nuclear weapons would be assured of victory.[14] One cannot but subscribe to this thesis, but the Pugwashites do not all seem to have drawn all of its consequences. Thus the commitment to 'No first use' of nuclear weapons had found much favour within the movement at the time when the Soviets had become propagandists of this idea in order to weaken NATO strategy, and American liberals saw in it an efficient way of avoiding crossing the nuclear threshold within the framework of 'controlled escalation'. But discussions between American and Soviet experts during the symposia on nuclear forces held in Geneva in the 1980s have demonstrated the flaws of a 'peace' policy based on the 'No first use'. None the less, and in spite of its ambiguities, the formula has continued to benefit from a favourable prejudice within the movement.

Finally, the signatories of the Russell–Einstein manifesto consider that a nuclear arms ban can have a positive value if it is in keeping with the pattern of a general arms reduction. Frédéric Joliot-Curie had expressed reservations on this point which are worth noting. According to him, the envisaged reduction had to be balanced, simultaneous and involve all armaments. The French scientist thus kept his distance from the Anglo-American approach which tended to privilege nuclear disarmament while conventional weapons continued to play a part in the calculation of military balances and were the sole instruments of national defence for states which did not possess the nuclear weapon. On the other hand, Russell and

Einstein emphasized the nuclear arms ban, from which were expected two positive effects – lessening East–West tension and reducing the risks of surprise attacks such as those mounted by the Japanese in Pearl Harbor. Now the elimination of nuclear weapons could not be adequately verified, and this obstacle had already been underlined during the negotiations within the London disarmament sub-committee in the spring of 1955. Some participants, notably the US, concluded that the aim of total nuclear disarmament was out of reach, and that other ways had to be found in order to avoid breaking the 'balance of terror'.

The Pugwash philosophy was thus stamped with a certain idealism, and showed the effects of the prejudices of nineteenth-century scientists. After the fashion of positivist philosophers who saw in the development of sciences the path to salvation, the authors of the Russell–Einstein manifesto have paid tribute to the religion of progress, being convinced that it made it possible to organize human societies in a rational manner. However, the tragedies of the twentieth century had taught them that science was not only a source of 'happiness and wisdom', but that the instruments of death that science had created might just as well lead to the extinction of humanity. Given the urgency of the nuclear peril, men thus had to silence their quarrels and forget their differences. By making the right choice, the path towards a 'new paradise' (*sic*) was open; otherwise, one risked total annihilation and the extinction of the human race.

The 1958 Vienna declaration is less flamboyant, but is inspired by the same principles. The nuclear arms race still continues, and the lack of progress in the negotiations to bring it to an end have made the Pugwashites even more convinced of the need for increased vigilance and the multiplication of efforts in favour of peace. For this purpose, they made recommendations which can be summed up in seven points:

1) Any war includes the risk of escalation, and the use of nuclear weapons would be probable in the hypothesis of a generalized conflict. Measures should therefore be taken to proscribe war in all its forms.

2) The arms race results from mistrust between states, and to a certain extent also contributes to this mistrust. Thus any measure which tends to slow down the competition for the procurement and modernization of armaments is welcome. The end of nuclear

testing would represent a step in the right direction, and the Pugwashites were pleased that scientists from East and West could agree on common conclusions about the feasibility of detecting test explosions (Geneva Expert Conference, 1–21 August 1958). In other fields, disarmament control raises delicate technical problems, and it is up to the scientists to contribute to their solution. However, it would be erroneous to limit the problem of disarmament to its technical dimension; its solution involves re-establishing confidence as well as active and diversified cooperation between states.

3) War waged with nuclear means would have disastrous consequences not only for the belligerent countries but also for other states because of the scattering of radioactive dust over the surface of the Earth. There would be millions of deaths, the main centres of civilization would be destroyed, and economic chaos would rule in the zone of confrontation. As far as long-term genetic effects are concerned, although they are hard to evaluate, they could be a serious handicap for the survivors. No distinction is to be made between 'dirty' and 'clean bombs' in the estimation of the consequences of a nuclear exchange. It is implied that limiting damage by using tactical nuclear weapons would only be a delusion. Their use on the battlefield would have collateral effects of which the civil population would bear the cost. And one cannot exclude the possibility of them being used against urban centres in order to break the enemy's will to resist.

4) The biological effects of nuclear arms testing have not yet been subject to a precise evaluation, but in doubt it is best to be cautious and to reduce to a minimum level the exposure of humanity to atomic radiation.

5) The free exercise of scientific research and international cooperation are key factors for the re-establishment of confidence and the strengthening of peace. Considering the importance of science in world affairs, it is up to the scientists to take upon themselves a special responsibility in the promotion of the common good.

6) Fundamental research and applied science are interdependent, and technical progress serves the interests of war just as well as peace. International cooperation should be established in order to put technology to the service of peace, in particular by promoting the development of poor countries.

7) Scientists are in a better position than others to perceive the dangers and the opportunities of scientific discoveries. Mistrust between nations and the resulting race for military supremacy have

led to mobilization of the scientific community for the development of arms. Such militarization of science goes against its vocation, which is disinterested research and mastery of the forces of nature for common good. Stable and lasting peace alone would be able to remedy this situation.

By implicitly or explicitly referring to this philosophy, the Pugwash movement tried to bring a contribution to solving the problems posed by the development, modernization and spreading of nuclear weapons.

THE PUGWASH MOVEMENT AND NUCLEAR ARMS CONTROL

From the very beginning, the debates within the Pugwash movement followed the meanders and the intricacies of the disarmament negotiations, and its leaders' ambition was to weigh on the decisions of the political actors by developing models likely to mobilize all states involved, and by helping solve technical problems raised by the arms regulations. For example, the Lake Beauport conference (1958) touched on the subject of nuclear testing directly in connection with the tripartite negotiations (United States, United Kingdom and the Soviet Union) which had started a little while before and, in spite of the fact that the scientific community disagreed on the evaluation of risks run by the human race and the environment as a result of these tests, a consensus emerged easily about the possibility and the ways of verifying their prohibition. Later on, the Pugwash movement made proposals on the subject which were taken into account during the talks that led to the Moscow Treaty (5 August 1963) which banned nuclear weapon tests in outer space, in the atmosphere and under water. Likewise, the theme of 'disarmament and global security' was at the heart of exchanges between Americans and Soviets during the Pugwash conference held in Moscow in December 1960. On this occasion, a profitable dialogue was initiated on the ways and means of stabilizing the strategic balance through arms control.

Since they had accepted the Franco-British plan of 'progressive, balanced and controlled disarmament' (September 1954), the Soviets had been in favour of general and comprehensive disarmament, and had made proposals for this purpose not only to the London conference of the subcommittee on disarmament, but also to the conference of the Ten Nations Disarmament Committee in Geneva (1960). The United States had moved away from this approach, and as early as the summer of 1955 President Eisenhower had suggested dealing with the problem of disarmament by introducing confidence-building measures and 'reserving' global plans until progress in detection techniques made it possible to discuss them in a useful way. After a Soviet artificial satellite was put into orbit in 1957, the Americans were concerned about averting the risks of a surprise attack. But the failure of the expert conference which met in 1958 in Geneva in order to examine conceivable answers to this challenge led them to develop a new concept – arms control – in order to promote peaceful coexistence between the two protagonists and prevent the destabilizing effects of their 'techno-strategic' competition.

The philosophy of arms control was presented in a systematic way in a special issue of the journal *Daedalus*,[15] and the concomitant election of J. F. Kennedy to the United States presidency led to expectation of a change in Washington's security policy. Of course the new administration did not deliberately break with the rhetoric of general and complete disarmament, as demonstrated by the McCloy–Zorine agreement of September 1961 and the proceedings of the Eighteen Nations Disarmament Committee from 1962 to 1964. But the American option in favour of arms control was irrevocable, and what remained to be done was to convince the Soviets of its merits. In this respect, the role of Pugwash was decisive. Key figures such as Walt Rostow, Jerome Wiesner and Paul Doty, who later became advisers of the American President, had taken part in the Pugwash conference held in Moscow in December 1960 and had seized the opportunity to establish contacts with their Soviet counterparts which would bear fruit in the following years. In addition, atomic scientist Leo Szilard played the role of a sharp-shooter in this event by throwing in the idea of a minimum deterrent, and denouncing the drawbacks of an anti-missile defence which would only boost the arms race and shake the foundations of mutual deterrence between the two great powers.

Asserting that Leo Szilard's suggestions of minimum deterrence inspired the arms control policy of the two protagonists would be hazardous. At the time, they were mostly concerned with adding more strings to their nuclear bow. But it does seem that the Soviets used the concept as a diplomatic argument in the 'game of disarmament' which was going on in Geneva. Andrei Gromyko, for instance, addressed the United Nations in September 1962 and suggested that the parties to a comprehensive disarmament treaty should keep during the first two stages of the process a minimum capacity of ballistic missiles, anti-ballistic missiles and anti-aircraft missiles. This was meant to allow them to be prepared for any outcome if the treaty concluded was violated. Later on, Semion Tsarapkin, Soviet representative at the Geneva disarmament conference, detailed Soviet conceptions on the subject (March 1963). But the idea of a 'nuclear umbrella' was abandoned when it became apparent that Soviet–American disagreements about the components of the balance of forces and the organization of security in a 'disarmed world' were insurmountable. It was not before the 1980s that the question was raised once again, but this time in the perspective of a reduction of nuclear arsenals following concessions made by Mikhail Gorbachev in order to facilitate the elimination of nuclear weapons from the European theatre (INF Treaty of Washington, 8 December 1987). This tendency has been confirmed by the signing of the so-called START agreements, and especially START II of 3 January 1993, which provided for a reduction by two-thirds of the strategic arsenals of the United States and Russia. Nevertheless, the uncertainties related to the implementation of the latter treaty render very hazardous any conjecture about the more or less long-term emergence of a deterrence based on 'sufficient means'.

At the Berlin Pugwash conference of September 1992, some had thought they could deduce from the agreed or announced disarmament measures that the possibility of a nuclear weapon free world was no longer mere theory. Others drew attention to the risks of instability which might result from total nuclear disarmament, and argued for a minimum deterrent. Still others underlined that the elimination of the nuclear weapons held by the Americans and the Russians raised delicate problems of a technical and political order, and that the START I treaty had still not been implemented (the exchange of ratification instruments only took place in December 1994). Therefore speculation about an acceleration of the 'disarmament race', or talk about the 'delegitimization' of nuclear weapons would be irrelevant. Even if drastic reductions of strategic weapons in Russia and the United States took place within the time limits set by the START II agreements, the two powers would each continue to have available over 3,000 nuclear warheads at the beginning of the new millennium. Would the resulting situation

correspond to a stable deterrence based on minimal capacities? Or
would further reductions be needed to meet this requirement? In
the meantime, Russians and Americans called their mutual relationships a 'strategic partnership', and displayed their intention
of persevering in the route to nuclear disarmament by opening as
soon as possible the so-called START III negotiations. Such an
approach corresponds to the proposals of the arms control theoreticians and to the recommendations of the Pugwash movement since
the beginning of the 1960s.

Although the 'minimum deterrence' urged by Leo Szilard in
Moscow in December 1960 only had a limited impact, Donald
Brennan's initiative to create a group of Soviet and American experts in which questions related to arms control could be freely
debated, and where common positions could be defined, immediately caught the Soviets' attention. In this respect, the role of some
of the members of the Academy of Science of the USSR, such as
Topchiev, Millionshchikov and Artzymovinshch was decisive. And
since they were in favour with the people in power, their recommendations to create the group were approved at the highest level.
On the American side, the project first gave rise to reservations
within the administration and the scientific community, and several years went by before the first meeting could take place in Boston
in June 1964. The meeting lasted two weeks and allowed the Soviets
not only to familiarize themselves with American conceptions regarding deterrence and strategic stability, but also to enjoy the hospitality of their colleagues and members of the Washington
establishment. Official contacts were suspended during the period
when the Vietnam war was intensified, but unofficial exchanges
continued within the framework of Pugwash conferences. In 1967
the question of counter-missile defence became crucial in Soviet–
American relations, and President Johnson suggested to the USSR
that negotiations be initiated with the aim of limiting anti-ballistic
missiles in order to stabilize the strategic balance. Such an initiative corresponded to the logic of arms control but went counter to
the Soviet tradition of a 'defence of the mother country' with their
own means, of which General Talenski was the harbinger. In order
to dispel these prejudices, the common expert group was once again
called upon, and a meeting took place in Moscow in December
1967. It had favourable repercussions, since the Soviet side finally
rallied the conceptions which Secretary of Defence Robert McNamara
held dear – i.e. deterrence based on second strike capacity – and

Andrei Gromyko accepted the following year that negotiations be opened with the United States for strategic arms limitation (SALT). These negotiations led in 1972 to the so-called ABM treaty which represents the core of arms control between the two great powers, and which determines progress on the route to nuclear disarmament.[16]

On a different front, Pugwash dealt very early with problems raised by dissemination of nuclear weapons, and at the conference of Udaipur, India (January–February 1964) the plan was drafted of a non-proliferation treaty. In September of the same year, the movement's leading authorities made recommendations on the same subject at the end of the Karlovy-Vary conference (Czechoslovakia). Finally, when negotiations for the non-proliferation treaty (NPT) entered a decisive stage, after the explosion of the first Chinese atomic bomb (October 1964), groups of experts met under the patronage of Pugwash to examine the technical problems of controlling the use of nuclear energy for exclusively peaceful purposes. They also made recommendations which tended to tone down the discriminatory nature of the treaty by developing a certain balance between obligations of states which possessed the nuclear weapon (the Haves) and those which did not (the Have-nots), but without questioning the aims of the treaty, i.e. sealing the strategic status quo and consolidating the status of the legitimate nuclear powers.

In this respect, the Marianske–Lasné declaration of 15 May 1967 is particularly significant. It states the priority of the obligation for non-proliferation without being much concerned about the 'unequal nature' of the treaty which endorses it. However, it acknowledges the fact that the non-proliferation regime would appeal more easily to countries which did not have the nuclear weapon if the Haves made firmer commitments in the field of disarmament than those of article 6 of the NPT, and offered negative as well as positive guarantees of security to states which had renounced the nuclear weapon. In spite of such imperfections, the non-proliferation treaty is still considered by Pugwash authorities as the core of a policy destined to contain nuclear arms proliferation. But the imbalance between obligations of countries which have the weapon and those which do not prompts reservations on the part of Third World scientists. At the Berlin conference in September 1992, for instance, some of them pointed out that a nuclear test ban would give some satisfaction to the non-nuclear states which were parties to the NPT and facilitate the extension of the treaty beyond 1995. Others considered that actual disarmament was the only effective way of reducing the incitements to nuclear proliferation, but that significant progress in this direction should not be expected before the opening of the conference for the review and extension of the NPT.

Since then, the NPT has been prolonged for an unlimited time, and a comprehensive test ban treaty has been opened to signature in September 1996 in accordance with the commitments undertaken by states which were parties to the treaty at the end of the review conference (New York, April–May 1995). However, India did not agree with this procedure and considered that a nuclear test ban without any firm commitment regarding disarmament would only consecrate the status of the nuclear powers. In this respect, the four members of the Pugwash leading authorities who had addressed a public letter to the French President to ask him to stop nuclear testing in the Pacific during the summer of 1995 used the same method on the Indian Premier, and urged him to act in order to bring negotiations for a comprehensive test ban treaty to a successful conclusion. This procedure was strongly criticized by Professor Udgaonqar, a member of the Pugwash Council, who stood up for the Indian government and suggested that its reasons were just as valid as those of the nuclear powers, which are satisfied with half-measures regarding disarmament. This incident demonstrates very well the diversity of opinions expressed within the movement, and no doubt also the difference of treatment in the exercise of the right to reply to initiatives taken by the leaders.[17]

It is difficult to express a view on the share of the Pugwash movement in the drawing up of the NPT. On the other hand, there is more or less reliable information available on the role which it played in the negotiation of the Limited Test Ban Treaty. This question had already been raised in 1958 at the Lake Beauport conference, but it was during the London conference of September 1962 that American, Soviet and British experts agreed on a remote verification method of underground tests. In order to get the debate out of the deadlock in which it was placed because of Soviet reluctance to agree to an optimal number of on-site inspections, they imagined installing on the territory of the involved states automated stations monitoring earth tremors. This device, termed a 'black box', was at the centre of the final communiqué of the London conference, and received a favourable reaction from political circles. Soon after, Kennedy and Khrushchev took this idea up again in an exchange of letters related to negotiations on banning nuclear tests, while the Secretary General of the Pugwash movement organized in London, in March 1963, a restricted expert meeting – 6 experts from the United States, 3 from the USSR and 3 from the United Kingdom – in order to examine the technical and political aspects of the problem. The common conclusions which they reached were passed on to the governments involved, which from then on had at their disposal a solid foundation to conclude 'a test ban treaty as soon as possible'.

In the opinion of many observers and actors, the Pugwash initiatives made a major contribution to the success of the tripartite negotiations which led to the conclusion in July 1963 of the Limited Test Ban Treaty which was open for signature in Moscow on 5 August of the same year. Thus Franklin W. Long, who had taken part in the expert meetings, was a member of the American delegation led by Averell Harriman. Lord Zuckerman, one of the main advisers of the British cabinet for scientific affairs, revealed in the autumn of 1990 that the intervention of Pugwash had been decisive in the event. And as far as the Soviets involved in this affair were concerned, although they seemed reluctant to share their views, their opinion most probably weighed on the choices made by the Kremlin leaders. It should, however, be noted that Pugwash recommendations on the verification of the underground test ban by 'black boxes' were not followed by the recipient states, who, for political reasons, preferred to leave this option open, as the safety of nuclear weapons depended to some extent on the continuation of their testing.

Lastly, it is worth noting the role played by Pugwash in the debate on the modernization of theatre nuclear weapons for Europe. The crisis brought about in December 1979 by Nato's 'double decision' and the invasion of Afghanistan led the leaders of the movement to convene a study group on 'nuclear forces' in Geneva as early as January 1980. It was within this framework that the ways and means of reducing 'intermediate-range nuclear forces' (INF) were examined, and it can be assumed that discussions between Soviet and American experts, as well as opinions expressed by the Europeans on this occasion, had an effect on the conduct of official negotiations which started in the same city in November 1981. Thus, the initial proposals of the United States and the Soviet Union – President Reagan's zero option and Mr Brezhnev's proportional reductions – gave rise to systematic presentations and compromise solutions were discussed in order to break the deadlock of negotiations or to help resuming talks after they broke off in the autumn of 1983. The discussions also helped clarify the conceptions of both parties on the balance of forces (taking into account the nuclear forces of third powers, comparison between aircraft and missiles, status of the INF deployed East of the Urals, etc.). Finally, regular contacts were established, outside the working sessions, between members of the study group on nuclear forces and Soviet and American negotiators. Of course it would be presumptuous to assert that all of the Pugwash suggestions were taken into account in the INF negotiations, but the group's regular meetings (twice a year on average) probably contributed to the creation of an atmosphere favourable to an objective analysis of the given information on the problem, and to the conclusion of the Washington Treaty in December 1987 which for the most part satisfied all parties involved.

The preceding observations do not allow the actual impact of the transnational activities of the Pugwash movement on disarmament and arms control negotiations to be measured. And the information available is too fragmentary to enable us to establish a cause and effect relationship between the informal seminars of Eastern and Western scientists and the states' adoption of measures destined to reduce the risks of the Nuclear Age. On the other hand, the exploitation of American records has helped to bring to light the major part played by Pugwash in setting up the group of Soviet and American experts who contributed to bringing the Soviet leaders round to the idea of arms control. Pugwash also contributed to the conclusion of the ABM treaty which remains to date the core of strategic stability and the condition for a more ambitious nuclear disarmament than that which has been reached in the past. Nevertheless, although the role of individuals in the event cannot be denied, the latter could act only if they were supported by the political authorities and if their views were coordinated with those of the people in power. The idea that the Pugwashites always behave as private persons without any national or governmental ties should therefore be questioned. Thus, most of the Soviet participants were members of the Academy of Science, which is known not to have been a neutral organization in the communist system. In the same way, key American figures such as Walt W. Rostow, Jerome B. Wiesner and Franklin W. Long were advisers of the Kennedy administration just before the signing of the partial test ban treaty, and it was difficult for them to disregard their official function when taking part in Pugwash activities. What is more, the proximity of

Pugwash members to the centres of power is considered to be a positive factor since the movement defines itself above all by the implementation of a strategy of communication and cooperation with political decision-makers.

Thus the Pugwash movement appears as a hybrid actor, which belongs to the network of NGOs and plays as well the game of parallel diplomacy. Although the movement was conceived by its founding members as a laboratory of ideas where scientists, acting on their own account, tried to influence governmental policies in favour of disarmament, it has now become an intergovernmental medium of communication outside traditional channels, and thus runs the risk of being used by states as an instrument of their own policy. Up to now, its credibility as a centre of autonomous reflection on the problems of war and peace has not been undermined, and it has persevered in the direction chosen by Einstein and Russell in the 1950s. Through its mediation, scientists try to leave their mark on international policy. But the traces of their action on history are not always discernible, even though their contribution to the cause of disarmament and arms control is undeniable.

NOTES

1. The press, for instance, largely echoed the remarks made by MP Pierre Lellouche (RPR), who declared he was 'scandalized by the fact that an organization which is known to have been openly manipulated by the Soviets should be rewarded today' – *La Croix*, 14 October 1995, *Le Monde*, 15–16 October 1995, and *Le Figaro*, 14–15 October 1995. This argument has been developed in extreme terms in François Lebrette's article 'Les non-dits d'un prix Nobel' – *Figaro-Magazine*, 21 October 1995. About the international role of Pugwash and the diversity of opinions expressed in the movement, Georges Ripka, President of the French group and physicist at the Study Centre in Saclay, has made his meaning perfectly plain. See 'Non, Pugwash n'est pas un mouvement anti-nucléaire' – *Le Monde*, 19 October 1995.

2. See the declaration of Jacques Rummelhardt, spokesman of the French Ministère des Affaires étrangères – *Le Monde*, 15–16 October 1995. Let us note that the requirement of a form of disarmament guaranteeing the security of all parties involved is a fundamental principle that President Valéry Giscard d'Estaing emphasized in his speech before the 10th extraordinary General Assembly of the United Nations on 25 May 1978.

3. See the text of the letter sent to President Jacques Chirac in *Pugwash Newsletter*, 33, no. 1/2 (July–October 1995), 19.

4. The corresponding passage from the letter addressed to the French President read: 'We hope . . . that you will proclaim the willingness of France to agree immediately to a comprehensive treaty forever banning nuclear-weapon testing.' This injunction could be interpreted in two different ways – France was asked either to subscribe in advance to a treaty in embryo, or to unilaterally proclaim an irreversible moratorium. There was little chance that France would follow this advice unless it relinquished all freedom of action in the conduct of its disarmament diplomacy.

5. The letter signed by Etienne Bauer, Jean Klein and Pierre-Frédéric Tenière-Buchot was published in the *Pugwash Newsletter*, 33, no. 3 (January 1996), 215. Georges Ripka, president in office of the French association, had accepted the terms of the letter. As far as the Secretary General of the movement, Francesco Calogero, is concerned, he justified the strong line taken by the members of the international council by referring to precedents. He also suggested that the 'best French experts' (*sic*) had been consulted and had found no flaw in the argumentation used.

6. The history of the Pugwash movement has been written down by its current President: Joseph Rotblat, *History of the Pugwash Conferences* (London: Taylor and Francis, 1962); and Joseph Rotblat, *Scientists and the Quest for Peace: A History of the Pugwash Conferences* (Cambridge, Mass.: The MIT Press, 1972). As far as the period 1972–92 is concerned, four special issues of the *Pugwash Newsletter* are available, dating back respectively to May 1977, July 1982, July 1987 and May 1992. Information about the activities of Pugwash is also to be found in *The Bulletin of the Atomic Scientists*.

7. See the articles by Philippe Breton and Jean Klein in Stéphane Courtois and Annette Wieviorka (eds), *L'état du monde en 1945* (Paris: La Découverte, 1994).

8. About the policy of the Third Reich in the field of military applications of nuclear force, see Mark Walker's classic work *German National Socialism and the Quest for Nuclear Power 1939–1949* (Cambridge: Cambridge University Press, 1989). See also the conversations of German scientists held in detention at Farm Hill near Cambridge (England) from July to December 1945, and monitored by British secret services – *Opération Epsilon: dix physiciens allemands aux mains des Anglais*, introduction by Sir Charles Frank (Paris: Flammarion, 1993); and Jeremy Bernstein's article 'The Farm Hill Transcripts: the German Scientists and the Bomb', *New York Review of Books*, 13 August 1993.

9. Joseph Rotblat, the current president of the Pugwash movement, was the only scientist involved in the Manhattan project to leave Los Alamos at the end of 1944. Having learnt that Germany had given up the nuclear weapon, he considered that the finalizing of the weapon was no longer necessary to overthrow Nazism. See Joseph Rotblat, 'Hiroshima und Nagasaki. Geschichte und Gegenwärtigkeit', *Wissenschaft und Frieden* (July 1995).

10. See in particular the declaration by the Council of the Pugwash movement adopted on 3 September 1988 at the end of the Conference of Dagomys in the USSR, *Ensuring the Survival of Civilization.*

11. Indeed, the 45th Annual Conference was held in Hiroshima from 23 to 29 July 1995 in order to move 'Towards a Nuclear Weapon Free World'. The theme had been attracting the attention of the movement for a long time, but the end of the Cold War had boosted reflection on this topic again, and a collective piece of work published in 1993 took stock of this question: Joseph Rotblat, Jack Steinberger and Bhalchandra Udgaonkar (eds), *A Nuclear Weapon Free World: Desirable? Feasible?* (Boulder: Westview Press, 1993). As far as the British group is concerned, it published in 1995 a report about the future of British nuclear force: 'Does Britain Need Nuclear Weapons?' by C. R. Hill, R. S. Pease, R. E. Peierls and J. Rotblat. The group advises in particular placing the question of nuclear weapons elimination on the agenda of the Geneva disarmament conference. But considering the uncertainties of control, some continue to doubt the virtue of a nuclear weapon free world, and believe that more advanced research is necessary before going down this route.

12. The theme of the 46th Annual Conference which took place in Lahti (Finland) from 3 to 7 September 1996 reflects this state of mind: 'The Unfinished Agenda for the 1990s'.

13. We particularly have in mind Horst Afheldt's works and his model of 'techno-guerrilla', proposed in *Defensive Verteidigung* (Reinbek: Rowohlt, 1983). A French version of this work has been published under the title *Pour une défense non-suicidaire en Europe*, preface by Jean Klein and postscript by General Georges Buis (Paris: La Découverte, 1985).

14. The relevant passage in the Russell–Einstein manifesto reads as follows: 'And so they hope that perhaps war may be allowed to continue provided modern weapons are prohibited. This hope is illusory. Whatever agreements not to use H-bombs had been reached in time of peace, they would no longer be considered binding in time of war, and both sides would set to work to manufacture H-bombs as soon as war broke out, for, if one side manufactured the bombs and the other did not, the side that manufactured them would inevitably be victorious.'

15. See the Fall 1960 issue of *Daedalus.*

16. The origin and functioning of the common Soviet–American group on arms control was subject to an extensive study by Bernd W. Kubbig: 'Kommunikatoren im kalten Krieg: die Pugwash Konferenzen, die US–Sowjetische Studiengruppe und der ABM Vertrag' – Report 6 of the *Hessische Stiftung Friedens- und Konfliktforschung* (1996).

17. See *Pugwash Newsletter*, 33, no. 4/5 (April–July 1996). An editorial by the Secretary General of the movement admits that the public positions taken by Council members raise problems which have to be discussed.

9 The Individual in the New Clothes of War

Dominique David

The word 'strategy' undergoes a significant number of definitions and of still more uses. Initially, for a soldier the word 'strategy' alludes to military manoeuvres covering a particular space and a given time. Yet this square relationship between will, means, space and time can also be extended to a broader purpose than just military manoeuvres. 'Strategy' is now used to refer to any action carried out in a resisting environment.

Whatever definition is retained, strategy cannot be devoid of manoeuvres: planning the manoeuvre and taking action being both uncertain and evolutionary, according to how well the environment resists. The instruments used in manoeuvres are either objects or men. The relation between these components of strategic action and the role of the individual as decider, citizen and soldier, is therefore not immutable. This role varies, depending on what period and society the action takes place in and on the various 'strategic cultures'.

Nothing could be said about the evolution of strategic cultures which we know, without mentioning the essential breaking point which led to technological war: total war.

TOTAL WAR AND UNKNOWN SOLDIER

The French strategic debates of the nineteenth century's last decades – launched by the 1870 defeat and the restructuring of military teaching – considered the individual as an essential element, especially the man who thinks out military manoeuvres. This is about the period when Napoleon was rediscovered in France. Indeed, the great man influenced the general shift towards an offensive strategy, which was to last until 1914. On the one hand, the zealous supporters of offensive manoeuvre, apparently due to Napoleon, recommended permanent forces largely led by professionals, ready to strike and move rapidly. On the other hand, Jaurès and his partisans believed in a defensive strategy based on the progressive mobilization of reserves. The terms of the debate were concerned in fact with different types of manoeuvres, whether the strategy should be in favour of or against the Napoleonic legacy – symbol of the quintessence of France for some, of historical defeat for others.[1]

Here the individual is not only the captain, or the strategist, but also the fighting-man. This is the period when Ardant du Picq studies the psychology of soldiers, and when Jaurès tries to liken the soldier to the citizen and refuses the necessity of the offensive[2] on behalf of civic conscience. Whether it be in the heroism of the fight or the morals of the citizen-soldier, everywhere the individual gives sense to the battle and guarantees its efficiency.

The opposition between these classical conceptions within the remarkable military debate of the nineteenth century disappeared into the revolutions caused by the First World War. Up to then, the fighting individual was easily identifiable: war space was clearly distinct from civil society, whatever the size of the armies involved. The break-point that took place concerning how to wage war was symbolized by the control of what is heavier than air, which annihilates the age-old distinction between civil space and military space – enemy lines can indeed be flown across. This break-point brings the spaces of civil society and war to the same level. In a few decades, from the first use of military aeroplanes to the first firing of inter-continental missiles, the ability to manage more and more massive destruction over broader and broader parts of societies will annihilate the opposition between military space and civil space, between the fighting individuals and the supporting rear.

From the beginning of the century, it becomes clear that the means with which war is waged are not merely military ones. Giulio Douhet's *guerra integrale*, and Ludendorff's *Totale Krieg*[3] produce a theory about this new idea: each social body and each individual are essential for the battle in their own role – soldiers, propagandists, women working in the home front industries, etc. Here starts the era of exhaustion wars. The enemy society must be exhausted at all levels of its forces. A manoeuvre which would merely break its military instruments is no longer sufficient.

Just as the Clausewitzian annihilation finally materialized in the mass destruction of the twentieth century, the mobilization of citizens decreed by the Revolution takes shape in the social mobilization of the First World War.[4] War becomes in its literal meaning a matter that concerns everyone. This somehow will not lead to the multiplication of heroes, but on the other hand to the virtual cancelling of individual fighting, which the myth of the unknown soldier will soon symbolize.

One man – a strategist, a soldier and an artist – sums up best the new dramatic effects of war and the protagonists' change of roles: the Italian writer, Giulio Douhet.[5] Right in the middle of the First World War, Douhet produces a theory about the massive use of air-bombing, no longer aimed at making the enemy fall back, but at breaking systematically the most vulnerable areas of the hostile society: towns, economic forces, civil populations and their morale, stability of political regimes. The pattern of this total war is presented in very different works, such as strategic and technical studies, but also fictional books. The latter type is undoubtedly the most interesting one. There Douhet describes war not merely as it now could be – a manoeuvre more subtle than others – but as it will be – the only possible manoeuvre. In a 1917 novel, *La vittoria alata*,[6] and what might be called a strategic fiction, *La guerra del 19...*, Douhet explains that airforce strategy substitutes all others, being the only manoeuvre in which land and naval forces, even if they mount guard, can only make an auxiliary contribution.

We know that Douhet's theories will lead to 'strategic bombings'[7] during the Second World War. These will constitute one strategic manoeuvre among many others. For Douhet, massive bombing, carried out by real airforce armies, was almost a unique act. What is interesting here is the intellectual nature of his work and what it reveals about the contemporary evolution of war. According to Douhet, the use of massive bombing can hardly be regarded as a strategy – a self-conscious, evolutionary choice between several hypotheses that can be examined again and changed. It is a manifest fact brought about by scientific progress. So much so that the future shall only be described to the enemy using tracts or other means, so that he must yield to scientific reason. Strategy tries to plan the future through successive choices. The future depends on scientific certainty, thereby causing a significant shift which resembles a kind of death of strategic reasoning.

This certainty about the technological crushing of the adversary constitutes indeed a great revolution in the way fighting is carried out. A mechanism and a machine now have to be perfected. Douhet describes at length the industrial power that might be able to produce its bombing aircraft in large numbers – waves of attacking aeroplanes that would be so numerous and close to one another that any aerial defence would not manage to reach them. As a consequence man is left aside. Strategy is giving way to the scientific evidence of bombing, in which the fighter is a robot programmed for one single kind of shot – perhaps the only possible kind. Paradoxically, the airforce gains as heroes are discredited, although at the beginning of the twentieth century this weapon was what contributed most to revalue personal heroism and chivalrous fighting between the 'aces' of the First World War.

The novel *La vitoria alata* consists of a double framework: the historical birth of the airforce, and on the other hand the death of heroes. The novel's main character,[8] the ace Rodolphe d'Adelsberg, fades as his heroism appears less and less useful. No room is left for a war thought through by the individual. Science is the leader. The 'last' strategist is an interpreter of scientific progress; no room is left for an individual – except in his temporary useful role of running the machines. The only men who do not die in Douhet's works are terrified victims becoming aware that their war is more and more useless, robots so frightened that they cannot avoid thinking and acting as has been planned by technology. One should there-fore not be surprised that at the end of the world war, Giulio Douhet should be, in the journal *Il Dovere*, the creator of the idea of the *Milite ignoto* – the soon famous and worldwide 'unknown soldier'.

In Giulio Douhet's books, what disappears is a certain concep-tion of war, of strategic reasoning, and of the role of the indi-vidual in war manoeuvres. Though he intended to prove that technical power restricts the hypotheses of future to only one, since it offers a compelling future, Douhet in fact kills the concept of manoeuvr-ing, and murders at the same time strategy to the benefit of tech-nology. Meanwhile the individual is excluded from 'strategy' – soon to be reduced to the application of a technical model.

Of course things will not happen exactly as Douhet had predicted. Many reasons may account for this. First Douhet refers to techni-cal objects which do not exist yet; then he overestimates the ef-fects of bombings, even massive ones,[9] and underestimates anti-aircraft defence, etc. Less than three decades after Douhet's reasoning was first formulated, his logic was renewed by nuclear arms. The hard core of Douhet's theory – the description of a fu-ture smothered by technology, in which any other form of war has no place, by the setting down of a total threat; then, since any war is regarded as unreasonable, the wreck of the hero facing the use of more and more abstract weapons – this logic of his theory is now at the very heart of reflections concerning nuclear strategy.

MARGINALIZATION OF CONFLICT AND THE INDIVIDUAL'S SPACES

As regards nuclear power, three different kinds of strategic reasoning can be considered possible. First, one could imagine a sort of pure nuclear strategy based on the radical innovation of nuclear power, where man's will can only intervene in two places: to show the visible technological means which contribute to giving credibility to deterrence, and in case of crisis, to carry out the deterrent threat with the best chances of success. This 'pure' way remains extremely close to Douhet's, since its efficiency is linked to the announcement of an uncontrollable destruction and the discrediting of any counter-manoeuvre. The second possible form is the conventional way. The conventional forces are not annihilated by nuclear power and are able to work on their own in some places and for some aims, even to the benefit of nuclear power. Finally, one might try to mingle the first two forms – the use of nuclear forces being considered as crowning a classic fight, or the nuclear weapons conceived as ordinary ones to which the same strategic and tactical reasoning as for so-called conventional weapons[10] could be applied.

Even in a nuclear era and for a nuclear power, there is therefore room for reasoning which allows the use of manoeuvres to be maintained in war – as underlined by the last two forms quoted above – and which leaves strategists and fighters a significant role: in the 1960s, the Sokolovski doctrine, which stressed that classic and nuclear forces could be united into one single global manoeuvre; in the late 1970s and early 1980s, the 'Air Land Battle' doctrine, which intended to give back to the American armies the ability to manoeuvre even in Europe – an over-nuclearized space; or even during Reagan's presidency, the theories which believed that they could explain how a nuclear war[11] could be won. All these examples testify to the survival of strategic logic, and therefore of the men entrusted with its materialization.

What could be said is that the more powerful a nuclear actor is, the more he can retain alternative strategies. The room which he can spare for classic strategic reasoning is therefore larger. The

United States is for instance sufficiently powerful to have concurrently one or several conventional strategies, whereas France has centred its strategy around the nuclear nucleus, around a single logic. This may account for the differences between the formulations and applications of the strategies of these two actors, as regards the way the individual is considered.

Numerous men have elaborated the successive steps of the American nuclear strategy.[12] They have then carried out their work in many establishments, institutes, foundations and centres devoted to the study of strategic matters. On the other hand, it seems very difficult in France to mark the establishments which have elaborated the strategies of the last thirty or forty years. This comment could also be applied to those who instigated nuclear strategy – a few military men unknown to the general public.[13]

Thought through by various people according to their own logic, the nuclear innovation, while allowing previous forms of warfare to remain, none the less globally redefines the status of war. Everyone knows that the East–West system, inseparable from nuclear power, has defined a specific geography which makes a distinction between a warless world and a world which remained ordinary. In the former, the refinement of the scenarios of confrontation acted mainly as a way to camouflage the impossibility of war. Elsewhere, war remained possible, and at times necessary, *a contrario*, to preserve the theatre which was free of war. In France, non-war was theorized in a model reflecting the heterogeneity of the so-called 'three circles' strategic theatres.[14] Some of the theatres were placed in a position of strategic and geographic marginality – the very ones where armed conflict remained possible.

Concurrently with the geographic marginalization of conflicts, their technicization changed the position of the actors – the military apparatus – in society. France, since it became a nuclear power, has only taken limited armed actions, and always with professionals or volunteers. This is obviously the case for Great Britain. The massive involvement of the boys in Vietnam gave rise in the United States to well-known movements of public opinion and resulted in the abolition of conscription. The closed Soviet society was practically the only one to have allowed itself, well into the 1980s, to use conscripts in an external war – the impact of the Afghanistan war on the evolution of Soviet opinion is now established. In fact the tendency is to develop a dual military instrument. At home, war has become impossible and security is guaranteed mostly by invisible and largely non-territorial technical systems. Elsewhere, the wars which remain are usually run by professional units.

In this nuclearized world, the individual's role is limited to a few frameworks, all very different from those in which he was intended to intervene in classic times.

The first framework is that of declaratory strategy. The less the efficiency of arms can be demonstrated by actual wars, the greater the importance of symbolic demonstrations – voting of required credits for budgets or multiannual provisions, development, as publicly as possible, of industries necessary to the defence of the country, permanent explanations of forces and the way to use them, etc. Serving the purpose of these elements of a declaratory strategy are many individualities, political rulers, industrialists, theoreticians, etc. Non-war is *par excellence* the business of everyone since, following its own logic, strategy ends henceforth with the start of war – the end of all reason.

The business of everyone theoretically, but in fact the privilege of a few, as the abstraction of the objectives as well as the postulates restricts it to a limited circle of rulers, soldiers and theoreticians. Such a restriction is nowhere better exemplified than in France. The country which produced the most theory about nuclear strategy – non-war – is also the country where the defence community (soldiers and civilian experts) and the defence debate are the smallest, whether one likes it or not.

At the top of the ladder is enthroned the supreme decider, the embodiment of individual will. The supreme decider combines the diplomatic function and the warrior function. He is the one and only interpreter for the national community *vis-à-vis* the outside world, the one who asserts the will, thus the ability to act. In pure logic, a simple mechanism, automatically triggered off, would produce the best effect. Distinguished theoreticians have been seen explaining that the nuclear decision should be, when the time comes, removed from the vagaries of public opinion.[15] It might just as well be removed from the uncertainties of decision – the enemy would know that the technical system, barring accidents, would leave him no way out. Keeping the supreme decider undoubtedly reflects the last defiance of the political individual facing a technicized defence, the wish to embody a will for defence while stating the continuity of responsibilities between diplomacy and war.

The contradiction remains that the man–decider, maintained in this position partly to demonstrate that there will always be a choice (to fire or not to fire), is required to reduce uncertainty to a minimum level and to display an unyielding determination. Let us consider the catastrophic effect of Giscard d'Estaing's admission about his resolution not to trigger nuclear fire.[16] Such an announcement could have been interpreted as the expression of a will to do anything in order not to be faced with such a choice. The fact remains that the configuration of nuclear doctrine did not allow such a reading. The decider holds an unprecedented position in the nuclear nation; he takes part as a special individual, an interpreter more than a creator.

Embodiment of the will to defend oneself, the decider proves the existence of a spirit of defence, the second framework assigned to the individual in the societies of industrial war redefined by nuclear capacity. The expression 'spirit of defence', the determination to defend one's right or existence by conflict, corresponds to the modern willingness to see wars as national undertakings, led by the peoples themselves. In this sense, the spirit of defence is nothing more than the spirit of the nation, the feeling of belonging. The assimilation of Nation and Defence is particularly strong in France, where the Republic created itself from an act binding the proclamation of popular sovereignty with the defence of the borders.[17] However, the simple awareness that a state is sovereign if it can defend its sovereignty, and that national wars are made by nations, is getting less and less obvious as real wars are left to peripheral theatres and appear there treated by professional units, whereas nuclear deterrence proves itself by limited manoeuvres conducted by a limited number of men. The spirit of defence turns into an incantation, a claim from the military, disconnected from civil society. From now on, the spirit of defence is no more than a mere feeling of belonging to the national community, to the Republic, with no particular duty of 'defence'. The commitment of the individual-citizen is still required, but in an abstract way. It is a question of supporting a policy, of sustaining, if necessary by keeping silent, the decider involved in the crisis, etc.

Hence the problems posed in France by the National Service, which should be the third framework for the individual in collective defence. However the problem is treated, universal military service has obviously lost in the last decades the bulk of its military significance. This significance used to be straightforward: the principle was to position a mass of men to counter a massive strike into the open geographic space of Northern France. Starting from the end of the late 1940s, France placed several hundred kilometres and a strong collective defence line between its territory and the potential enemy. From the 1960s onwards, it centred its strategy around nuclear force, in a logic which only assigned conventional forces to a deterrent pre-manoeuvre role. From this moment on, the conscript army no longer had a military meaning corresponding to its importance. A real shift in the significance of national service then took place. The idea was no longer to respond to a military necessity by lining up soldiers, but to prove to the other party that the French people remains involved in matters of defence,[18] and to prove to the people itself that the defence apparatus, a weighty component of the nation, however technical and abstract it may seem, does not intend to act independently from the nation.

The individual, the citizen, thus still have a military definition, but essentially for political reasons. Assertion of the ability to mobilize people for their own defence and assertion of national cohesion are the arguments most heard lately to defend national service. This new definition obviously brought other theories into question too. For instance, the argument that the cohesion of French society still depends on national service, as it has since the beginning of the century, is highly debatable. For better or worse, the educational system or mass media are playing this role from now on.[19]

Fourth and last framework assigned to the citizen: that of protest. Let us simply point out that if organized or individual protests might have affected in some way the action of this or that armed force in a particular conflict (Vietnam, Afghanistan maybe), they do not seem to have ever seriously influenced strategy or defence system choices. With one exception – the question of the American neutron bombs which were to be deployed in Europe at the end of the 1970s. And even that example is wrong since the pressure of opinion, inspired by the Soviet Union, had no effect on the German government which ended up accepting the principle of deployment. It was the Carter administration that finally cancelled it. The French peculiarity should also be mentioned in this context, that no large-scale movements of opinion and even no fundamental debate about defence questions have been recorded in our country for several decades.

THE RETURN OF WAR

The system which had secured the balance of power in the developed world for 45 years has shattered. We learn at this juncture that war was not blocked by the atom itself but by a shared and controlled atom, organizing a strategic space where any conflict involved the two super-powers. Although nuclear arms remain, the structure of power has changed, thereby altering the status of armed conflict in Europe itself.

War is coming back to Europe. The rigid East–West game, controlled by two major players, has given way to a myriad of actors. A strategic actor is a group of people who identify a common plan leading to a collective action based on specific means. The existence of such a will and such a group used to occur with great difficulty – the system would stifle any deviant reaction. The situation is now very different. The empire which used to silence half of Europe has collapsed. The destructuring of the empire logic leads to a systematic fragmentation of political will in Europe. This has an obvious consequence – in a set which has no more common rules, where states are getting weak, any strategic actor, even the weakest, has an uncontrollable capacity to harm. And this capacity is first of all marked by the multiplication of armed confrontations.

In a way, war is getting closer to individuals, politically as well as technically. Politically, because entry into war can now be decided by limited communities – be they Yugoslavia, the Russian community of Moldavia, or tomorrow the many units inheriting a possible Russian implosion. In most of the examples given in central and eastern Europe, a real 'communitarization' of states is taking place. Through this movement, war is coming back to basic units, so to speak. Technically, these conflicts are often led by small groups with local military efficiency, in operations looking more like guerrilla warfare[20] than manoeuvres of large conventional forces.

All of this, which may be considered as a reappropriation of war by communities frustrated by the self-definition allowed by conflict, is developing in a dangerous and complex framework. Yesterday the nuclear forces used to block any conflict. Tomorrow they will only be able to block a small part of the conflicting hypotheses of the continent – mainly those which would include nuclear powers. A blockage power remains, thereby guaranteeing (if nuclear arsenals remain controlled by strong political powers . . .) that local conflicts in Europe will not degenerate into large-scale confrontation.

But from now on this blockage power will have to coexist with real wars.

We will therefore remain a nuclear world. Even if some tendencies seem to make us regress back to a pre-nuclear situation, such as the risk of a certain 'lebanization' of the continent. As state legitimacies are being questioned, as infra-state communities are getting organized, the military machinery might be subject to regional or local appropriations – an inevitable feudalization if the central state splits up or shows its inability to ensure the survival of the army. This regionalization of conventional forces is already in progress here or there. The United States' haste to dismantle the huge contingent of Soviet short-range missiles in Europe simply shows that the same process can be feared for nuclear weapons. This is just a hypothesis. But, above all, what has been undermined by the prolonged economic impotence of the Russian state is the Red Army.[21] Considering the amount of weapons at stake, no one can swear that they will remain under control. The same could be said about all types of armament, including nuclear weapons, whose reduction process will at best be slow.

All of these prospects point to an atomization, a fragmenting of the fact of war in Europe. The return of armed conflict to elementary political units (regions, communities, villages, clans) revalues the place of the individual, of the warrior in the development of wars which can only multiply.

For France, the situation is curious. The country has always been in contact with the adversary, even if the latter changed throughout the centuries, and has now been abandoned by the enemy for the second time in fifty years: Germany in 1945, the Soviet Union in 1990. While war is coming back to Europe, it is physically moving away from us: it is no longer two stages of the Tour de France away and does not involve us directly anymore. Conversely, while it is physically moving away, it is getting politically closer: we can no longer believe we are living in a warless world.

This double observation will lead to a total rethinking of the concepts of French strategy. Conventional forces, whose structures and deployment are based on the paradigm of mass defence on the Eastern line, will need to adjust to hypotheses of more distant intervention, for different objectives and with different means. The participation of the French people in its own defence, already relatively marginalized by the nuclearization of French strategy in the 1960s, is even more radically called into question.

Intervention scenarios of the French armed forces (direct threats on territory, combat or humanitarian interventions in central Europe, interventions outside Europe) do not involve use of conscripts. The explicit exclusion of conscripts from any operation which would not be protection of national territory was confirmed by the French President himself at the end of the Gulf War. And operations of protection of the territory requiring a large non-professional army are ever less conceivable.

A new geography of war in Europe, but also outside Europe. Up to now, the frozen situation of the blocs called for a distinction between the frozen central zone and the zones where war was still possible. Then, in the past few years, for a distinction between areas of priority interest (for different reasons, Latin America or the Middle East, for instance) and other areas, 'free' zones with limited danger where the super-powers intervened to defend private realms or to block the Other's movement (Africa for instance). Only in so far as it was excluded from the nuclear world could war survive. Tomorrow, these conflicts will be to us even more external, or maybe closer.

Even more external in some cases, because the geography of power is being reshaped. The end of East–West rivalry, the internal difficulties of the American power, the need to save half of Europe from economic wreckage and social and political chaos, in short the temptation for the rich North to restrict itself to its own problems has brought about the expulsion of a great part of the Third World towards the darkness of barbarism, towards the absolute exterior. Whole sections of the poorer world will not account tomorrow either for the economic interest or for the strategic interest of the powerful, i.e. developed, world. Real black holes,[22] modern *terrae incognitae*, are on the brink of formation. Wars which will take place there – consider for instance Africa – are very likely to be seen as wars between 'savages', external to our interests and culture, and in which the citizen of our countries will be able to intervene only by resorting to individual or humanitarian action. In such spaces, external to the rivalries of the great powers, some northern states may well still proceed to a few interventions, relating to traditional obligations, historical and cultural bounds with some local actors. But in this case operations would remain very limited and technical, led by professional bodies, according to the model of surgical action of French troops in Africa.

Some 'special' zones, however, continue to hold the attention of the powers; those where stakes are most important and common to almost all great actors of the planet – this is typical of the Mediterranean and the Middle East. There like elsewhere, the Moscow/Washington couple has lost all power to block the spiral of local oppositions. Moreover, the considerable amounts of weaponry spread about the region thanks to the exporting grace of the great powers,[23] the great jumble-sale following the collapse of the Soviet empire, the production capacities of local and regional arms industries, South/South arms transfers in constant progress, including in sensitive sectors such as ballistic armament, all explain why, while the barriers of the East–West system are being brought down, those regions have more means to make war, and why these war means are getting more sophisticated. The American Gulf War demonstrated the absolute technical domination of America. But the latter was in fact compelled to intervene at very high political and technical power levels.

The Gulf conflict also showed that peoples did not hold a very important place in this kind of operation, whether in the political debate or in action. Everything happened as if the evolution of public opinion and the decision to use the weapons had not been on the same wavelength. In the United States, where the support of public opinion was massive, the decision was only just reached in Congress. In France, where the support of public opinion was tepid before the beginning of military operations, it suddenly switched massively in favour of the head of state as soon as the firing started, to reach a most exceptional level of support, including in those circles which are traditionally refractory to the image of the military world (the intellectuals, the young), and with a remarkable degree of tolerance among the immigrated or recently integrated community.[24]

In action itself, the share of the individual soldier was always concealed by the deliberate emptiness of media coverage – i.e. absence of information – and by the technical nature of the warfare (intelligent weapons, etc.). So much so that the victimology of the Gulf conflict is still to be done, since allied victims were hidden by the image of the 'zero-victim-war'[25] and Iraqi victims were never subject to a serious evaluation. This war was indeed made of manoeuvres, in the classic strategic sense, but these manoeuvres remained abstract movements, as if they no longer involved men.

War, brought to its highest point by the first half of this century, had been blocked between major powers, consequently opening space up for peripheral conflicts. The strategic deadlock on the nuclearized space necessitated manoeuvres elsewhere. The more the individual was theoretically concerned with war in its progressive totalization, the more it seemed foreign and distant to him. And now war is coming back, close to us although not directly threatening. It cannot be a question of regression and Europe will not return to the great pre-nuclear wars. We will rather be confronted by an extremely complex situation and geography.

The return of real war, inside or outside Europe, has little chance of reversing the tendency of marginalization of the individual in developed countries' defence systems. The theoretician, the military strategist will undoubtedly more than ever have to finalize special military equipment and operations – organization of the modularity of military systems at national level and in cooperation, projection of forces, limited intensity conflicts... Operations of a new kind will require new operational strategies. But they will most likely involve, as far as man is concerned, only the army's technical and professional sectors.

Should we believe, then, in the end of war, which has been announced by many commentators since the beginning of the 1990s?[26] According to them, war is no longer possible in the North in its state-to-state confrontation form, and will go bankrupt in the South at the same time as state structures, thereby dissolving into a multitude of confrontations with unsettled actors, objectives, spaces and means. Future conflicts, returning to the barbarian struggles from before the modern age 'civilized' warfare, will involve the individual in the sense of a largely depoliticized atom, acting only in the scope of fugitive coalitions of interests. The great age-old Western movement, in which war was the privilege of ever more structured and rational groups and which made the individual appear only as a legitimating member of the group, has come to an end and is turning into new savagery.

More than the end of war, what we are undoubtedly experiencing is the end of the particular kind of war we have theorized about and put into practice for two centuries in a so-called 'Clausewitzian'[27] world. War organized within the iron bounds of Trinitarian logic: a people for passion, a strategist state for decision, a policy for Reason. This war is most likely, for a future whose end remains unknown, to become marginal – save for an exceptional operation to put order into a theatre of some importance, where power will easily outdo the local trouble-maker.

An obvious consequence of this: the military apparatuses of the powers seem more and more out of phase with future conflict hypotheses. In the South, they will have difficulty keeping diffused, urban and irrational conflicts under control (see the Somalia example). In this respect, the last few years have asserted a tendency to a disengagement of the powers and not to the all-out engagement that may have seemed final following the Gulf War and the 'UN spring': inadequacy of armies, growing indifference of public opinion towards ever more distant stakes, will join to advise abstention. In the North, security of the developed states is not guaranteed forever, but it could be questioned by means very different from those that Clausewitzian wars taught us to fight. Of course, the hypothesis of a resurgence of major classic-type threats has to be sustained, but is inevitably marginal. More important from now on are hypotheses of an explosion of more or less close regions, new threats of a transversal and non-state kind (drug trafficking, development of illegal economy, terrorism, etc.), risks affecting vulnerabilities specific to developed societies, which were not yesterday called into question in a rather stable and 'civilized' world order but which might tomorrow be in a more anarchic context.

The change here is radical, even though it has many heads. These hypotheses of an undermining of security cannot be dealt with by the military instrument alone – and even the role of the military as such is relatively marginal. All the hypotheses of fighting against these scenarios of insecurity are indeed collective. What is therefore at stake is fundamentally the relationship between individuals and the defence system, and more broadly the relationship between individuals and their national framework.

The disruption of the relations between individuals and the war system – symbolized by the virtually general tendency to the professionalization of armies in Europe – is only here the epiphenomenon of a more profound uncertainty. What should indeed be revised is their relationship with politics, embodied by the state. The planned military reforms, although they avoid reflecting on sovereignty, on the place of the military in national or collective strategies, on action in a globalized and yet fragmented world, will reshape mechanisms with no sense, ever more distant from perceptions and interests of the citizens. The spirit of defence automatically produced by the growth of threats, mobilization in acts of war expressing the very existence of the national community –

all this belongs to the past or to a still distant future. What remains to be dealt with is the transition.

NOTES

1. As regards the terms of the debate, see Raymond Aron, *Penser la guerre, Clausewitz, II. L'âge planétaire* (Paris: Gallimard, 1976).
2. See Jean Jaurès, *L'Armée Nouvelle* (Paris: Editions sociales, 1977).
3. Giulio Douhet speaks of 'guerra integrale' in *La difesa nazionale*, published in 1923; Ludendorff's *Der Totale Krieg* was published in 1935.
4. Carnot had already advocated the total mobilization of men to fight, of women, of old people to harangue the home front in public places, etc.
5. Concerning Douhet's global logic, see Dominique David, 'Douhet ou le dernier imaginaire', *Stratégique*, 49 (1991).
6. *Come fini la grande guerra – La vittoria alata*, written in 1917, and published at the end of the Great War. *La guerra del 19...* was published in 1930.
7. See Alain Joxe, *Le cycle de la dissuasion* (Paris: La Découverte, 1990), pp. 74–83.
8. The novel is analysed in Dominique David, 'L'invention de la guerre', *Etudes polémologiques*, 25–6 (1982).
9. One of the presupposition about Douhet's model was that defending oneself against poison-gas air attacks would be completely impossible. Yet this presupposition eventually proved to be wrong during the Second World War when the enemy's means of navigation were muddled up, when the DCA demonstrated its efficiency, when different kinds of deception were settled, industries were scattered, etc.
10. This was precisely where the ambiguity of the strategy of 'flexible response' adopted by NATO in 1966 lay with regard to the atomic weapon as 'the last step' in the progression of violence. Hence the argument with France, for whom there could be no slow progression in the use of violence, but only an immediate threat of escalation to extremes through nuclear threats.
11. Concerning the Sokolovski doctrine, see Jean-Christophe Romer, La *guerre nucléaire de Staline à Krouchtchev* (Paris: Publications de la Sorbonne, 1991). Concerning the theories of victory, see Colin S. Gray, *War, Peace and Victory* (New York: Simon & Schuster, 1990).
12. See Fred Kaplan, *The Wizards of Armageddon* (New York: Simon & Schuster, 1983).
13. See François Géré, 'Quatre généraux de l'apocalypse', *Stratégique*, 53 (1992).
14. The 'three circles' model – sanctuary, national territory, external space – was theorized in Lucien Poirier, *Essais de stratégie théorique* (Paris: FEDN, 1982).

15. This is specially the case for general Gallois. See Pierre M. Gallois, *Stratégie de l'âge nucléaire* (Paris: Calmann-Lévy, 1960).
16. V. Giscard d'Estaing, *Le pouvoir et la vie, tome 2: L'affrontement* (Paris: Cie 12, 1991).
17. This is of course the meaning of Valmy, whose bicentenary was celebrated in 1989, whereas the gunfire dates from 1792.
18. This is the bulk of Jean-Pierre Chevènement's argument, for instance. See Pierre Messmer and Chevènement, *Le Service militaire* (Paris: Balland, 1977).
19. The small amount of debate brought about in 1996 by the French President's professionalization of the army says much about this loss of meaning of the national service.
20. See the confrontations between Azeris and Armenians, or the war in Bosnia, whose outlines made the military intervention of Western forces so difficult.
21. See Alexis Chkolnyi, in 'Le débat sur le budget de la défense', *Politique Etrangère*, 4 (1996); and Dmitri Trenin, 'Stratégie russe: une difficile naissance', *Politique Etrangère*, 1 (1997).
22. This is especially the argument of Jean-Christophe Rufin, *L'empire et les nouveaux barbares* (Paris: Lattès, 1991).
23. Let us simply note that in the mid-1980s, 80 per cent of French arms exports went to Third World countries, and that among them 80 per cent went to the Middle East – which displays remarkable geographic focusing.
24. With reference to the opinion polls taken during the month of January 1991. See in particular Elisabeth Dupoirier, 'De la crise à la guerre du Golfe: un exemple de mobilization de l'opinion', in SOFRES, *L'état de l'opinion 1992* (Paris: Seuil, 1992).
25. General Pierre M. Gallois believes that this idea of the 'zero-victim-war' will prevail in great-powers interventions, and that it will thus compel them to adjust their strategic choices to such a requirement. See Pierre M. Gallois, 'A la charnière des siècles, de bouleversements en turbulences', *Défense nationale* (June 1992)
26. See in particular Martin van Creveld, *On Future War* (London: Brassey's, 1991).
27. On these questions see Dominique David (ed.), 'Stratégies et Conflits: l'après-demain', *Politique Etrangère*, 1 (1997).

10 Individuals and Humanitarian Law: the Geneva Paradox

Jean-Pierre Colin

Is the individual at the heart of international law? The answer to this question is not as obvious as we could believe it to be in an international society composed above all of states. Indeed, since the very origin of the international system in which we live, most authors, referring to international practices, have considered that international law only regulates relations between states and that the individual should therefore not be considered as a subject of international law. Given the way the system functions, they would seem to be right. One only has to think of the institution of international responsibility in a system lacking compulsory sanctions yet trying to be legal. Traditional law defines only the responsibility of one state to another. It can be applied only by one state against another state. It aims only to repair the damage caused by a state. If the outrages are committed against the person of one of its citizens, it is the state which ultimately remains in control of the indemnity that the citizen may receive after an international procedure. Case law is constant: The State's decision to intervene in international responsibility is an act of state, not subject to appeal. It is the state that is compensated, not its nationals.

This doctrinal vision of a judicial universe composed exclusively of abstract entities has, in reality, never been unanimously accepted. On the contrary, certain authors have always considered that in reality the individual is the only subject of international law as he is, more generally, of every legal rule. That was the case, in France, according to Georges Scelle, but his very original view was in many respects not so isolated. In Russia at the end of the last century, the great Russian jurist of Estonian origin, Frederic Frommhold de Martens, whose role was so important during the Hague Conferences of 1899 and 1907, wrote – perhaps as a good Lutheran – 'the degree of consideration, given to the human being as such, always indicates, for a given period, the level of development of international relations and of international law'.[1]

While the new rules concerning the protection of human rights nowadays constitute a major part of positive international law, and are at the same time a justification – although sometimes ambiguous – for intervention in the internal affairs of other states, the traditional rules have also protected the individual, while at the same time very gradually allowing him to get personally involved. Apart from the law applicable in times of war (*jus in bello*), these traditional rules were only apparent in, for instance, the radical banning of slavery. That principle was laid down by the Treaty of Paris in 1814, restated by the final act of the Vienna Congress in 1815 and later on by the Conferences of Aachen (1818) and of Verona (1822). Even so, this rule only acknowledged the right of warships, mainly British, to inspect merchant ships whatever their flag may be and even in times of peace . . .

It is therefore within the laws relating to warfare that a legal system was established, which may be applied directly to the individual, whether for his protection or to establish his responsibility. It is an extraordinary if little-noticed fact that states, who are so jealous of their sovereignty that they can envisage defending their own citizens only in their own name, are ready to admit a system of direct protection of individuals. Moreover, they are led to recognize that an individual, whether a political or military leader, could be held personally responsible for an action undertaken in the name of the state. In modern times things have without doubt taken this turn progressively. By adopting the first Hague Conventions in 1899, states were aware that they were codifying 'the ways and customs of war', and they took the precaution of foreseeing, in the famous 'de Martens clause' included in the Preamble to the Hague Conventions, that 'in cases not provided for by the Convention, private individuals and soldiers in fighting units [would remain] under the protection and the authority of the principles of the law of nations, as it results from established customs, humanitarian principles and the requirements of public conscience'. The principle would be restated, not only in the Hague Conventions of 1907, but later on in the four Geneva Conventions of 1949, with their famous common article 3, and more recently in the additional Protocol of 1977 and the Convention of 1980 on the prohibition or the limitation of the use of certain traditional arms of warfare. In the name of principles superior to the transitory will of states, here is a real case of individuals being given legal protection, although it is still held that the application of humanitarian law has no effect on the legal status of the parties to the conflict.[2]

This clear understanding of the existence of rules superior to the will of states is surprising in a world in which, during the eighteenth century, positivism prevailed in general international law for a long time. The idea of the existence of a natural law older than, and superior to, positive law still remained at the heart of the law of nations for Grotius, who, however, no longer confused it with divine law but made it proceed from the principles of 'right reason'. With Vattel, the state became the sovereign interpreter of natural law and positivism finally assumed a dominant position, practically up to the Second World War. The only exception to this was in the domain of the law of warfare, a fact which is well worth thinking about.

Basically positivism expresses, in international law, a fundamental reality: legal rules binding states are no more than the expression of an agreement between themselves. One of the first positivist authors, Georges Frederic de Martens, Prussian homonym of the above-mentioned – and no less famous – Frederic de Martens, published, in 1788, his *Précis du droit des gens moderne de l'Europe fondé sur les traités et sur l'usage*, and it was in making an inventory of the practices of states that he identified the applicable rules. Among the fundamental principles that he singled out in his exhaustive study, two can receive our attention here. First, only states are in a position to appreciate what they must or must not do, and international law, having a purely inter-state character, does not apply to individuals. Second, concerning relations between sovereign states, war is allowed.

Such a vision is therefore based on the dual nature of the legal system. In times of peace, positive rules apply to the relationships between states, who run the risk of exposing their international responsibility if they breach these rules and cause other states damage. This responsibility will be progressively widened and become a way to measure the effectiveness of the international legal system. In times of war, most of the normal rules are abolished, or at least suspended,[3] and exceptional measures are applied. The legal situation is in that case doubly exorbitant. The passage from peace to war is generally the result of a unilateral act which conventional warfare law surrounds with a maximum of precautions, such as vigilant regulations for the declaration of war. In the new relationship between belligerents, agreement is hardly possible any more since communications are theoretically cut off. What neither states nor jurists wanted is precisely that no more rules should then be applicable at all and that war should mean a pure and simple return to barbarism. If we consider the facts, it is clear that this goal has hardly been attained, even though the rules of *jus in bello* have often attenuated much suffering. What prevails here for us is their approach from a philosophical as well as political point of view. Indeed, such rules imply that, in its position of absolutism, the state still needs to attach its legitimacy to superior principles when it goes to war. But they also lead to an unprecedented transparency of the 'international society', and the individual becomes, or returns to being, the real objective of legal rules concerning either his protection or his responsibility.

From the mists of time comes the idea of 'the just war'. The concept has certainly been the object of many interpretations from St Augustine to Grotius, including St Thomas Aquinas, and it is not the prerogative of Christianity, since the Koran itself regulates the *Djihad*. Furthermore, in our times, this concept is experiencing new developments, particularly since it was put forward by Mao Tse-tung.[4] Obviously the concept responds to the need to justify an enterprise becoming more and more remote after centuries of common ethics. The Sixth Commandment, 'thou shalt not kill', can therefore be put into perspective: 'thou shalt not kill, except in a war'. The concept of a just war has not, however, developed in a permissive way. Theologians have sought to give it a positive meaning and one has finally arrived at the triple condition of a just cause, a just right (the famous competence to make war) and a just conduct. Massacres and pointless suffering were therefore condemned, by Suarez as well as by Vitoria; violence unnecessary to victory was not justified. 'Violence, no longer regarded from the angle of punishment, stops being an end in itself. It becomes a means that one uses with increasing and calculated moderation', wrote Pierre Boissier.[5] In his *De Jure Belli ac Pacis*,[6] Grotius detailed these *temperamenta belli*, thereby contributing to the foundation of modern law, whose rules have been inscribed in human conscience more deeply than is generally assumed. When Louis XV was asked, on the evening of the battle of Fontenoy in 1747, how the wounded enemy should be treated, he answered: 'But exactly like ours because being wounded, they are no longer enemy.'[7] It is true that during the seventeenth and eighteenth centuries war was often a battle between professional armies with reduced numbers. Civilians were no longer automatically involved because the troops had catering structures at their disposal and looting was forbidden. War became 'an art', a war *'en dentelles'*, where treacherous and cruel methods were quite willingly banned because they exasperated the adversary and reinforced his combativeness. Since the end of the sixteenth century 'cartels' have been concluded, most of the time between army commanders before the battle, in order to lay down the terms and conditions concerning the fate of the prisoners and the wounded, the burial of the dead, etc. These provisional agreements constituted the foundations of customary law, given that from 1581 to 1864 there were 291[8] of them, the first ones dating back to 1393.[9]

Not only did this effort respond to a necessity but it also followed a certain logic. On the one hand, the main necessity was to protect individuals, who, being prisoners, wounded, abandoned by their army, defeated on the battlefield, or civilians fallen under the power of the enemy, could no longer count, at least momentarily, on the guarantee of the state on which they depended. It was not merely a humanitarian necessity, because ardour in battle partly stems from the feeling that the belligerents as well as their families might have to be protected. On the other hand, the fact that they abolished between themselves the rules which they had agreed upon led the belligerents to submit to laws superior to their will. The logic was therefore to incriminate those who had violated these rules, firstly before internal courts (the military courts of the belligerents), but also before *ad hoc* international courts which may have foreshadowed a permanent international penal court, today officially called for by states. It is significant that these requirements have continued to be valued in a world that thought it had abolished the competence to make war by regulating the *jus ad bellum* in such a way that war would be banned from then on. One knows that this was not the case and that the resort to force remains, in many circumstances, the *ultima ratio*, not only of states, but also of other human groups, since the principle of self-defence has become the cardinal point of the new system, although its application depends on subjective criteria.

THE PROTECTION OF THE INDIVIDUAL IN THE *JUS IN BELLO*

Before putting forward the fundamental principles of the humanitarian law applicable in armed conflicts, it is necessary to keep in mind the developments that have marked the fact of war, because these have had an influence on the application of the legal rules, although without altering their essence.

The ideology of human rights has played an ambiguous role here. Obviously the American and French revolutions of the end of the eighteenth century strengthened citizen's rights, in times of war and peace alike, but they also brought back a just reason to make war at a time when it had declined. As Boris Mirkine Guetzevitch wrote,[10] the men of 1789 thought that wars could only be wished for by Kings. That is why, in the conscience of Assembly members, the constitutional rule which allowed the Assembly to retain a decisive role in the declaration of war was synonymous with the adoption of the principle of eternal peace. The men of 1789 sincerely thought that an assembly of representatives of the people would never want a 'war of aggression'. Indeed, the decree of 22 May 1790 – reaffirmed by the Constitution of 1791 (title VI: Relations of the French Nation with Foreign Nations) – stipulated: 'The French nation forgoes undertaking any war with the aim of conquering and will never use its forces against the freedom of any people.' The question came up again when, on 20 April 1792, the Legislative Assembly declared war on Austria. The fatherland was declared to be in danger and Hérault de Séchelles, speaking in the name of the military and diplomatic committees of the extraordinary commission, expressed the revolutionary fervour in most modern terms: 'The war that we have undertaken does not at all resemble those common wars that have so often distressed and torn apart the globe: It is a war of equality against a coalition of powers intent on modifying the French Constitution, because they dread the establishment of our philosophy and the lights of our principles in their countries. This war is therefore the last of all wars between them and us.'[11] This idea would endure and the calling of 'the war to end all wars' still exalts belligerents on battlefields.

The updating of the concept of a just war, as far as its ideological foundation is concerned, was unfortunately not associated with an improvement in the humanization of war, quite the contrary. It was indeed characterized by the institution of conscription – compulsory military service for all – and at the same time by a change in the nature of battles. From then on, they would become mass wars between whole peoples standing up against one another, having assembled all their material resources and mobilized all their spiritual energy. They fought 'for ideas', but paradoxically this brought about a terrible human decline: Field Marshal Foch was to speak of 'unleashed wars.'[12] As early as the First Empire principles fell into obscurity again, cartels were much less frequent, and field hospitals were once again the target of fire. Whilst still a general, Bonaparte ordered the execution, by gun and by bayonet, of the 4,000 Turkish soldiers of the garrison of Jaffa although they had surrendered after being promised that their lives would be spared . . . Later on, French prisoners could be seen dying slowly on British vessels, where they were crammed together without being able to get off. It was only with Henry Dunant and the creation of the Red Cross that a powerful return of humanitarian rules was possible. In the preceding years, during the Crimean War, a young English nurse, Florence Nightingale, had already distinguished herself by organizing military field hospitals. However, out of the 300,000 men from the French-British expeditionary force, 83,000 died of illness. After that, Great Britain profoundly reformed its medical service.

While the efforts of the militant English woman continued during the American Civil War and the Franco-Prussian War, it was on the battlefield of Solferino, on 24 June 1859,[13] that Henry Dunant was seized by a prophetic inspiration. He immediately wrote a short book, *Un souvenir de Solferino*, in which he expressed the double wish that a voluntary aid association be constituted in every country in order to be prepared, even in times of peace, to help army services in the event of a war; and that states subscribe to the 'conventional and sacred principle' that provides legal protection to military hospitals and medical personnel. From the first wish originated the institution of the Red Cross, a federation of national associations. From the second, the first Geneva Convention of 22 August 1864, 'for the improvement of the situation of the military wounded in campaigning armies', and from then on these two institutions were inextricably linked. That was to be the starting point of the rapid growth of contemporary humanitarian law.

Humanitarian law continued to be improved over the course of the years with a double series of regulations – the Hague Regulations, above all devoted to the conduct of war and resulting essentially from the Conventions of 1899 and 1907,[14] and the Geneva

Regulations, more specifically devoted to the humanitarian protection of contending forces and non-combatants. A new problem appeared, however, with the distinction between international armed conflicts and non-international armed conflicts. Owing to decolonization and the multiplication of liberation wars, the distinction often appeared invalid, null and void, and led to laborious negotiations, notably at the time of the updating of humanitarian international law applicable to armed conflicts which resulted in the adoption, in 1977, of two additional Protocols to the Geneva Conventions of 1949.

In the eyes of Third World states, who constituted a large majority at the Diplomatic Conference that met four times in Geneva under the Red Cross's patronage between 1974 and 1977, the protection of the contending forces was, in any case, illusory in an armed conflict defined as an internal conflict, even if new competencies were recognized for international organizations such as the International Committee of the Red Cross. This was above all a political question and the legitimacy of the struggle undertaken by peoples against oppressive state authorities had to be recognized. It was under such conditions that the qualification of these conflicts was modified by paragraph 2 of article 1 of the first Protocol relating to international armed conflicts. From then on, 'are included in the category of [international] armed conflicts the armed conflicts in which peoples fight against colonial domination, foreign occupation and racist regimes'. However, from the moment that a second Protocol relating to non-international armed conflicts was put to discussion, Third World states adopted a very restrictive attitude, going so far as to denounce, in the case of representatives from India, a text aiming at giving protection to criminals that used violence against the state. This second Protocol, though prepared with the greatest care by Geneva experts, was finally emptied of all substance and subsequently considered as a title restricting the interpretation of earlier rules.[15]

Undeniably, the individual tends to be sacrificed to the cause of the combatant. These Geneva discussions, between 1974 and 1977, were very significant. Humanitarian law was not always applied in practice and from a historical point of view, it appeared as an official recognition of war. A new meaning was forced upon humanitarian law because the actors did not intend so much to apply or draw benefit from it for their combatants as to use it as an instrument of differentiation. It allowed them to distinguish legitimate conflicts, liable to suitable qualifications, from others, rejected as criminal enterprises.

Having said that, the rules protecting the individual increasingly elude, in principle, the particular will of states. This state of things is firstly due to the large number of conventions that, by binding most states, enact rules in humanitarian affairs. It also results from the fact that, over and above these particular provisions, a certain number of principles are acknowledged as applying to the whole field, although some of them were never actually formulated by the states. It is above all within the framework of the International Committee of the Red Cross that these principles have been affirmed,[16] first of all by those who govern the national Red Cross associations. These latter associations first appeared in 1921 and were visibly impregnated by the experience of the Great War. They postulate impartiality, political, religious and economic independence, universality, and equality within the national Red Cross, and today Red Crescent,[17] associations. Later on, the fundamental principles that inspired the movement prompted numerous resolutions, notably on the occasion of the International Conferences of the Red Cross, particularly in 1952 in Toronto,[18] or in 1977 in Geneva. The first of these principles, the so-called principle of humanity, whose scope is very general, can be formulated in the following way: 'The military requirements and the maintaining of public order should always remain compatible with the respect for the individual's rights.' From this general principle ensues the principle inspiring the Hague regulations ('the parties in conflict will not cause harm to their adversaries out of proportion to the aim of the war, which is to destroy or to weaken the military potential of the enemy') and the principle inspiring the Geneva regulations ('persons put out of action and those who do not participate directly in the hostilities will be respected, protected and treated with humanity'). From that also followed numerous universal rules, among which mainly the principle of inviolability. Besides these necessities suited to combat, the individual has a right to the respect of his life, his physical and moral integrity, and the attributes inseparable from his personality. The man who falls in combat is inviolable and the enemy who surrenders will have his life spared. No one will be submitted to physical or mental torture, nor to corporal punishment, or to cruel and degrading treatment. Everyone has a right to the respect of his honour, his family rights, his convictions and his customs. Retaliation, collective punishment, the taking of hostages, and deportation are prohibited. In the same way it is stated that humanitarian assistance is never to interfere in a conflict, even if, as counterpart to the immunity that is given to them, the medical personnel must abstain from any hostile act. In the same way, nobody will be harassed or punished for having given aid to the wounded or the sick, and nobody will be forced to give information about the wounded and the sick in his care, if it might be prejudicial to their interests. The state must ensure the national and international protection of those fallen under its power. The prisoner is not to be left under the control of the troops that captured him, but of the Power to whom the troops are responsible. The enemy state is responsible for the fate and the support of those it holds in custody, and, in occupied country, for the maintenance of public order and public life. The victims of conflicts will be provided with an international protector from the moment that they no longer have a natural protector. As far as civilians are concerned, they benefit from general protection against the dangers of military operations, so that the contending forces must, at every moment, make a distinction between combatants and non-combatants. The civilians must never be the object of attacks, even retaliation. Acts or threats of violence chiefly aimed at spreading terror amongst civilians are forbidden, but only members of the armed forces have the right to attack the enemy. Attacks must be strictly confined to military objectives. Attacks on undefended localities are therefore forbidden. No hostile act may be directed against edifices devoted to science or charity, against historical monuments, works of art or places of worship that constitute the cultural or spiritual heritage of peoples. In the same way, attacks on constructions and installations that might set free forces dangerous for the population are forbidden. The population may not be used to shelter military objectives from attacks and looting is banned. Finally, special arms and methods of war are forbidden for everybody, namely those arms and methods which might by nature cause unnecessary losses or excessive suffering. Acts of war founded on betrayal and perfidy are prohibited, being traditionally distinguished from authorized war stratagems. More recently, with the Protocols of 1977, new regulations were added, relating to the protection of the natural environment and artistic heritage.

Of course all these rules are based on the existence of an international armed conflict. They could surely be applied, after adaptation, to non-international armed conflicts, but it will be difficult to get people to accept the protection of the 'combatants' under the law of warfare. The attempt of the ICRC to make people admit that men and women engaged in a non-internationally recognized struggle, should benefit from the legal rules applying to combatants (status of prisoners of war, etc.), failed with the adoption, in 1977, of a very restrictive Protocol concerning non-international armed conflicts.

A new attempt is presently being made to extend the usual framework of humanitarian law, because contemporary forms of war tend to include conflicts that are difficult to qualify using traditional concepts. Within this new humanitarian approach, the protection of the individual should be enlarged in situations of internal trouble and tensions by adopting a 'Declaration on Minimal Humanitarian Norms' that could be the first step towards the codification of these new rules.[19] The project, on which the International Committee of the Red Cross has not yet defined its position, deals with 'situations of violence, internal troubles, internal tensions and exceptional public danger' in which 'any derogation from the obligations relative to human rights ... [should] remain within the limits provided for by international law', given 'that certain rights must not suffer from any derogation'. Such provisions are compatible with the new rule of the internationally ensured protection of human rights. At a time when blind violence is once again being unleashed in many regions of the world, international society is undoubtedly at a vital turning point. It will overcome the difficulties by which it is assailed only if it shows audacity in this field. After all, if the international community, especially regional organizations, had prevented after 1981 the capture of Kosovo, Yugoslavia would have changed without any doubt, but it would perhaps not have disappeared in the turmoil of war ...

THE RESPONSIBILITY OF THE INDIVIDUAL IN THE *JUS IN BELLO*

In traditional humanitarian law, the repression of offences only falls under the internal mechanisms that states, bound by modern Conventions, committed themselves to organize. Separate legislation is what is generally provided for in this respect, and the behaviour of states is very variable, many of them showing little concern for the respect of their obligations.[20] In times of war, the offenders will normally be tried by military courts, an obligation when a prisoner of war is prosecuted.[21] Naturally this situation imposes limits on the system of protection. The latter may depend on the goodwill of states, who would hardly want to test it in a period of war. An internationally ensured repression would constitute the only credible guarantee in this field. This repression is only gradually being introduced, at least for the worst offences.

Historically, there are few precedents. In his treaty, Georg Schwarzenberger called attention to the proceedings instituted against Peter von Hagenbach at Breisach in 1474. Nominated Governor of the territory of the Upper Rhine, von Hagenbach had been left behind by the Archduke of Austria in order to protect Charles the Bold. While strictly executing the orders of his master, he had devastated the region, allowing homicides, rapes and looting. Made prisoner after a revolt, he was tried by an international court composed of 28 judges, of whom 8 had been nominated by the town of Breisach. During the trial, the accused put forward the excuse of superior orders that had been given to him, but the court condemned him to death for having violated divine law.[22]

Much more recently, articles 227, 228, and 229 of the Treaty of Versailles[23] provided for the creation of an International Court of Justice instructed to try Emperor William II for 'offences against international morals and the sacred authority of the treaties', as well as for the creation of national courts in order to try enemy citizens guilty of war crimes. William II is known to have found refuge in the Netherlands, which remained neutral during the war. Being the grandson of Queen Victoria and related to all the European royal families, he was not handed over to the Allies. Besides, the international court was never actually brought into operation. As for the national courts, their activity was greatly reduced.[24]

It was only after the Second World War that a real international system of repression became apparent. During the conflict, the Allied governments, facing an unprecedented situation due to the violation of human rights by Japan and especially Germany, on a scale hitherto unknown, had already announced their intention to punish war criminals at the end of the war. That was the object of the 'Declaration of St James Palace', made by the governments of the Allied countries occupied by Germany, on 13 January 1942, and especially of the 'Declaration of Moscow', made by the Allied Powers on 1 November 1943, with Germany and Japan at the back of their minds. Many courts were therefore created, some of them under the authority of the Allies in their respective zones of occupation in Germany, others, mostly North American courts and military tribunals, instructed to judge crimes committed in the Far East. But the most spectacular decisions were the London Agreement of 8 August 1945, creating the Nuremberg Tribunal that had to try 'the great European war criminals of the Axes whose crimes defied a precise geographical localization', and the Tokyo Agreement of 19 January 1946, creating the International Military Tribunal for the Far East, instructed to try Japanese war criminals according to principles and rules almost identical to those of the Nuremberg Tribunal. These *ad hoc* tribunals were based on a new definition of crimes submitted to their jurisdiction, defined in terms that, much later, were to create case law: crimes against peace, war crimes and especially crimes against humanity.

Without lingering here on the exceptional importance of these new categories of international penal law, it will be noted that the responsibility held up was above all individual.[25] It was operative whatever the internal laws might be. The accused could put in a plea, and there was no remission, the court being able to pronounce any punishment deemed necessary, including death penalty. An *ad hoc* procedure was set up by the London Agreement. The signatories reserved themselves the right to establish, if needed, other international military courts with identical composition, competence and procedures – an option that they used for the crimes committed by the Japanese in the Far East.

This was a complete innovation, as far as its principles were concerned. Neither internal law nor superior orders were capable of exonerating the individual from his personal responsibility. State mediation was no longer operative. As for internationally organized repression, it was based on a superior law established by an international legislator. The advocates of the accused once again put forward the traditional exoneration clause, drawn from the existence of a superior order, but the Nuremberg Tribunal considered 'that the international obligations, that are imposed on individuals, outweigh their duty of obedience to the State of which they are citizens. He who has violated the law of warfare cannot, in order to justify himself, allege the mandate that he received from the State, given that the State, by delivering this mandate, has outstripped the powers recognized by international law.' We can add that, for the first time, the accusations were expressly aimed at public agents of the State, some of them being of the highest officials. Furthermore, many internal courts, in particular French tribunals, consider that the London Agreement implied that crimes against humanity were not subject to prescription (an idea restated by the French Law of 26 December 1964). At an international level, on 26 November 1968, the United Nations General Assembly adopted a similar convention applicable, without distinction, to war crimes as well as to crimes against humanity.

The mission of the *ad hoc* tribunals was rapidly completed and finalized on 1 October 1946 in Nuremberg, and on 12 November 1948 in Tokyo. But the effort of codification continued and since then an important movement has been pushing for the creation of a permanent international criminal court. Crimes against humanity especially are the object of particular attention. Thus, on 11 December 1946, the United Nations General Assembly pointed out that genocide is 'a crime under international law'. On 9 December 1948, it unanimously adopted a 'Convention on the Prevention and Repression of the Crime of Genocide' that came into force in 1951. The international character of the offence is indisputable: the offence is defined by the Convention as any act committed with the intention to destroy, in whole or in part, a national, ethnic, racial or religious group. Its authors must be punished, whether they are private persons, civil servants or rulers. The crime is punishable whether it is committed in times of war or in times of peace. Responsibility for this falls jointly on the national courts of the victim state and on an International Criminal Court which has still not yet been created.

Likewise, the International Law Commission requested by the General Assembly on 21 November 1947 adopted, in 1954, a Draft Code on Offences against the Peace and Security of Mankind.[26] The Assembly had however decided to adjourn the discussion of the Draft Code[27] while waiting for a definition of aggression to be adopted, which occurred in 1974.[28] The question has therefore been raised again since the 32nd Session of the General Assembly, this time on the initiative of Third World States.

In fact, the efforts to create international regulations in this field were for a long time hampered by specific problems. The new states, which came into being with the decolonization movement, rightly put the crime of *apartheid* in the same category as crimes against humanity. They obtained on 30 November 1973 the adoption of a Convention on the Elimination and Repression of the Crime of *Apartheid*, which defined a new category of offence when it came into force in 1976. According to the terms of its article 2, the notion included 'the policies and practices. . . . of racial segregation and discrimination' and led to a list of inhuman acts committed with the intention of maintaining the domination of one racial group over another. It appeared extremely likely that the risk of seeing the policy of *apartheid* eventually attacked by an International Criminal Court had at that time curbed the ardour of Western states linked to South Africa to promote a new international criminal tribunal.

The question has been redefined by the changes brought about by the collapse of communism. *Apartheid* has been replaced by new conflicts, causing the shadow of new genocides to hang over whole peoples, in Africa, in Asia, but also at the heart of Europe. In virtue of Resolutions 808 and 827 of the Security Council (1993) an International Tribunal was thus instituted to prosecute individuals presumed responsible for serious violations of international humanitarian law committed on the territory of Former Yugoslavia since 1991.[29] It has been active since 1991 and seems destined to create jurisprudence '[constituting] . . . the beginning of an innovative and on the whole coherent *corpus juris*'.[30] Since then, a new tribunal has been created, the International Penal Tribunal for Rwanda, which has also been asked to adopt the regulations of the International Tribunal for Former Yugoslavia.[31]

Will these courts bring about new developments in international penal law? It is still somewhat early to answer in the affirmative even if the first rulings have already been given. They were in fact created by the Security Council only within the general framework of its peacekeeping mission. Outside this very precise context, a unanimous decision of the states to create an international penal tribunal with a general vocation remains very unlikely in the foreseeable future.

None the less, individuals guilty of crimes against humanity appear openly in public, whatever their level of responsibility – simple agents or commanders in chief. Furthermore, as the first debates before the International Tribunal for Former Yugoslavia have shown, the defence questioned, right from the first case, the legality of Resolutions 808 and 827 of the Security Council. The framework adopted – the peacekeeping context as well as the genuine sanctioning power of the Council – ensures the legitimacy of the new courts. In addition, the Agreements of Dayton and of Paris, which were supposed to put an end to the war in Bosnia-Hercegovina, did not abolish, as some had feared, the *ad hoc* International Tribunal, but on the contrary, reminded the Parties of their obligation 'to co-operate with the inquiries and with the prosecutions relative to war crimes and other violations of international humanitarian law'. Article IX of the Constitution annexed to the Agreements prohibits any person, condemned or accused by the Tribunal, from being a candidate for, elected or nominated to, any post of public responsibility whatsoever.

CONCLUSION

1. From a practical point of view, international humanitarian law, applicable in armed conflicts, has proven itself, to such an extent that states have become prudent. France, for instance, refused to sign Protocol I of 1977, while the United States and Great Britain signed it but abstained from ratifying it.[32] An important part of this diplomatic instrument was devoted to the protection of civilian populations in the light of the lessons of the Second World War, and the Korean and Vietnam Wars. The Great Powers acted with courage here. They knew perfectly well what they were doing. At the time of the Gulf War, it was thus clear that, bound by Protocol I of 1977, they would no longer have the free hand they used to have regarding the means of prosecuting war.[33]

2. This is where one can judge the paradox of a law formalized at the Hague in 1899 and 1907 and that has since then been developed in Geneva.

The states or parties involved in a conflict rarely have the opportunity to agree on anything at all during the conflict because they are isolated. Modern war, with its technical sophistication and its ideological radicalism, has not, from this point of view, made the situation any easier. If nevertheless one can hope to see humanitarian law applied, this will be done by giving its rules an unusual strength, inspiring respect from the most ferocious, and by making them independent from the immediate will of the states. Thus although at first the law of warfare was very difficult to introduce, to apply and therefore to sanction, it has nevertheless progressively been surrounded by the strongest guarantees, to such a point that it can now be considered as the premise of a general mandatory law, which is still very dubious in other fields of international law.[34]

The legal expert can draw his own conclusions. Humanitarian law applicable in armed conflicts is to a large extent made up of general principles. The implementation of Conventions is as flexible as can be imagined, whereas their denunciation is most often rendered very difficult. Furthermore – and this resembles to a large extent the famous *jus cogens* – Conventions forbid special agreements which do not go as far as the protection given by the common article 42 of the Geneva Conventions of 1949. To that can be added a control led by structures exterior to the states, whether the International Committee of the Red Cross, the protective Powers, or even today non-governmental organizations; but most of all the creation of sanctions that can have a penal character.

3. From certain points of view, the states now find themselves caught in a trap. While they have agreed to see their freedom of action limited in times of war, this has rarely been through philanthropy, but merely in order to respond to objective requirements linked to the morale of the troops, who are keen to know their probable fate if they are taken prisoner or wounded, and to the morale of their families. To go too far along this route may, however, paralyse the belligerents. Henceforth an armed conflict, during which all humanitarian rules were strictly and constantly applied, could hardly develop 'normally' and the armed forces would often be like so many Gullivers on the terrain, hindered by a thousand links, very small and invisible – but none the less effective. It is therefore with extreme prudence that the Powers continue their efforts. This can be seen clearly when they refuse to ratify the new Conventions or also when they limit beforehand the future effects of an agreement which might appear modest to the layman. They have thus neither succeeded in forbidding fragmentation bombs, except in the particularly horrible case of the multiple fragments undetectable by X-rays, nor in prohibiting napalm bombings, nor in agreeing on a general ban on making people blind as a means of war,[35] although certain restrictions exist nevertheless to limit the use of laser arms which cause permanent blindness.

4. These difficulties illustrate the fears of states, including the most advanced democracies, about the use of outright bans that are often efficient. Indeed they fear these bans might weaken their means of defence at a time when (although no more than in the past) future forms of war are not really either known, or even imaginable. This legal system is, however, paradoxically superior to the will of the

states, because it is destined to control their behaviour during the hostilities and because no appeal is then conceivable except for a return to barbarism, which was precisely what both sides sought to avoid. Universalism is also in the very nature of humanitarian law,[36] and the questions linked to the repression of war crimes in former Yugoslavia have been among the first opportunities for jurisprudence to affirm the existence of general mandatory rules, from which states will not be able to extract themselves, without seriously involving their responsibility, including on penal grounds.[37]

NOTES

1. Quoted by Jaan Kross, *Professor Martens' Departure*, a novel translated from Estonian by Anselm Hollo (New York: New Press, 1994).
2. See, for example, Jean Pictet, *Développement et principes du droit international humanitaire* (Paris: Pedone, 1983), pp. 74ff.
3. Diplomatic and consular relations between belligerents will thus automatically be suspended, each party instructing a third state to defend its interests on the territory of its adversary or adversaries, but the building and the property of the embassy will continue to be covered by inviolability.
4. During the first session of the Geneva Conference on the reaffirmation and the development of humanitarian law in 1973, the Chinese delegation affirmed: 'Wars are divided into just wars and unjust wars; imperialism is at the origin of all aggressive wars.' See CDDH/SR 22, pp. 113–14, and Jean-Pierre Colin, 'Guerres et luttes armées ou le droit introuvable', *Revue Belge de Droit International*, 1 (1981–2), 209–42.
5. Pierre Boissier, *From Solferino to Tsushima: History of the International Committee of the Red Cross* (Geneva: Henri Dunant Institute, 1985).
6. A book that the Roman Catholic Church kept under the Index up to 1899.
7. In actual fact, the chronicle says that, immediately after the end of the fighting, 1,200 vehicles evacuated 3,790 wounded French and 2,368 enemy to different hospitals, of whom only 583 died during the following weeks (reported by Boissier, op. cit.).
8. Certain wars remain very cruel of course and decimate civilian populations. This was the case, for example, of the wars of Religion and also of the war of the League of Augsburg where the Palatinate was ravaged by the French Army in 1689, Louis XIV pretending to defend the rights of his sister-in-law Charlotte-Elisabeth de Bavière – the famous Palatinate Princess.
9. The famous 'Covenant of Sempach', concluded between the Swiss Cantons, and which notably imposed respect for the wounded and the women,

from where originates the name of 'Frauenbrief', still remains today.
10. Boris Mirkine Guetzevitch, 'La guerre juste dans le droit constitutionnel français', *Revue Générale de Droit International Public* (1950) 2, 228ff.
11. Cf. the re-issue of the old *Moniteur*, volume XIII (1847), 118.
12. Quoted by Pictet, op. cit., p. 33.
13. The battle was a real slaughter with nearly 40,000 deaths, 60 per cent of the wounded having lost their lives because of the lack of care.
14. The Hague Conventions had been preceded by the St Petersburg Declaration (1868), that presently still binds seventeen states and by the Brussels Declaration (1874) which had not been ratified. The Institute of International Law, founded in 1873, adopted in 1880 the Manual named 'of Oxford', that was written by Gustave Moynier, one of the founders of the Red Cross, and that formulated the principles of the law of warfare and inspired the work of the Hague in 1899.
15. The delegate of the Holy See even went so far as to consider that a simple restatement of article 3, common to the four Geneva Conventions of 1949, was preferable. This article stipulates – in the spirit of the Martens Clause – that in the case of a non-international armed conflict, each party must respect a minimum of rules, treat the wounded, prisoners and non-combatants with humanity, while humanitarian organizations, such as the ICRC, are permitted to offer them their services. See Colin, op. cit., pp. 214ff.
16. The doctrine has also played a certain role in the assertion of these principles, with G. Moynier and E. Boissier, already quoted, and also Max Huber, whose reflection especially turns to the principles of humanity and neutrality. See notably Max Huber, *La pensée et l'action de la Croix-Rouge* (Geneva: CICR, 1954).
17. National associations of the Red Crescent appeared very early, as early as 1868 for the Ottoman Empire.
18. See CICR, *Manuel de la Croix-Rouge internationale*, 12th edn (Geneva: CICR, 1983), pp. 565–8.
19. See Hans-Peter Gasser, 'Un nouveau projet de déclaration sur les normes humanitaires minimales', *Revue Internationale de la Croix-Rouge*, 789 (May–June 1991).
20. See José-Louis F. Flores, 'La répression des infractions individuelles au droit de la guerre', *Revue Internationale de la Croix Rouge*, 789 (May–June 1991). It must be noted that France has still not ratified the first Protocol, by far the most important. In answer to a questionnaire of the IRCC it stated: 'Numerous articles of the Penal Code and the Code of Military Justice, that do not specifically relate to offences against the Geneva Conventions, allow one to ensure the repression of crimes and offences that they prohibit.' A similar attitude can be observed with the states that did not ratify the first Protocol, while other countries are much more respectful of the requirements of humanitarian law, Spain for example, or also within the European Community, the Netherlands, Great Britain and Denmark.
21. 'Unless,' specifies Article 84 of Geneva Convention III of 1949 relating to prisoners of war, 'the legislation of the detaining power

specifically authorizes civilian tribunals to try a member of the armed forces for the same offences as that for which the prisoner of war is prosecuted.'

22. See Georg Schwarzenberger, *International Law as applied by International Courts and Tribunals – Volume II – The Law of Armed Conflict* (London: Stevens, 1968), pp. 462–6.

23. It was as early as 11 November 1918 that an Interallied Commission was created, instructed to establish the responsibilities of those called 'war criminals' for the first time.

24. In fact, the Allies abandoned their call for the extradition of German criminals by accepting that they should be tried by the Leipzig Tribunal. Of the 896 criminals demanded by the Allies at the beginning, only 45 were tried and condemned.

25. Including for the persons having acted 'as members of organizations', paragraph 1 of article 9 of the Nuremberg Charter provided that 'when proceedings are brought against any member of a group or of an organization whatever, the Tribunal will be able to declare (on the occasion of any act for whom this individual could be recognized as guilty) that the group or organization to which he belonged, was a criminal organization.' See H. de Touzalin, 'Réflexions à propos du délit d'appartenance sur un essai d'unification des règles de répression en matière d'infraction aux lois et coutumes de la guerre', *Revue de droit pénal militaire et de droit de la guerre*, IV-1 (1965), 133ff.

26. See the report of the ILC on the Proceedings of its 6th Session, Doc. of the General Assembly, 9th Session, Supplement n. 9 (A2693), pp. 11–12.

27. Resolutions of the General Assembly 897 (IX) of 14 December 1954 and 1186 (XII) of 11 December 1957.

28. Resolution of the General Assembly 3314 (XXIX) of 11 December 1974.

29. See, for example, J.C. O'Brien, 'The International Tribunal for Violations of International Humanitarian Law in the Former Yugoslavia', *American Journal of International Law* (1993), 639–59.

30. See Hervé Ascensio and Alain Pellet, 'L'activité du Tribunal pénal international pour l'ex-Yougoslavie (1993–1995)', *Annuaire Français de Droit International* (1996), 101–36.

31. Resolution 965 of the Security Council, dated 8 November 1994.

32. In the United States, the question was the target of a lively controversy, the Reagan administration having at its arrival sharply criticized the American negotiators of the Treaty, 'accused to have accepted a document contrary to the interests of the United States, legitimizing international terrorism – in the name of international liberation struggles – and containing unacceptable clauses from a military point of view'. See M. Aldrich, 'Prospects for United States Ratification of Additional Protocol I to the Geneva Conventions', *American Journal of International Law* (1991), 1.

33. See on this point the reasoning of Philippe Bretton, 'Remarques sur le jus in bello dans la Guerre du Golfe', *Annuaire Français de Droit International* (1991), 145ff.

34. See Jean-Pierre Colin, 'La place de l'individu dans le jus in bello', in Michel Girard (ed.), *Les individus dans la politique internationale* (Paris: Economica, 1994), notably pp. 286ff.
35. See, for example, on this subject, Mario Bettati, 'Examen de la Convention sur l'interdiction des armes classiques produisant des effets traumatiques excessifs', *Annuaire Français de Droit International* (1995), 197ff.
36. See Yves Sandoz, 'Humanitarian Law: Priorities for the 1990s and Beyond', 2nd Regional Conference of the ICRC on International Law (Geneva: ICRC, 1994).
37. See notably Ascension and Pellet, op. cit., p. 120.

Index